watching wildlife in london

10 9 8 7 6 5 4 3 2 1

ISBN 978 1 84773 520 1

Although the publishers have made every effort to ensure that information contained in this book was meticulously researched and correct at the time of going to press, they accept no responsibility for any inaccuracies, loss, injury or inconvenience sustained by any person using this book as reference.

Publisher: Simon Papps
Editor: Ian Woodward
Colour artwork: Cy Baker, Stuart Carter, David Daly, Sandra Doyle and Bridgette James
Line drawings: Marianne Taylor
Cartography: Stephen Dew
Design: Paul Turner/Stonecastle Graphics
Production: Melanie Dowland
Publishing Director: Rosemary Wilkinson

Reproduction by PDQ in the UK. Printed and bound in India by Replika Press PVT Ltd

Cover images: Red Deer in Richmond Park by George Kay, Great Crested Grebe with perch, Comma and Common Blue Damselflies by Robert Cardell
Page 1: Firecrest
Page 3: Water Vole
Page 4: Honey Buzzard passing Canary Wharf

watching wildlife in london

MARIANNE TAYLOR

NEW
HOLLAND

Contents

Introduction

EVERYONE HAS an opinion on London, whether they live there, work there, visit there or avoid it as much as possible. Fans will speak enthusiastically of the vibrancy and elegance of central London and the unrivalled variety of culture and colour to be found in its various districts, while detractors will point out the astronomical house prices, worrying crime rates and notoriously cold-hearted attitude of the natives. The truth is that with a conurbation of this size (London is the most populous city in the European Union) generalizations will only take you so far. Perhaps the most accurate single adjective for London is 'diverse' – in its architecture, history, ambience, prevailing culture, ethnic mix, prosperity or lack of it, even its topography, the capital of England has something for everyone.

One thing that most would agree is lacking in London, however, is wildlife. Built on the lush floodplains of the country's longest river, what's now the London area was once a wonderful haven for wildlife. Now, with concrete soaring into the sky on all sides, the diversity of living things seems minimal – just countless hurrying humans and, above their heads, swirling flocks of pigeons. The parks are little better with their grassy patches covered in deckchairs and footballers – just pigeons, geese, gulls and squirrels dominating the scene. Even in the outlying boroughs, things don't seem much better – cars everywhere, gardens attracting little but Magpies and mangy Foxes, the few streams running through beds of concrete, the parks home to nothing but a few ducks and yet more pigeons and squirrels.

Despite these discouraging initial impressions, many ordinary Londoners could potentially see far more wildlife every day than they realise, and those with a keener interest have made numerous exciting discoveries in the most unexpected places. More than 350 species of birds have been seen within a 20-mile radius of St Paul's Cathedral, and Hyde Park and Kensington Gardens have racked up 188. The other groups of animals and plants are also, without doubt, more diverse than the average Londoner would suspect.

The aim of this book is to show you that there is indeed far more to London wildlife than first meets the eye. If your idea of wildlife-watching is a Kenyan safari then you'll have to adjust your expectations a little, but with patience, know-how and a little luck you can enjoy some of the best wildlife spectacles Britain has to offer without going beyond Zone 6. From rutting deer in Richmond Park to Peregrines hunting massed flocks of wildfowl over the Thames marshes, from adorable baby Tawny Owls in Kensington Gardens to skulking Bitterns at the Wetland Centre, London is as much a place for wildlife as it is for people. The key wildlife-watching areas in central London are the Royal Parks and the River Thames, though even the most urban areas can also produce interesting sightings from time to time. Beyond the centre of the city, the most exciting general areas to visit are the large rambling parklands of the south-west, the wonderful London Wetland Centre, the Lee Valley with its string of lakes and reedbeds, and the marshes on either side of the Thames out to the east of the city. Besides these areas, there are any number of parklands scattered across the outer boroughs of the city, all of which can be interesting to visit.

What do you need to be a London wildlife-watcher? To begin with, just your eyes and ears and a willingness to wander and take your time. As your interest grows, though, you are bound to want to get a closer look at a bird in a treetop or a zooming dragonfly, and then it's time to invest in some binoculars. Try out a few pairs before you buy, to make sure what you choose is comfortable to carry and easy to use. Binoculars come in sizes like 8x32, 8x42, 10x42 or 10x50 – the first number is the magnification factor, the second the diameter of the objective lenses, which affects how much light the binoculars gather and how bright the image is. Bigger 'bins' are heavier and powerful ones are more difficult to hold steady, so it's

Introduce yourself

Throughout this book, you'll notice quite a few mentions of 'introduced' or 'non-native' species. This may require some explanation – basically, these are plants or animals which have been brought here from other countries and set loose, sometimes deliberately and sometimes by accident. Introduced species tend to either disappear very quickly, or do extremely well and spread rapidly into new areas.

London is full of examples of introduced species – including some of our most familiar and best-loved plants and animals. There's the Grey Squirrel, the London Plane Tree, the Canada Goose and the Ring-necked Parakeet, to name but a few.

Does it really matter whether a species is native or introduced? Yes... sort of. Introduced species that are successful sometimes do well at the expense of native species. We all know the sorry story of Grey versus Red Squirrels – the American Greys are bigger, tougher and better at exploiting habitats than Reds, and to top things off they carry a disease that's lethal to the Reds. Many people would agree now that it was a terrible mistake to bring Grey Squirrels to Britain, and some feel that we should be doing all we can to eradicate them. There's a wealth of similar examples in the UK – American Signal Crayfish vs native White-clawed Crayfish; Harlequin Ladybirds from Asia vs various native ladybirds; Japanese Knotweed vs all other plants.

Other non-natives seem to have a much less severe impact on native species. The Little Owl, for example, was brought here from Europe in the late 1800s and seems to have blended seamlessly into our native fauna. Others, like Golden Pheasants, don't really thrive and spread but have maintained a few small, inoffensive populations in a handful of scattered woodlands.

It is illegal to release non-native animals into the wild, but ill-informed or careless people still do it all the time, and of course pets sometimes escape. The morality of what we should do with these animals once they are at large is a vexed question. For now, many are part of the London wildlife scene and seem likely to remain part of it for a long time to come.

always a compromise. Compact binoculars have much smaller objective lenses (they come in sizes like 8x21) and so are lightweight and highly portable. You may feel self-conscious at first when you use your 'bins' in places like the Royal Parks, but don't worry, there are bound to be other people doing more embarrassing things in your immediate vicinity at any given time.

The next tool you'll want is a notebook. Here you can record what you see, but also take notes on anything that confuses you, so you can look it up in the books when you get home. If it's an unfamiliar animal, notes on its appearance and behaviour plus a sketch or two (however rudimentary) should help you identify it later. With plants, you might want to take measurements as well as sketches – you could even trace around a leaf outline.

You can spend a fortune on field guides, although you probably don't need to. This book has a quick-reference species guide beginning on page 111, which should be a useful starting point. Investing in a field guide or field guides that cover most or all of the common plants and animals in the UK will help you identify most of the species you'll find in London and find out a little more about them. See page 97 for some suggested titles on a range of different types of wildlife. If your interest really takes off, your Christmas list will soon fill up with specialized field guides on every group of living things you can think of, from birds and trees to moths, molluscs and mosses.

If you are interested in photography, there are far worse things to point your camera at than London wildlife. While you usually need a giant telephoto lens to take good wildlife photos, in the city parks the birds and other animals are often so used to people that you can get close enough to them to photograph them well with an ordinary zoom compact. In contrast to binoculars, a camera is virtually expected when walking in the more scenic parts of the city.

Protecting biodiversity in London

You probably remember the concept of a 'food chain' from school. Plants get their energy from the sun, soil and air. Herbivores eat the plants. Carnivores eat the herbivores. Voila – the food chain. In real life, things are more complex than that. Some herbivorous insects only eat specific plants. There are carnivores that eat herbivores, carnivores that eat other carnivores, and omnivores that eat everything. There are parasites, that live on other animals but don't necessarily kill them, and scavengers that eat only animals that are already dead. Put it all together and the result is a web, not a chain, with each node representing a species. The more nodes there are in the web, and the more individuals in total, the greater that particular environment's biodiversity.

So, in a nutshell, the more species we can look after, the better job we're doing of conserving biodiversity. It goes beyond that though – if we can encourage new species into the web, we can build biodiversity, and that makes our environment a better place – for wildlife and for us.

The London Biodiversity Partnership brings together a whole range of organizations, from the London Wildlife Trust to the London Transport network, to help improve London's habitats and to ensure that redevelopment work takes into account the needs of wildlife. Specifically, there is a 26-part Biodiversity Action Plan aimed at improving the condition and extent of 14 important habitat types, and boosting the population of 12 species or groups of species. The work includes surveys, habitat creation, establishing nature reserves and increasing public awareness of biodiversity issues.

As the projects develop, we are slowly but surely seeing a greener and more wildlife-rich London emerge. Just as importantly, Londoners' attitudes are shifting too, with a growing interest in and awareness of environmental issues in general and the special wildlife of London in particular.

For those who are really keen to give something back to London's natural history, there are almost unlimited voluntary opportunities to help, through one of the many conservation organizations that are active in London. Among numerous options, you can fundraise for Buglife, do species surveys for the London Natural History Society, lead wildlife walks for the London Wildlife Trust or look after trees in Kensington Gardens with the Royal Parks. If you're interested in a career change and willing to undertake the necessary training, there are also a wealth of paid employment opportunities working with wildlife and habitats in London.

So there is no need to pine for the open countryside when you spend most of your time in London. You just need to look at things in a different way, and you'll soon learn to appreciate all that London has to offer as a place to see and enjoy wildlife.

The Streets of London

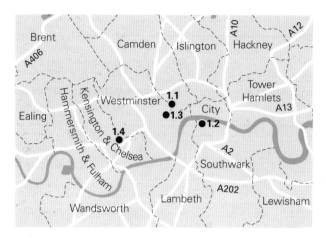

1.1 Centre Point
1.2 Tate Modern
1.3 Soho Square
1.4 Natural History
    Museum

IT'S DIFFICULT to imagine a more modified environment than the most built-up parts of London, whether you're among the gleaming towers of Canary Wharf, struggling past the throngs of shoppers along Oxford Street, or negotiating the raucous warren of side-streets in Soho. With greenery limited to rows of trees sprouting out of neat holes in the pavement and the occasional tidy little formal garden or square, and everywhere constantly seething with human life, wildlife-watching potential seems extremely limited.

Living alongside humanity in a city centre is a feat that only a few plants and animals can manage. With the earth concreted over, plants can only grow in the scattered small parks and gardens, and with so few plants there is little natural food or shelter for animals. However, most of those that do live in this environment do it very well. Many are simply blessed with resilient and adaptable natures – plants with the ability to take root in marginal habitats like a blocked gutter or the earth at the base of a pavement tree; animals with the ability to exploit new and unnatural food sources like dropped ice-creams. For some of the urban birds, which are able to fly far and wide in search of food, the cityscape of tall and sheer-sided buildings is not so different from their natural nesting habitat – sea cliffs.

Imagine being a bird, prepared by your earliest experiences and hard-wired instincts for a life living on a sea cliff. A narrow ledge on a high building is safe from predators and far above the roar of traffic which isn't so different to the crashing of the sea. Of course, if you are a bird which steps off your cliff every morning and plunges straight into the sea to hunt fish, for you the analogy breaks down rather quickly. But if all you want from your artificial cliff is a nesting place and you don't actually need the sea to be there, then city life could suit you rather well. Feral Pigeons, gulls and Peregrine Falcons are all cliff-nesters by tradition, and all have prospered in the heart of London.

We may not elect our city mayors solely on the basis of their pigeon policies, but Londoners do tend to have rather strong feelings about Feral Pigeons, seeing them either as charming and characterful delegates of the wonderful world of nature, or as filthy, disease-ridden vermin. Either way, the Feral Pigeon is the most visible wild creature living on the streets of central London, and if you want to learn to love them the best way to start is by understanding them.

Feral Pigeons are intensely sociable, feeding and breeding in large gangs whenever they can. In any given flock of pigeons, you can usually pick out a couple of males which are trying their luck with the females – strutting around their object of desire, bowing, high-stepping, tail-fanning and delivering the familiar cooing 'song'. The females usually appear less than interested, deftly sidestepping the would-be suitor while continuing to search the ground for crumbs. Yet when a female does decide to accept a male's advances, the climax of their courtship is a tender – and mutual – affair, the birds sitting together and gently grooming each other's head and neck feathers. Next, the male takes the female's bill in his – a ritualized version of the feeding of chicks that will follow when the pair becomes parents, and the origin of half of the phrase 'billing and cooing'. Finally, the female crouches down, the male hops carefully onto her back and mating occurs in a quick flurry of flaps and almost-overbalancing.

The pair stay together, often for life, going through the business of nest-building, egg incubation and chick-rearing as a team. Almost invariably two eggs are laid and two young reared. If there is enough food around (and there usually is, given our own species' wasteful habits) a pair can keep on churning out baby pigeons through the winter as well as the summer, producing six broods a year.

One of the classic London questions about wildlife is: 'Why do we never see baby pigeons?' It's a question that baffles many a naturalist – not because it's difficult to answer but because the answer is so obvious. Like many land birds, young pigeons (known as squabs) stay in or near their nests until they are almost fully grown and can fly. By this time, they are approximately the same size as the adults and look similar to them. Perhaps we are so used to seeing ducklings, cygnets and goslings on the park lakes that we expect the pigeons to also escort broods of fluffy chicks around on the ground. Unlike ducklings, squabs cannot feed themselves and so remain in the relative safety of the nest, rather than leaving it and facing an increased risk from predators. Instead, the parents feed them on the nest, vomiting up a nutritious goo called 'pigeon milk' straight into their bills.

You can still see very young pigeons if you find nests that are low enough and are not hidden from view. The undersides of railway bridges are popular settings for pigeon colonies. Listen for a shrill, insistent squealing – nothing like their parents' soothing coos – and you could see the gawky youngsters in the nest. When they are older they clamber out and pursue their parents along the ledges around the nest sites. Once they can fly with confidence and feed themselves, they join the adults in the local flock. It's still possible to tell them from the grown-ups for the first few weeks after they fledge. They have no purple-green gloss about the neck and are scruffier, their eyes are dull mid-brown rather than bright orange, their legs are a duller shade of pink, and their ceres (the waxy bare bump at the top of the bill) are smooth and greyish, rather than bumpy and white.

Feral Pigeons – why they're all our fault

Pigeons we all know – but why feral? The fact is that the city pigeon's route from the noble, wild bird of remote sea cliffs to the much-maligned 'rat with wings' of our city streets has been via dovecotes and pigeon lofts – all the street pigeons you see in London today are descended from domestic birds, which themselves are descended from a wild species called the Rock Dove.

Look up 'pigeon breeds' on the internet to see what staggering diversity of form has been squeezed out of the humble Rock Dove through selective breeding. Pigeons with massive inflated crops, looking as though they've swallowed balloons; pigeons with long plumes like second wings sprouting out of their feet; tiny pigeons; huge pigeons; fan-tailed pigeons; long-necked stork-like pigeons; short-billed and fluffy owl-like pigeons... and all of them in a great array of colours from pure black to pure white with every shade and pattern of grey and red-brown in between. The average flock of Feral Pigeons doesn't exhibit much variety in terms of shape and size, but retains the varied colour palette of its domestic ancestors.

Left: Feral Pigeon at Nelson's Column

Rock Doves were initially caught and kept for food – their domestication dates back at least 5,000 years and precedes that of any other bird. If captured young and confined in their dovecote for a few weeks, the birds would quickly accept their new home and would not usually stray when granted their liberty, instead forming an enthusiastic breeding colony in the dovecote and providing the homeowner with a constant supply of plump youngsters for minimal upkeep. Over the years, the hobbies of pigeon breeding and pigeon racing developed. Inevitably, a few birds did stray or escape, and from them the street pigeons descended.

Wild Rock Doves sally forth from the cliffs in flocks to forage in cliff-top fields for seeds and other plant matter. It's easy to see that replacing 'cliffs' with 'tower blocks', 'cliff-top fields' with 'streets' and 'seeds and other plant matter' with 'discarded chips and other edible rubbish' is not much of a stretch for Feral Pigeons. Not only did we bring them here, but we've also provided them with a habitat so rich in food supplies and nesting places that it's hardly surprising that they are doing so well. Some urbanites have a great affection for these tough and feisty birds, while others loathe and revile them – wherever you sit on the scale of pigeon-love, it's worth remembering just why they're here.

The Peregrine Falcon is a recent city success story. These powerful predators are much appreciated and encouraged by many Londoners, as much for the fact that they eat Feral Pigeons as for their beauty and high-octane charisma. Seeing one is always exciting – a big, anchor-shaped and fast-flying bird with an aura of high drama. Like all British birds of prey, Peregrines' numbers were hit hard in the 19th and earlier 20th centuries, as gamekeepers and pigeon-keepers shot them and the use of pesticides poisoned the food chain. Now, all birds of prey enjoy strict legal protection, although surreptitious illegal persecution regrettably still occurs now and then.

On the rise again after those decades of persecution and pesticide poisoning, Britain's burgeoning Peregrine population includes many city-centre pairs, often choosing to nest on the most impressive building they can find, e.g. Chichester Cathedral; the Clock Tower on Cardiff city hall. It's unlikely that they are selecting them because they admire the architecture! The buildings that we ourselves admire happen to be good for Peregrines as they often resemble tall cliffs, with ledges to build a nest and a good view to look out for prey.

The most famous of London's 13 or so pairs have opted to set up home at a site near the Tate Modern. After the young have fledged, the adults and juveniles regularly perch on the chimney of the Tate Modern, from where the juveniles can learn the art of hunting. You can often see them from the new and no longer wobbly footbridge across the Thames – the RSPB has volunteers with telescopes on site through the summer to give you a closer look and furnish you with Peregrine facts. The current pair are known as 'Misty' and 'Bert' (rather more imaginative than the famous Dutch pair 'Ma' and 'Pa'). In 2008 they produced four chicks, though sadly one was fatally injured soon after fledging after flying hard into a glass building, a hazard that urban Peregrines need to learn about as early as they can.

Late 2008 saw a pair of Peregrines holding territory on the Houses of Parliament, a handsome building with many suitable nesting spots and a riverfront position that should suit the birds very well. Given that certain minority groups are constantly lobbying parliament for the right to, once again, legally kill these wonderful birds, the building seems an especially fitting choice, lest our politicians forget the shameful history of Britain's treatment of her most magnificent native wildlife.

The Kestrel, a red-brown falcon and little cousin to the Peregrine, is a bird we associate very much with 'proper countryside' – green fields studded with trees and rich with small mammals to hunt. However, there are Kestrels breeding in central London too, most famously on that soaring landmark, the Centre Point block at the corner of New Oxford Street and Charing Cross Road. Adapting to city life is a much bigger deal for the Kestrel than the Peregrine. Rural Kestrels catch mostly rodents but city Kestrels eat a much higher proportion of birds – often stashing partly eaten corpses for later consumption.

In Shakespeare's time, 'kites' apparently soared above the London streets and scavenged for scraps on the ground alongside the crows. What kind of kites they were is unknown. They could have been the Red Kites that were exterminated as breeding birds in England in the 19th century, or the Black Kites which don't breed in Britain but are common in cities on the continent. Most experts plump for the former. Today, Red Kites are seen over London every spring, in increasing numbers, as a reintroduced population in the Chilterns prospers and spreads. Some may even be migrants from the continent. The chances of them breeding in the outer London boroughs are increasing every year, but as the streets in central London are so much cleaner than in Shakespeare's day, it's doubtful that we'll see Red Kites coming down to feed in Trafalgar Square.

Two long-distance migrant raptors may also be seen occasionally in London skies – a big fish-catcher and a small falcon. The Osprey is increasing as a breeding bird in Scotland and has now started to nest in England and Wales too. Ospreys travel to Africa in autumn and return in spring, visiting good fishing lakes on the way. Though still fairly rare in London, lucky observers might spot one overhead in either season. Regrettably the park lakes seem not to be tempting enough to persuade one to stop off for a longer stay. The Hobby has a rather Peregrine-like colour scheme and a graceful flying style. Unlike Ospreys, Hobbies can be seen all summer in some outlying parts of London, though sightings of them travelling over the city centre tend to be fleeting.

Two of our most familiar city birds have undergone severe population declines during the late 20th century. One of them, the House Sparrow, is all but absent from central London now – a shocking turn of events given their great abundance as recently as the 1980s. The other, the Starling, is still around in reasonable numbers and is one of the birds you're most likely to notice around the London streets. Starlings nest in crevices and aren't fussy whether those crevices are in trees or buildings. They also have wide-ranging dietary tastes and a utilitarian approach to foraging – essential attributes for city wildlife. Nevertheless, higher standards of street hygiene and building maintenance take away feeding and nesting opportunities for Starlings, and they are

Birdwatching in Soho Square

From our fourth-floor office in Soho Square, my colleagues and I had a great view into the tops of the London Plane trees that mark out the four quarters of this fairly typical central London square. Quiet moments would often see one of us standing at the window, scanning the branches with the office binoculars – all new sightings were meticulously added to the office bird list. Among the birds we saw and heard every day were Blue Tits, picking their way through the twigs in search of tiny insects.

One day we ordered a bird feeder – the kind that sticks to the window glass with suckers. We filled it with sunflower seed kernels, stuck it in place and scattered a few seeds on the windowsill as extra encouragement. We didn't really hold out much hope that the Blue Tits would spot the new addition on one of the thousands of windows overlooking the square, nor that London-bred Blue Tits would even recognize a bird feeder or be sufficiently

intrigued to fly from the trees to the building to investigate. We were wrong – within days the first Blue Tit had visited and soon we had a pair of them coming regularly.

Through summer, the square filled up with sunbathing office workers every lunchtime and the Blue Tits came back and forth every day. Then one day a fluffy, yellow-cheeked baby Blue Tit arrived. We were over the moon – 'our' Blue Tits had successfully nested in the square. At least three pristine youngsters were soon visiting with their tired and heavily moulting parents. But that wasn't all – we started receiving visits from Greenfinches (also with youngsters) and Great Tits. Our little window feeder was now busy through much of the day. The other people working in the building would come and marvel at the spectacle, often remarking that they never realized there were any birds at all in London, except pigeons.

commonest in the city parks and the more unkempt parts of town.

London's small green spaces don't compare to the Royal Parks as wildlife habitat. The most exciting wildlife spectacle you're likely to see in one is the fine statue of a Lioness taking down a Lesser Kudu in Grosvenor Gardens, near Victoria station. However, these little oases do make it possible for a handful of other species to survive in the heart of the city. Even the most closely cropped square of grass harbours insects and other invertebrates, as do ornamental flower beds. However, shrubs or trees are needed to make a green space attractive to birds. The trees may be dwarfed by surrounding buildings, but birds can rise above it all and see a map of greenery scattered across the city. With enough insects around, supplemented by the usual scraps and crumbs discarded by human visitors, a small population of songbirds can get by in London's small squares and formal gardens. The species you're most likely to see are Blue Tit, Great Tit, Greenfinch, Wren, Blackbird and Robin.

Robins are extremely good at finding little insects and other small creatures to eat on the ground – their big eyes enable them to start foraging at the crack of dawn and carry on long into the evening. As long as a city garden has enough suitable bare earth it could easily provide a permanent home for a pair of Robins. They are responsible for most of the birdsong you're likely to hear in the city, giving a sweet and rather melancholic twittering song throughout the year and often well into the night, especially where strong street lighting exists. The Nightingale that sang in Berkeley Square was, in all probability, a Robin (real Nightingales like rich, tangly woodland and don't live in central London). The same is almost certainly true of the Nightingale that was reportedly heard singing in Downing Street by Margaret Thatcher one February (real Nightingales not only shun central London, but are also migratory and are in Africa in February).

Blackbirds can find food in almost any grassy or earthy area, so you're likely see one or two in any of the city gardens. They are superficially similar to Starlings, but the latter are short-tailed and usually stand quite upright. Only the male Blackbirds are black, a rich and velvety-soft black, quite unlike the shiny and speckled black of a Starling. Male Blackbirds have bright yellow bills – so do Starlings, but the Blackbirds accessorize their yellow bills with matching yellow eye-rings that make their dark eyes stand out in their dark-feathered heads. Females are browner and spottier, often mistaken for thrushes but much darker than any thrush. You'll see Blackbirds bouncing in neat two-footed bounds across the grass (Starlings walk), pausing every so often to listen carefully and then perhaps rapidly attack the ground and haul a wriggling earthworm from its burrow. Like most urban birds, London's Blackbirds are used to people and will often happily hop within a couple of metres of passing pedestrians. They usually nest in bushes – the bushes on offer in London's formal gardens may sometimes be a bit more manicured than would be ideal, but the lack of nest-robbing predators makes up for it. This species is the other main city songster, delivering rich and fluty melodic phrases from dawn well into the evening.

Crows and their relatives do quite well in London, as befits their opportunistic ways. Carrion Crows are probably seen most – big black birds which some people insist are actually Ravens, escaped from the Tower. It's not true – there are no wild Ravens in London, but Carrion Crows can look discomfortingly huge at close quarters. They scavenge the streets for scraps, sometimes joining in Feral Pigeon scrums in popular feeding areas

Eyes to the Skies

At the end of September 2000, many London birdwatchers were glued to the windows of their high-rise offices or spending every possible moment out on the highest ground they could reach, scanning the skies for something really special. From 20th September, large numbers of Honey Buzzards were being seen along the east coast of Britain, and many of the birds were heading inland. Many of us were lucky to see one or more of the spectacular raptors over the next 10 days, as dozens overflew the centre of London.

The Honey Buzzard is a rare bird in Britain, but commoner on the near continent and in Scandinavia. Like many birds they migrate south in autumn – a combination of unpredictable weather conditions plus large numbers of young birds migrating for the first time means that autumn is a great time to find unexpected visitors crossing the skies above. Springtime can be equally good, as migrating birds return northwards.

It's worth looking overhead at any time of year, though, because all kinds of birds overfly London without ever touching down, while others commute between the parks or lakes. Over the course of a year I saw six species of wildfowl flying overhead close to Victoria station, and most of my London sightings of Sparrowhawks and other birds of prey have been overflying birds glimpsed between rows of buildings. The first Swifts of the year will be streaming above from the end of April, while on October nights it's a case of 'ears to the sky' to listen for the thin calls of the first Redwings of autumn.

Some of the birds that live in central London forage mainly around the tops of the buildings and are not often seen at street level, so listen for their calls – among them are Grey Wagtails (which say *'chissk'*) and Pied Wagtails (which say *'chissick'*… yes, they are rather similar).

Below: Honey Buzzard passing Canary Wharf

like Trafalgar Square, but also indulge in occasional predatory behaviour. A badly injured Feral Pigeon won't last long once the crows have spotted it.

Magpies are also fairly common in central London, though they are more confined to the parks than the Carrion Crows are. They too are generalist, opportunistic feeders. In some instances, they have even been recorded eating dog faeces, which doesn't sound great for them but is obviously good news for us, as not everyone is considerate enough to scoop.

There is one city bird that is a real rarity in Britain, although it's a common town bird just across the Channel and it's a bit of a mystery why it is so scarce over here. The Black Redstart is a handsome bird, Robin-sized and shaped, with a striking red tail. Males are otherwise mostly black with a prominent white wing patch, while females are grey-brown. Like many city birds, Black Redstarts occupied cliffs and other rocky habitats before there were any cities, but found suitable habitat among the buildings as they appeared. They first bred in London in 1926 but only really thrived after the Blitz, nesting in bombsites in the City and foraging among the weeds that sprouted among damaged, neglected and derelict buildings. Today they are much rarer again, as many of their preferred nesting places have been patched up and redeveloped – you're most likely to see one in East London. Today, regeneration of areas that have Black Redstarts is carried out in a manner that's sympathetic to the birds' needs. When buildings are redeveloped, incorporating 'green roofs' (sown with grass or other plants) or 'brown roofs' (covered with bare soil and allowed to develop a natural vegetation) into the design are effective ways of ensuring Black Redstarts and other birds have places to forage for insects.

How typical it is of humankind that we decide gulls should be called 'seagulls' and then berate them whenever we see them away from the sea. Gulls are water birds, of course – their webbed feet attest to that. However, they are the most general-purpose of water birds. They are strong fliers and perfectly competent walkers. Their utilitarian bills are just as good at hoovering up bread crusts as they are at snapping up fish. Most of London's gulls do spend time on or by the water every day, whether the Thames, the park lakes or both. But some pairs do nest on buildings far from either, and can be seen circling high over the streets. St Pancras station has for some years provided a lofty home for nesting Herring and Lesser Black-backed Gulls.

Not surprisingly, mammals in London are few and far between. At street level, the terrain is much too hostile for earthbound animals. Unless you can escape up a tree, down a drain or into the sky, the streets are far too dangerous, to say nothing of the difficulty of finding food or a place to live. Grey Squirrels abound in the parks but are rarely seen in the smaller gardens. Even Foxes, common in the suburbs, generally avoid the streets of the city centre – gardens and other safe hiding places are just too few and far between. A handful of pipistrelle bats may roost in city centre buildings, but they too are very scarce except in the parks and the suburbs. The only mammals (apart from ourselves) which can really cope with inner-city living are the ones that alarm us the most – rats and mice.

The urban rat is the Brown Rat, the urban mouse the House Mouse. The two are easily told apart by size. A couple of mice would sit easily in the palm of your hand but you'd need both hands to hold a rat – not that you'd necessarily want to. Otherwise, they are similar – brown-furred with long bare tails, smallish round ears and beady black eyes. Although both are common in central London, living in hollows in buildings and eating anything they can find, they are also a great deal shyer and more retiring than their horror-fiction alter-egos. You're not particularly likely to see either as you go about your business in London – the exception being the mice that live on the London Underground.

Tube life

Many a commuter will have whiled away the minutes between the tube train they just missed and its successor by watching the mice scooting up and down below the tracks, sniffing out burger remnants and other tasty snacks thrown or dropped there through the day. They are House Mice and there are around half a million of them roaming the tube network – the Piccadilly and Northern Line stations in central London are particularly good places to see them. If you have a very long wait for a train, you could observe many chapters of 'tube mouse' life – watch them playing chase, carefully grooming their fur (which nevertheless seems to remain a darker and dirtier colour than that of 'surface' mice) or shrilly squeaking in a scuffle over the ownership of half a kebab. There are tube rats too, but they are much more rarely seen.

making predictable journeys, boarding and disembarking at the same stations and same times each day, conducting themselves en route with every bit as much aloofness as any human commuter. It's proved rather difficult to verify these tales, though I have personally seen a pigeon taking a ride on an overground train in London. It's difficult to imagine how a pigeon would find its way up and down to the platforms on stations below ground-level, though they are without doubt intelligent birds. Pigeons are vigorously discouraged from loitering in stations – perhaps pigeon-commuting would be a more common phenomenon were this not the case.

Perhaps the most interesting underground animal is the mosquito *Culex (pipiens) molestus*. This insect is a fascinating example of evolution in action, for it descends from the surface mosquito *Culex pipiens* but over the last 100 years has become a distinct subspecies, that can be differentiated from *C. pipiens*. It lays its eggs in puddles and the adult females then roam the networks, biting rats, mice, pigeons and humans with voracious abandon. The story is ongoing, too, with signs of three genetically distinct subpopulations occupying the Victoria, Bakerloo and Central lines. Perhaps a modern-day Darwin would have refined his ground-breaking theory while waiting on a Tube platform scratching his mozzie bites, rather than cruising around the Galapagos Islands.

Above: House Mice on the Underground

There are many apocryphal stories of Feral Pigeons travelling on underground trains. These include tales of certain individuals

Have you ever looked up on a sunny day to see a dragonfly zooming purposefully down Oxford Street, or noticed a beautifully patterned moth resting on a brick wall in Islington? Quite possibly not – though it does happen occasionally. A general scarcity of insects on the London streets is no bad thing in the eyes of many, but however you feel about them, insects are key to a healthy ecosystem and without them the other wildlife tends to be sparse or absent. Insects are closely associated with plant life and most are nowhere near as mobile as birds. They are mainly confined to the city's green spaces, especially those that have water bodies. Even tiny ponds will add a major new dimension to a city garden's wildlife.

The Natural History Museum's exhibits are mostly of creatures that have long since breathed their last, but it's a different story in the museum garden, which you can visit between April and October. Here, many native British plants and insects thrive, in a network of mini-habitat patches including heathland, woodland, meadow and wetland. A busy hive of Honey Bees is a star attraction – the nest is inside a hollow tree, with a glass panel so you can watch the bees coming and going, building their waxy honeycomb hexagons and performing their famous 'waggle dance' that codes precise co-ordinates of good nectar sources for other bees to follow. Honey Bees from here and other city hives travel widely across London, visiting window boxes and hanging baskets as well as flower beds and the meadowland patches in the big parks.

The museum garden is also home to a mysterious creature, discovered here in 2006. It is a 'true bug' – yes, 'bug' is a proper scientific classification for a specific group of insects – and rejoices in the name *Arocatus roeselii*. Or does it? If you are going to discover a new species, the garden of the Natural History Museum is a good place to do it, and researchers soon found that the mystery bug was a very close match for specimens of *A. roeselii* – but *A. roeselii* is more colourful, lives no closer than Nice in the south of France and lives on Alder trees (the museum's bugs were on London Plane trees). Nevertheless, *Arocatus roeselii* or a variant of it is the best guess so far – research is ongoing. If you visit the museum, you could easily find the mystery bug for yourself – it's the commonest insect in the garden. It has also been found in other parts of London, but nowhere else in Britain.

By and large, London is not a great place for butterflies. If you look at the UK distribution maps for some otherwise common butterfly species, the London area forms a conspicuous blank hole while other smaller cities are fully coloured in. These butterflies tend to be species that have rather poor powers of dispersal, rarely venturing very far from their birthplaces, where they form colonies. On the other hand, a few species are great wanderers by nature, and these are the ones you're most likely to find in central London.

The group of butterflies called the vanessids include some of the most familiar and colourful species – Red Admiral, Peacock, Painted Lady and Small Tortoiseshell. All are big, bright and strong on the wing – in fact Painted Ladies and (to a lesser extent) Red Admirals migrate to Britain from continental Europe and even North Africa, sometimes in very large numbers (for example in spring 2009). For butterflies that can take a sea crossing in their stride, the streets of London represent no significant obstacle to their travels. They hibernate in their adult form, but the British winter is normally too cold for Painted Ladies, so any that of these that you see in early spring are likely to be migrants. The same was true until recently of Red Admirals, but with warmer winters it is now believed that some do manage to survive, and they can sometimes be seen on milder days in mid-winter. As soon as the warm spring days arrive they take wing, looking for others of their species to get on with the business of courtship and mating. Through mid-spring and early summer their eggs hatch, the caterpillars grow and eventually pupate. A new generation of adults is on the wing by mid-summer. Some species, such as Small Tortoiseshells, may have a second brood. Others are now totally disinterested in the opposite sex but instead stuff themselves with as much nectar as possible, building fat stores for the hibernation ahead.

One of the most ubiquitous city plants happens to be one of the best nectar sources, a real boon for the butterflies of London. The Buddleia is sometimes called the 'butterfly bush', so attractive are its long drooping flower clusters to butterflies. The species that flourishes so well in Britain is *Buddleia davidii*, and is actually native to China and Japan. It's an extremely popular garden flower, as much for its butterfly-attracting properties as its pretty purple flowers and sweet scent, and the large London population descends from the wind-blown seeds of garden specimens. It's not unusual to see Buddleias sprouting out of guttering far above street level, while alongside railway lines outside the main London terminals it self-sows to form dense thickets.

Its attractiveness to butterflies and other nectar-feeders masks the real story of the Buddleia. Like many of the most familiar living things of London, is a non-native and therefore not necessarily good news for our 'own' wildlife. Its flowers provide nectar for passing butterflies but its foliage goes uneaten by our native insects. Compare this to the humble Common or Stinging Nettle, which is a vital food source for 40 insect species, including Small Tortoiseshell and Peacock butterflies. Unfortunately, in London's formal gardens the unassuming native 'weeds' are often ruthlessly dug up and colourful non-natives are planted – only in the Royal Parks and a few other larger parks is there room for 'wildlife areas' where native plants are encouraged.

Common native plants – or 'weeds' as we often unkindly characterize them – do keep up a constant assault on the streets of London. On a recent walk from Cannon Street to Islington I paid particular attention to the greenery sprouting out of pavement cracks and around the bases of street plane and rowan trees. I noted Dandelions, Chickweed, Groundsel, Stinging Nettle and numerous anonymous tufts of grass, all fighting for a foothold in this concrete jungle. It is comforting (to some, at least) to reflect how quickly these pioneering plants would carpet the city if one day all the humans packed up and left, ushering in a new era of urban wildlife.

Meanwhile, the 'brown roofs' and 'green roofs' schemes for redeveloping buildings, endorsed by the London Biodiversity Partnership, provide places for the windborne seeds of such plants to grow and flourish. This environment will in turn encourage invertebrates to become established and birds to visit and perhaps nest on them. The kinds of wild flowers that will hopefully prosper on these vegetated rooftops include Ragwort and various thistles as well as those already mentioned – their seeds could easily settle and take root on a rooftop as long as enough earthy, nutritious substrate was available. Plants like this would, when mature, provide a home and nectar for insects, and an autumn crop of seeds for birds. The website www.blackredstarts.org.uk has a great deal of background information on how the schemes work, and how they can help Black Redstarts in particular and wildlife in general. It's perhaps regrettable that all this conservation effort is happening so far above our heads, where we won't be able to see the rooftop wilderness blossom – but it can only be good news for the wildlife of the city as a whole.

As you begin to head away from the city centre and into more residential areas, things don't change very much on the face of it. Huge swathes of London, in all compass directions from the city centre, are essentially urban sprawl, with rows and rows of houses, busy shopping streets and not much else. There is still a preponderance of concrete and an apparent lack of green spaces. However, with houses come gardens, and even the

London Plane

The most familiar plant of all in London is not native to our country. Nevertheless, it is extremely well-established here, as its English name attests. The majority of trees in the city centre, and a large proportion of those in the great parks, are London Plane trees. The species, which has the scientific name *Platanus x hispanica* (sometimes *Platanus x acerifolia*), is distinctive, with bark that peels away in chunks, giving the trunk an attractive variegated pattern, broad leaves with multiple points, and largish, spiky, spherical fruits that dangle in small clusters from the twigs like Christmas decorations.

The 'x' in the scientific name indicates that that the London Plane is a hybrid, probably between the Oriental Plane and the American Plane, while the 'hispanica' reveals that the form first arose in Spain. Numerous varieties exist within the species. A good example of 'hybrid vigour', the London Plane's resistance to the often awful air quality in city centres meant that it was widely planted in conurbations. Even though city air quality is now much improved, there is a real fondness for the London Planes that have survived where lesser trees could not, and many fine, tall old specimens exist in the London parks, especially Green Park.

The London Plane also copes well with 'root compaction', which is why it is so popular as a roadside tree. These trees are sometimes pollarded or otherwise cut back to keep them from becoming dangerously enormous. You may notice that where a plane tree's twigs grow very close to a street light, the leaves on those twigs remain alive and well in winter long after the others have dropped. They form a perplexing little cluster of green around the light-source that serves as a surrogate sun through the night and artificially extends the lifespan of the leaves.

These trees, as non-natives, are of limited value to wildlife, but they are better than nothing – they provide shelter and a limited food supply for a variety of insects and birds. As the years go by, London's native wildlife may adapt and evolve ways to exploit the plane trees more effectively – if so the trees could help support a more diverse ecosystem in the future. For now, they provide a breath of green colour and natural beauty in the most concreted and sterile parts of the city.

Below: *London Plane tree*

Unexpected encounters

One morning I was walking to work along Shaftesbury Avenue when I noticed a House Mouse scampering up the pavement ahead of me. It was fairly early and the streets were still quite quiet, but it was still a surprise to see the animal out and about in broad daylight. Ahead of me, up the street, a large motorcycle courier stood in a doorway, checking his paperwork. When he noticed the mouse scuttling towards him, he gave a surprisingly girlish shriek and jumped up onto the nearest doorstep, from where he stared down in great alarm as the rodent went past. Maybe he was phobic – but then few of us are prepared for a close-up encounter with a wild animal in the middle of London.

I've been hit in the face by a flying pigeon – in a way it's surprising it's only happened once, though I'm not complaining. A colleague of mine witnessed something similar – an office worker heading up Charing Cross Road was hit in the chest, but as she recoiled from the bird, waving her arms at it, my colleague realized that it wasn't a pigeon but a male Kestrel.

Every so often, in hard winters, large numbers of Waxwings reach Britain from northern Europe and beyond, and the flocks systematically search out berry-bearing trees, shrubs and bushes and strip them of their crop. These spectacular, colourful and very approachable birds often draw quite a crowd, especially when they pick somewhere as public as the corner of Warren Street and Fitzroy Street, as a 100-strong flock did in March 2005.

All of which goes to show that, if you're interested in wildlife, keep your eyes open wherever you are, even in the busiest and most built-up parts of the city, because you never know what you might see.

smallest and dullest garden can make a difference. Add together lots of small, dull gardens, and you have a large patch of habitat that, in terms of wildlife potential, is far greater than the sum of its parts. Even the greyest London suburbs can provide interesting wildlife-watching.

If you live in such an area, you can do a great deal to improve things for wildlife. Use any outside space you have to cultivate native plants. If you hate gardening, that can work too – just let the weeds flourish, and soon you'll have a garden that will be very inviting to wildlife, albeit perhaps less so to any human visitors you may have. You can plant native herbs in window-boxes or hanging baskets, and you can fix bird feeders and nest boxes to your walls. It will all help.

The variety of birds you'll see in open spaces increases the further you get from the city and becomes more typical of the mixture you'll find in the big central London parks. Dunnocks, which don't seem keen to live in the very centre of London, are more frequent. House Sparrows, once found everywhere in the city, remain common in some parts of the suburbs. Greenfinches are joined by Goldfinches, Blue and Great Tits by Long-tailed and Coal Tits, Blackbirds by Song Thrushes, Woodpigeons by Collared Doves. There is also a chance of something more exotic – okay, not a huge chance, but much better than in the city centre. Take the American Robin found in a Peckham garden in 2006 – a migrant blown very, very far off course – or the confused Nightjar which set up home on top of a Teddington lamp post rather than a Surrey heath, and gave several streets of residents insomnia with its incessant night-long churring song.

There will still be Brown Rats and House Mice about, hopefully not living actually in your house. There will also be Foxes, the controversial stars of the urban wildlife scene – in some parts of London they are incredibly common. If your council does not provide wheelie bins, you probably have good reason to curse the urban Foxes – they will happily spend the night before collection day shredding any bin-bags unwisely left out and scattering the contents across the road in their search for anything edible. They also do other unsociable things such as marking gardens with their acrid urine (and worse), setting up home in unattended garden sheds, and having loud sex at 5am in the morning. As neighbours go, they leave rather a lot to be desired.

Nonetheless, city-dwelling Foxes have many fans, and when you see a healthy, bright-furred adult relaxing in the sun or watch a litter of cubs at play, it's easy to see why. They might live on our doorsteps but they are real wild animals, with size and attitude, intelligent eyes and pointed teeth, and (although they do mostly eat left-over takeaways) the unmistakeable aura of the predator. The urban Fox may be a far cry from its rabbit-chasing country cousin, but every Fox carries in its genes the adaptability and resourcefulness to succeed where so many others cannot – on the streets of London.

Above: *An urban Fox forages in typical fashion*

The Royal Parks of Central London

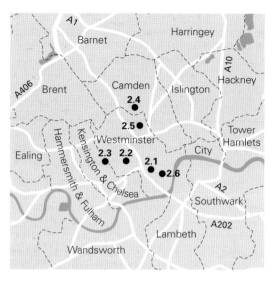

WHAT IS a city without its green spaces? London's parks are as much appreciated by its human workforce as they are by its wildlife, and the fact that Regent's, Hyde, Kensington Gardens, Green and St James's Parks form an almost unbroken chain through the centre of London makes them much more valuable as a whole than they would be individually if the distances between them were greater.

Of these five parks, four have sizeable bodies of water (Green Park is the exception), and all have significant 'wild areas' which are not closely manicured but allowed to remain in a more or less natural state. The Royal Parks Agency, which manages all the parks, belongs to the London Biodiversity Partnership, and wildlife is always on the agenda when management plans are devised.

Regent's Park (officially 'The Regent's Park'!) is the most northerly of the four. It is adjacent to Primrose Hill, which for management purposes is actually a part of the park, and which itself is close to the much wilder Hampstead Heath (see page 88). London Zoo occupies a northerly segment of this big, squarish park, and has

contributed in a small way to the wildlife of the park as a whole over the years. In 1965 the unimaginatively named Golden Eagle 'Goldie' escaped from the zoo and spent several days at large in the park, preying on the ducks and even trying his luck with a couple of small dogs while the zoo-keepers struggled to find a way to return him to custody. He was eventually caught after being distracted with a dead rabbit. More recently, a population of Aesculapian Snakes, perhaps descended from escapees from the Reptile House, has become established on the banks of the Regent's Canal. Aesculapian Snakes are native to southern Europe, are adept tree-climbers and rat-catchers and, happily for us, are non-venomous.

The park has lovely formal rose gardens, some sizeable areas of flat grass used as playing fields, a famous open-air theatre and the usual scattering of bandstands, playgrounds and eateries. The main wildlife interest is centred around the large, three-armed boating lake taking up most of the south-eastern corner, which is home to an assortment of ducks and other water birds and has a wildlife garden at its far end.

Hyde Park and Kensington Gardens form a large continuous area, the two parts being divided by a road that crosses the long, narrow lake. Although actually two parks, the whole area is often referred to as just Hyde Park. West of the bridge, in Kensington Gardens, the lake is the Long Water, eastwards of there, in Hyde Park, it is the Serpentine. The Serpentine is larger and wider, and has a wooded island, but it is used for boating – the Long Water is quieter. Kensington Gardens also has the much smaller Round Pond. Both parts of the park, like Regent's Park, have pleasant formal gardens (mainly close to Hyde Park Corner in the south-east and at the north-eastern corner of Kensington Gardens) and large areas of undulating grassland with many scattered trees – London Planes, Horse Chestnuts and an assortment of others. With no wildfowl collection, the ducks, geese and swans here are all 'wild', or at least free-flying. There are bird-feeding areas north of the Serpentine, which attract many small garden birds.

Green Park (officially 'The Green Park') is waterless with no really 'wild' areas, and therefore is not as good for wildlife as the others, but it does include some really magnificent London Plane trees which may attract woodpeckers, and in early spring there is a wonderful show of Daffodils. It adjoins Buckingham Palace Gardens, which has a small lake but is not normally open to the public.

St James's Park is mostly taken up by its large lake. The rest of the park is close-cut grassland with rows of large trees, and a few shrubby areas. It is a rather small and much manicured park but there are a few corners that are dedicated to encouraging wildlife. For example, parts of the lake are mid-way through a reed bed development scheme, which should make it more attractive to wildlife. From the bridge, you can get great views of large Mirror Carp and assorted smaller fish swimming through the shallow water – there are other fish too although they are not so easy to see. The eastern end of the park is quite well-wooded, as is the large island at this end of the lake. The park's five pelicans tend to make the biggest impression on visitors, although, like some of the lake wildfowl, they are not wild and are wing-clipped to prevent them from flying away.

The most striking lakeside birds in Regent's Park are probably the Grey Herons that nest in trees on islands in the lake. They also visit Hyde Park and St James's Park but are less common there. Most of us imagine herons to be shy and wary birds, so it can be a little disconcerting to see them standing impassively on the path by the boating lake among throngs of squabbling pigeons, paying no heed to the passing tourists. Herons nest earlier than most species. In late winter, you'll see adults standing on their massive stick nests, and in spring they will be feeding their growing chicks on a tasty diet of regurgitated fish. The young herons are loud, amusingly coiffed, and embody the concept of 'gawkiness'.

On the park lakes, Coots, Moorhens, Greylag and Canada Geese, Mallards, Tufted Ducks and Pochards are all easy to see. If you've always thought that any bird floating on the water is a duck, it's time to think again. The classic duck of parkland ponds is the Mallard – the big one with the glossy green head and curly tail (the males) or dappled brown plumage (the girls). The other two common ducks are the Tufted Duck and the Pochard. The 'Tuftie' male is a dapper black, yellow-eyed duck with white flanks and a dangling back-of-the-neck crest. The male Pochard has borrowed the colour scheme of an old-style Duracell battery – copper-coloured head, and a body that's black at both ends and silver in the middle. The diving duck females are both brownish. The Tufted Duck is darker and the Pochard greyer, and the female Tuftie has the same yellow eyes as her mate, while the Pochard's are dark. Look at the size and shape as well – the Pochard is larger with a distinctive sloped forehead. Hyde Park, which has no captive wildfowl collection, also has regular visits from four other kinds of ducks – of which the males are described – Gadwall (silvery-grey with a black rear end), Shoveler (green-headed with a white breast and deep chestnut flanks – both sexes have giant comedy bills), Red-crested Pochard (a bouffant orange hair-do and a brown, black and white body) and Mandarin Duck (small, absurdly flashy and colourful, with long orange whiskers and 'sails' in the wings).

If it floats like a duck but is three times the size, it's going to be a goose. Greylags are, helpfully, grey-brown all over with orange bills and pinkish legs. Canada Geese have brownish bodies but black heads and necks with neat white chin-patches. I've heard it said that they migrate here from Canada, but this is not the case (occasional transatlantic vagrants are seen in Britain, but are unlikely to occur in London). The species is indeed native to Canada and the USA, and the populations there they do migrate south for the winter, but the birds we see here around our city parks and many other places are descendants of captive geese and wouldn't recognize Canada (or indeed migration) if you showed them a photograph. What they do recognize is the bite-size chunks of Hovis, handed out in abundance by tourists every day. With foraging this easy throughout the year, it's hardly surprising that the migratory instinct has lost its edge.

Mute Swans live on all the lakes, belying their serene looks by a distinctly ferocious and paranoid disposition when there are cygnets to protect. An overprotective swan papa (known as a 'cob') will launch himself at geese, ducks, other swans, dogs and even people to keep them away from his

Duck dilemmas

It has long been a Royal Parks tradition to keep a collection of captive exotic wildfowl on the lake for visitors to admire – a kind of livelier version of a lovingly tended rose garden. There are many similar collections across the country. The assortment of 'ornamental' ducks, geese and swans are prevented from flying off by wing-clipping (cutting the flight feathers on one side) or pinioning (amputating the top joint of one wing when the bird is very young). Pinioning is permanent, but clipping has to be done every year, as the new flight feathers grow after the main annual moult.

Of course, birds sometimes manage to fly away before they're caught for clipping, which is why we now have 'wild' Canada Geese in this country, as well as Egyptian Geese from Africa, Red-crested Pochards from southern Europe, Ruddy Ducks from America and Mandarin Ducks from China. All of these have officially self-sustaining populations in Britain, albeit originally descended from escapee birds many generations ago. The Ruddy Duck is currently the subject of a costly eradiction programme funded through Defra, as birds from Britain have reached Spain where it is feared they will interbreed with the internationally endangered White-headed Duck. This has divided the birdwatching community with many holding strong opinions either for or against the programme.

In the central parks, the free-flying London birds just rub shoulders too closely with the captives. London's Red-crested Pochards are still not regarded as officially 'wild', although many of them are free-flying and they now breed in Hyde Park. It's not always easy to tell whether the bird you're looking at is a genuine

water check for metal or plastic numbered rings on its legs – this usually indicates captive origin (though wild birds are often trapped and ringed for research purposes as well).

Above: *Common Pochards (two males, one female) with one male Red-crested Pochard (top left)*

wild one, a captive, a wild-born member of a feral population or a recent escapee, especially in Regent's and St James's Parks, which both have collections of wildfowl exotica. The collections include several species that are found in the wild elsewhere in Britain, such as Eider, Goldeneye and Long-tailed Duck. Even some of the Tufted Ducks and Pochards in Regent's Park are actually captive birds. Welcome to the murky and confusing world of 'what counts' when you are a birdwatcher keeping a list.

If it isn't one of the species already mentioned it is probably not even slightly wild, but other wildfowl do visit the parks from time to time. In February 2009, for example, a wild Smew appeared in Regent's Park and birders looking for it wanted to be sure that they had seen the wild bird rather than one of those in the collection. The first thing to check is the wings. If the bird has its full complement of feathers, you'll see two pointed wing-tips crossed above the tail. This isn't easy to see on some of the diving ducks, so you might have to wait until the bird stretches up in the water and has a good flap – luckily most do this rather frequently. If you see the bird out of the

If the bird is full-winged, there's every chance it arrived at the lake by flying there rather than in a box. That still doesn't necessarily make it wild, though. Birdwatchers often refer to something called the 'bread test' when trying to assess the origins of a suspect duck. If the duck is shy of people then it's more likely to be wild. If it greets you like a long-lost friend and rushes to your side as soon as you take out the sliced white loaf, it probably recently hopped the fence at a local wildfowl collection. However, in central London where all the birds are fairly fearless, the bread test is unreliable, as a single lost wild duck joining an established flock will tend to quickly adopt the habits of that flock.

The ornamental wildfowl collections are great places to hone your identification skills, and also just to enjoy watching a great variety of species, with Regent's Park's collection especially diverse – you'll find them mostly in the northern arm of the boating lake, but also on the small Queen Mary's Gardens lake and in a loop of water at the far end of the western arm of the boating lake. On a recent visit I saw more than 30 species of ducks there. If your timetable makes it possible to visit frequently, you're more likely to spot a new arrival, and that may be something very unusual and genuinely wild, like the male Lesser Scaup (from North America) which visited Regent's Park in winter 2003.

young ones. While it may not be true that a blow from a swan's wing can break a man's arm, you still wouldn't want to get in a fight with one. The 'I mean business' posture of an angry swan is distinctive – the wings are raised and their feathers puffed up, doubling the size of the bird's body. When it is really irate, it will tuck back its neck within those pumped-up wings and will paddle fast towards whatever has upset it with powerful alternate swipes of its massive webbed feet. On the main lake in Regent's Park there are also non-wild Whooper Swans – told from the Mutes by their slighter physiques, and their knob-less yellow-and-black bills.

The other two common floating birds are both black and smaller than the ducks. The Coot is the one with the white bill, sneezy call and insanely argumentative attitude. The Moorhen is smaller, shyer, has a red bill with a yellow tip and a charming jerky tail action as it swims. These two are related to each other but not to the ducks – they belong to the rail family.

In springtime all will be busy with courtship and nest-building – you may see Coots engaging in furious, kicking and screaming, territorial battles, Mallards performing their quaint, head-dipping courtship displays (and, less endearingly, drakes sometimes forcing themselves upon unwilling ducks), and Moorhens discreetly constructing an untidy heap of a nest by the waters' edge. Ducklings and other babies will be out and about from mid-spring – the ducks, geese and swans usually produce a whole flotilla of fluffy youngsters while the Coots and Moorhens tend to have only up to a handful each. It was revealed on a natural history documentary that Coots often begin with half a dozen or more babies, but the parents sometimes inexplicably kill all but a couple when they are very young. Moorhens seem more family-minded, with youngsters from earlier nests often helping their parents to take care of the second brood of the year.

Among these stocky waterfowl drifts an altogether more elegant creature – the Great Crested Grebe. In spring, these grebes perform a rightly acclaimed courtship display as breeding pairs affirm their commitment before nesting begins. You can see this on any of the central park lakes in early spring. The two birds perform synchronized dives and dances, climaxing with the 'weed dance' in which the birds dive towards each other, surfacing breast to breast and treading water, each with a bill-full of water weed. Later on in the year, you could see them giving their cute, stripy chicks piggy-back rides across the water.

Other swimming fish-eaters that you may see are Cormorants and Little Grebes. The former are long-necked, blackish, big and primitive-looking, the latter are tiny, with round, fluffy 'powder-puff' behinds. They don't have the lavish head ornamentation of their larger cousins, but are attractive nonetheless in their blackish and burgundy breeding colours. Like their relatives, they also have stripy chicks which they carry on their back. Both grebes become paler and duller in winter, with the Great Cresteds losing their frills of orange whiskers.

If you've ever wondered why all the male ducks disappear in late summer and only dull females are around, you've been deceived – that's just what they want you to think. In fact, the males are still there, but they are in drag. Every autumn, ducks undergo a full moult, and this includes dropping all or nearly all of their flight feathers at once. As a result, they completely lose the ability to fly and are therefore suddenly much more vulnerable to predators. To help minimize the risks, the males grow a new body plumage at this time, which is dull and camouflaged, closely resembling that of the females – it's called 'eclipse' plumage. You can still spot the male Mallards by their bright yellow bills, and you'll notice once the bill gives him away that even an eclipse male Mallard is that little bit brighter and more strongly patterned than a female. The new breeding plumage is in place by the end of autumn, and the birds have grown new flight feathers and are once again able to fly.

Feed the birds

Feeding the pigeons in Trafalgar Square is now outlawed, but in the parks bird-feeding continues unabated and brings delight for many a visitor, as well as for the birds themselves. The Royal Parks authorities discourage the feeding of Carrion Crows, Feral Pigeons, geese and Grey Herons (the latter probably won't be interested anyway, unless you've brought a bucket of fish with you), but have no problems with us throwing our crusts to the ducks.

Bread isn't the optimal diet for ducks. Seeds, cooked grains or even specially formulated duck pellets are much better, but bread (especially wholemeal) isn't that bad, and the ducks do supplement their bread rations with natural foods too so you're unlikely to be contributing to a wildfowl health crisis if you do feed them bread now and then. However, on sunny weekends so many people have exactly the same idea that it can, by lunchtime, be extremely hard to arouse any interest from the ducks and the water is a veritable sea of soggy bread scraps.

In winter, when Black-headed Gulls are numerous on the lakes, much fun can be had by lobbing bread fragments high in the air and watching the gulls try to catch them, a feat at which they're remarkably adept. The larger and less manoeuvrable gull species rely on their bullying skills to commandeer any pieces that fall to the water.

Some of the small birds in the parks have also wised up to the willingness of humans to provision them with food. Up until the 1980s, great flocks of House Sparrows would come and take seed from the outstretched hands of people on the bridge in St James's Park. Sadly the sparrows are no more – not for want of feeding, it seems. However, tits and Robins will still come to the hand, though they're more tentative about it than the sparrows were. Try the south side of the Long Water in Kensington Gardens on a quiet weekday: take along some peanuts, placing one or two along the railings, and keep your eyes open for Great Tits watching you with interest. If you see one, proffer a few nuts in an open palm and with luck and patience the little bird will touch down on your hand before long.

Starlings here will also come and take food from your hand – as will the pigeons, of course, given half a chance. And the park squirrels have no problems whatsoever in clambering all over you and searching your pockets, the moment they suspect there might be something there for them.

Gulls visit the park lakes throughout the year, though are most numerous in winter – most adults leave for breeding colonies in spring. It is usually easy to see four different species – Black-headed, Common, Herring and Lesser Black-backed in Hyde, Regent's and St James's Parks. Some of the Black-headeds have leg-rings which reveal them to be visitors from the Baltic Sea – many make the lengthy trans-European journey every year. Uncommon species show up from time to time, and as nobody keeps captive collections of ornamental gulls, their origins are never questioned. Great Black-backed and Yellow-legged Gulls appear quite frequently, while rarer treats have included Mediterranean Gulls, which are very beautiful as gulls go, with a German bird bearing a green ring now a regular winter visitor to the Round Pond in Kensington Gardens. Even more unusual was a gull showing plumage characters of the 'Azorean Yellow-legged Gull', that was on the Serpentine and Long Water in winter 2006/07 – this one a rather grimy-faced and unprepossessing individual but it got many birdwatchers very excited.

In addition to its wild and captive wildfowl, St James's Park has a quintet of captive pelicans – four Great Whites and one Louisiana Brown – which occasionally and notoriously supplement their fish diet with the odd unwary pigeon, with film of one such incident becoming a hit on the internet.

Alongside the lakes in all of the parks that have them are variable amounts of shrubs and bushes, which offer shelter to small and not-so-small birds. The usual common species are normally easy to find – Blue, Great and Long-tailed Tits, Dunnock, Wren, Robin, Blackbird, Starling, Greenfinch, Chaffinch, Goldcrest, Magpie, Carrion Crow, Jay, Woodpigeon and Ring-necked Parakeet. A bright day in early spring is a good time to come and look for 'little birds', which are busy singing and establishing territories, and are often very approachable. Later in the year they become much more secretive, all their energies taken up with incubating eggs and then tending chicks in a (usually) well-concealed nest.

Learning what birds look like is only half of the story when it comes to becoming a confident bird-identifier – songs and calls are just as important. The parks are good places to hone your skills, as they have a good but not bewildering variety of species. Some noises are easy – the nails-down-blackboard screeching of Ring-necked Parakeets, the yelping laughter of Green Woodpeckers. Others are not. It takes practice to tell the songs of Robin, Dunnock and Wren apart as on first listen all three are just pleasant twittering noises, and many little birds give near-identical rattling alarm calls when danger threatens – a universal language of anxiety. Your best bet when you hear a song or call you don't recognize is to track down the bird that's making it – this might take a while but that should serve only to fix the association between sound and bird more firmly in your mind. You can buy birdsong CDs, which are a great way to learn, or listen to recordings on the internet. Thoroughly learning the common bird sounds will help you to recognize a more unusual one – by virtue of the fact that you don't recognize it, so it must be unusual.

Summer visitors are few and far between in the parks. Chiffchaffs and Blackcaps breed in small numbers but most other species of warblers that visit the parks do so only fleetingly, before continuing their journeys. Swifts, Swallows and House Martins all chase insects over the lakes, especially the Serpentine. Most of them are also just passing through – albeit sometimes in impressive numbers. A few House Martins do still breed near Kensington Gardens and can be seen throughout the summer. Because of the chance of finding migrants, mid-spring is an exciting time to watch birds in the Royal Parks. Keen birdwatchers regularly find the unusual, often by frequently scanning the skies. In May 2008 birdwatchers in Hyde and Regent's Parks saw a cornucopia of

Take a closer look

Visitors to the London parks will invariably notice the creatures that want to be noticed – cheeky Grey Squirrels that hurry up to you if they suspect you're harbouring nuts and have been known to climb up people's legs; the St James' Park pelicans that square up to you on the narrow footpaths; the ever-hungry pigeons clamouring for a bite of your lunchtime sandwich. However, the parks are also home to a wealth of shyer and less showy creatures, and you'll need a little more time, care and luck to spot them.

To get the most out of a wildlife-watching visit to one of the Royal Parks, pick a day and time when there won't be so many people about. Only the most emotionally robust animals can cope with the volume of human traffic that a sunny weekend afternoon will bring, but you are likely to see much more if you go on a weekday morning. Head off the beaten track and explore the quieter parts of the parks – Kensington Gardens, the rough grassland of Hyde Park, the wildlife gardens in Regent's Park.

In Kensington Gardens, you could find Song Thrushes nest-building in the dense bushes at the western end of the Long Water. The birds that come to the feeders in Regent's Park's wildlife garden include Coal Tits, Chaffinches and Goldfinches. The Long Water attracts wild Shoveler ducks in winter – look for them resting on the shore, screened off from casual viewers by overhanging vegetation. You could find a Green Woodpecker searching the soil for ants in Green Park, or even see a Tawny Owl

asleep in the treetops. Migrating songbirds may visit the parks early on in the day before moving off later on.

On summer days, look out for insects. Hyde Park and Regent's Park have 'wild' areas of grassland where native wild flowers are encouraged, and they in turn attract bees, grasshoppers, butterflies and hoverflies. Where natural wetland vegetation is allowed to grow by the lakes, you could see dragonflies and damselflies. Regent's Park has a few Hedgehogs, and all of the parks have Wood Mice and Common Pipistrelle bats. We are straying into the realm of the very-difficult-to-see now, but if you really want to experience the breadth and depth of the Royal Parks' wildlife, spend plenty of time in them in all seasons.

Below: Song Thrush

migrants including Red Kite, Honey Buzzard, Common Sandpiper, Turtle Dove, Ring Ouzel and Sedge Warbler.

All of the parks have large areas of what's often called 'amenity grassland' – short turf suitable for ball games, picnics and general recreation. Important though all these things are for people, it does mean the grassy open areas are often devoid of wildlife, especially when the sun comes out and the entire local working or resident population decamps to the nearest patch of green. There are a few birds that use the grassy expanses though, and your best chance of seeing them is to visit early in the morning, before the crowds gather.

The Green Woodpecker is a handsome bird, of the calibre that would draw an admiring gaze from even the most jaded wildlife non-enthusiast. The largest of our woodpeckers, its bright yellow rump and pointy shape in flight are eye-catching, while with a close view the gimlet eyes set in a black bandit-mask, fearsome stabbing beak and crimson mullet hairstyle make for an unforgettable face. Rough grassland often harbours colonies of ants, and ants are a Green Woodie's favourite thing, so it's not unusual to see these big woodpeckers hopping about on the ground like thrushes, using their insanely long tongues to flick up mouthful after mouthful of hapless ants. You can often get quite close to them in the parks, certainly the parkland Green Woodies are much less wary than their super-cautious country cousins.

In spring, migrating songbirds on their way up north may stop off in the parks. Two species, the Wheatear and the Meadow Pipit, enjoy areas of grassland and if you visit early on a spring day you might bump into one of them. The Wheatear is a perky, pastel-coloured little bird with a white rump, dark wings and (in the male) a black mask – its name is a sanitized version of the old English 'White-arse', which aptly describes the view of a retreating Wheatear. Meadow Pipits, or 'Mipits' as birdwatchers affectionately nickname them, look like mini thrushes. Actual thrushes forage on the grass year-round – Blackbirds are the commonest of the family, then Mistle Thrushes, with Song Thrushes rarer. Autumn and winter may bring their northern cousins into the parks to forage the amenity grassland and berry bushes – Redwings, with their distinctive white eyebrows and rusty-red flanks, and Fieldfares, grey-rumped and grey-headed, chestnut-backed and dark-winged.

Dedicated park birdwatchers find all sorts of oddities during the autumn migration – more so than in spring because a) there are more birds migrating overall, as all the young birds born that year will be joining their parents, b) those youngsters are migrating for the first time, and so are more likely to get lost and end up in a city park and c) birds tend to take more time in autumn as they are not in a rush to claim a breeding territory and find a mate. Spotted Flycatchers and warblers like Common and Lesser Whitethroats and Garden Warblers are found in most years, while terns may overfly the lakes along with the returning Swifts, Swallows and martins.

Winter brings Siskins – pretty green finches which travel in often large flocks and may settle for long spells to feed in suitable trees. Their calls are distinctive drawn-out nasal tweets – a tree full of Siskins can make an amazing racket. They have a special liking for alder trees which can be found at the edges of some of the park lakes. Other finches that make occasional appearances in winter include Bramblings and Lesser Redpolls, which may sometimes using the bird feeding stations.

Parkland trees offer shelter and feeding opportunities for many birds. Green and Great Spotted Woodpeckers drill neat nesting holes in the trunks – these are often taken over in later seasons by other birds, including tits, Starlings, Nuthatches, Stock Doves and Ring-necked Parakeets. With so many birds fighting it out to use the relatively few tree-holes, the provision of nesting boxes by the park staff is much appreciated, especially by Great and Blue Tits,

London's missing sparrows

If this book had been written in the 1970s or 1980s, it would be unthinkable to have got this far through discussing the Royal Parks without making more mention of House Sparrows. Times have changed, though, and the disappearance of the iconic 'cockney sparras' from central London is one of the most shocking, perplexing and saddening of the city's wildlife stories.

The decline has been underway for a lot longer than many realize. Annual sparrow counts in Kensington Gardens show a fall from more than 2,500 House Sparrows in 1925, to just under 550 in 1975. Today, a few remain in Regent's Park, but seeing even one sparrow in any of the other central Royal Parks would be remarkable. It is not just in London that the species has suffered, though. House Sparrow populations in other UK cities and towns have fallen too. Whatever the problem is, it's clearly something that goes beyond the particular factors of London life.

Those who recall the sparrow-feeding scrums on the St James's Park bridge would be quick to say that the problem could not be anything to do with a shortage of food. However, while it's true that adult sparrows manage well on a diet of birdseed, their young do not – they require plenty of insects.

There can be no doubt that both central London and the wider countryside have fewer insects around than they did a hundred years ago, thanks to more 'efficient' methods of managing crops and gardens. However, other insect-eaters like tits and Robins still seem to be thriving in city centres.

A shortage of nest sites is another possible cause of the decline. The kinds of places sparrows like to nest – crumbling walls covered with ivy, holes between roof tiles and broken guttering – have become harder to find as run-down and damaged buildings are renovated. Another theory put forward is that, with the increase in traffic noise, male House Sparrows can't make themselves heard when advertising their territories with the familiar monotonous chirrup, and so fail to attract mates. The fact that House Sparrows are still doing well in rural gardens lends support to all three of these ideas, and indeed there probably is no single factor behind the decline but a combination of several which, added together, have spelled catastrophe.

It could be that we will never again see House Sparrows dodging neatly between the pigeons' feet for crumbs in the parks, and it's a great shame to reflect that there is a whole generation of young Londoners who may never have seen a sparrow at all. However, the priority now is to look after the sparrows where they still survive, which does include many London suburbs, and to try to figure out what's going wrong so we can turn the tide.

Left: House Sparrows (male and female) feeding from the hand

which find the woodpecker holes a bit too large. Nuthatches are small birds too, but solve the problem of over-large nest-holes by plastering up the edges with mud, narrowing the opening to exactly the size they want.

Other birds build cup or bowl-like nests in dense tangles of vegetation – often close to the ground. The prettiest nest belongs to one of the prettiest birds, the Long-tailed Tit. It constructs a ball of moss, cobwebs and other delicate materials, stuffing the insides with thousands of tiny feathers and camouflaging the outside with lichens. Long-tailed Tits are much in evidence through most of the year in the parks, travelling in noisy family parties and often remaining apparently oblivious of onlookers as they systematically flit from twig to twig, searching each for tiny insects. Only in mid spring do they seem to disappear, throwing their time and energies into the business of reproduction.

In Kensington Gardens, a pair of Tawny Owls nests regularly in a Horse Chestnut tree, and from mid-March both the baby owls and their parents spend their daytimes sitting out in full view on branches close to the trunk. They are by no means the only Tawnies nesting in the Royal Parks but they are probably the best known, and visitors in the know have taken some great photos of the handsome adults and the utterly charming fluffy chicks. Tawnies – the biggest British owls – may be seen in all of the parks. They hunt rats, mice and other small animals by night, and hide in the trees in the daytime unless they are busted by a gang of songbirds, which will ruthlessly mob and harass any owl they find, often forcing the poor sleepy Tawny to decamp to an alternative roosting spot.

By the end of April, the Kensington Gardens Tawnies are harder to see, partly because the young owls are more mobile, but also because the trees are coming into full leaf and obscuring the birds. Nevertheless, it's worth checking the big trees within the triangle between the Round Pond, Speke's Monument and the Physical Energy Statue. The Tawnies are well camouflaged against tree bark with their beautiful mottled brown plumage – they need to be, to protect them from the 'songbird police' – but with patience you could find one at any time of year.

Surprisingly, Tawny Owl is not the only owl species that can be found in central London. A pair of Little Owls has also taken up residence in Regent's Park in recent years. This enigmatic species sometimes uses more open perches than Tawnies and can be seen more easily during the day if it remains undisturbed. Unfortunately this is unlikely here in London, as so many people visit the park every day.

The other birds of prey that live permanently in the parks are the Sparrowhawk and the Kestrel. They are superficially similar – both smallish with long tails – but their lifestyles and hunting tactics are quite different. The Sparrowhawk is a stealth missile, sneaking up on its prey by flying just below the tops of hedges or walls, then appearing from nowhere at tremendous speed and scattering panicking small birds in all directions. Birdwatchers nickname it the 'Sprawk' – perhaps because by the time you've finished saying to your companion or companions: 'Look, there's a Sparrowhawk' the fast-moving bird has usually disappeared so a strangled cry of 'Spraaawk!' is often a better bet. The exception to this is in early spring, when on fine days Sparrowhawks circle high in the sky, perhaps enjoying the weather while advertising their presence to potential mates. Look for an outline shaped like a capital 'T' – long tail, straight, shortish wings and a not very projecting head – that moves with a lazy flap-flap-glide flight pattern. If the bird comes low enough you could also see the neatly barred pattern on its belly and the undersides of its wings.

A pair of Kestrels nests in a purpose-built nest-box in a tree overlooking the ornamental wildfowl collection in Regent's Park, and elsewhere often on buildings. City Kestrels eat more birds than their country equivalents, but the Royal Parks do have a

Above: *Male Kestrel surveying Hyde Park*

supply of little furry critters, which suits the Kestrel's palate and hunting skills rather better. The familiar hovering behaviour is not often demonstrated by central London's Kestrels, as it renders them too visible to avian prey. The city Kestrels' method when bird-hunting is the wait-and-pounce tactic, with hovering more often used when looking for small mammals in the long grass.

The ubiquitous mammal of the Royal Parks is the Grey Squirrel, which here has reached a pinnacle of cheekiness. Most of them are completely fearless and practically mug passers-by for handouts. While squirrels in less busy town parks are grateful for any scraps they can find, a Hyde Park squirrel will shun a bread crust and instead hold out for the monkey nuts which someone will eventually provide. For every squirrel skipping about in the park on a sunny weekend, there will be half a dozen or more people pointing a camera at it while making adoring noises – no wonder these pampered rodents behave as if we are but a race of big, bald, nut-carrying slaves.

Although the North American Grey Squirrel is responsible for the near-extinction in England of the rather prettier native Red Squirrel, Grey Squirrels enjoy, at least in London, rather good PR. Perhaps this is because London seems much too hurly-burly a place to ever have been home to delicate Red Squirrels, and so the Grey Squirrel's greatest crime is seen as an irrelevance here. Instead, as practically the sole representatives of free-ranging cuteness and fluffiness in central London, they provide Londoners with a major link with all that's appealing in the world of nature – something that mammals have always and will always do better than birds ever can. Those who wish to eradicate Greys from the UK will have the mother of all battles on their hands if it ever comes down to a situation where the Royal Parks' Greys come under sentence of execution. Invasive aliens they may be, but they possess inalienable charm from their twitchy noses to the tips of their bushy tails, and their fans are numerous and passionate.

A tale of two tails

If you spend time feeding the birds and squirrels along quieter parts of the Long Water, you'll probably spot another furry creature darting in now and then to grab a morsel of food, but it is unlikely to elicit the same coos and sighs of appreciation from any onlookers. Instead, it's likely to provoke exclamations of disgust, because it's a rat.

But wait, are the Brown Rat and the Grey Squirrel so very different? They are about the same size, they're both rodents, they both have soft fur, gentle dark eyes, cute whiskered noses, little paws and small, rounded ears. Why, then, does one make us want to give it a cuddle while the other makes us want to throw things and run away screaming? Even people who keep pet rats and adore them, acknowledging their intelligent and affectionate natures, often have the same uncompromisingly hostile attitude towards the wild ones.

The difference between the two is partly attitude. The Grey Squirrel is fearless (so we kid ourselves that it's friendly) and perky, often sitting up on its hind paws and gazing around. The Brown Rat is furtive, scuttling. It's afraid of us because we throw things at it, but we think it must have something to hide – disease, probably, and perhaps a primal urge to swarm over us and eat us alive, à la James Herbert.

It's famously been said that squirrels are just rats with better outfits, and this for me hits on the crux of the issue – it's all about tails. If you've ever seen a tailless Grey Squirrel, you were perhaps surprised at how dramatically the absence of the tail dents the animal's overall cuteness. Rats, however, are in our eyes worse than tailless, their tails are long and *bald*. Better no tail at all than one that looks like a stuck-on worm – there's something disturbing about bald bits on an otherwise furry animal. If the squirrel's full, bushy tail is the equivalent of a really sharp suit or pretty dress, the rat's tail is like a lime-green mankini – an affront to all that's decent, and it takes away any charm the rat might possess. That is my theory, anyway.

Below: Grey Squirrel and Brown Rat

The park rats mostly keep a low profile in the daytime, as do the mice. There are Wood Mice here as well as House Mice, so if you do see a mouse you may want to know which kind it is. Wood Mice are longer-tailed with bigger eyes and ears – their fur is also a richer brown than the greyish House Mice. To see them you should visit early or late in the day, explore the quieter and less cultivated parts of the parks and move quietly and carefully. Leaving bait in the form of peanuts and dried fruit around the bases of trees with particularly gnarly root systems could also be worthwhile. Unfortunately, behaving like this could bring you some unwanted attention from the park police. There are, however, easier places to see Wood Mice outside of central London.

Bats are much easier to see, and watching them hunting insects over the lake in St James's Park is a pleasant way to spend a summer evening. The commonest bat is the tiny, fast-fluttering Common Pipistrelle. The bat known until relatively recently as 'Pipistrelle' has now been shown to be three separate species. All look identical to our eyes, but they call using different pitches and this is enough to keep them from interbreeding, warranting their status as different species. The commonest is, fittingly, known as the Common Pipistrelle, but the rarest, Nathusius's Pipistrelle, has been found over the St James's Park lake. Dedicated bat enthusiasts use a gadget called a 'bat detector', which not only picks up the higher-than-we-can-hear sonar squeaks the bats make as they move about and hunt, but also helps the expert assign a bat to the correct species. Bat detection reveals that the pipistrelles that hunt over the Regent's Park lake include both Common and the third species – Soprano Pipistrelle. If you see a much bigger bat, with a straighter, high flight and a call so low that some people are able to actually hear it, this will be a Noctule. Serotines and Daubenton's Bats have been observed in Regent's Park as well. The Daubenton's has a distinctive flight as it hunts very low over water,

often appearing to skim the surface. All bats hibernate through the winter, but will be out and about again as soon as the air is warm enough for insects to fly.

Bats breed and roost in tree hollows and sometimes buildings. All species enjoy exceptionally strict legal protection – you are absolutely forbidden from touching or disturbing a bat that takes up residence in your loft, or blocking off its access. The Bat Conservation Trust has a wealth of information and advice on every bat issue you can think of.

A friend told me a while ago that he saw a Rabbit in Kensington Gardens, but then the same friend insists there is a very hairy man who believes he is a lion living in the rough grassland north of the Serpentine, so I was sceptical. My mistake, as I later discovered there is indeed a small Rabbit population north of the Long Water. Regent's Park is the only one of the central Royal Parks which has Hedgehogs, though in their case it's certain that they are not new arrivals but the remnants of a disappearing population. Hedgehogs get through a massive quantity of worms, slugs, beetles and other creepy crawlies, so it's not surprising that they should manage to hang on only here, in the wildest of the central parks.

Foxes are active in the Royal Parks mainly by night – even the toughest urban Fox has not yet reached Grey Squirrel standards of boldness. Here they mainly scavenge but will hunt rats, mice and any birds that get within their reach. The early-morning commuter is much more likely than the midday tourist to see a parkland Fox.

Only the commoner British amphibians live in the Royal Parks. All of them have to come to water to mate and release their eggs, which will develop into tadpoles, but otherwise they spend a fair amount of time away from the water. They need damp and sheltered places to hide during the daytime, which can be few and far between in the parks. In Regent's and St James's Parks the new schemes to create naturalistic 'wetland' areas will

Scaly aliens

Reptiles and amphibians are not well represented in Britain in general. We have just six species of native reptiles (three snakes and three lizards) and not many more amphibians (three newts, two toads and two frogs). However, because both reptiles and amphibians are frequently taken on as pets but then dumped in the wild when they prove too much to cope with, we now have large numbers of non-natives at large. Several of these have done rather well, establishing successful and flourishing colonies, and Britain is now in the rather bizarre position of having as many species of non-native reptiles and amphibians as it does natives.

Two of the reptilian exotics can be seen in London's parks. The Aesculapian Snakes that live alongside Regent's Park canal have already been mentioned. There is a second colony in Colwyn Bay in Wales, so the species has a foothold in Britain already – the Colwyn Bay snakes are, like the Regent's Park ones, descended from zoo escapees, and have

thrived there since the late 1960s. It remains to be seen what will become of the so far very small London population and what impact they could have on native wildlife.

Around the shores of Long Water, you might see another alien relaxing in the sun beside the ducks – there is at least one and probably more well-grown Red-eared Terrapins living here. These handsome freshwater turtles are popular pets when tiny, but grow to the size of a generous dinner plate and develop a fearsome bite, which is why so many have ended up in park lakes up and down the country. The terrapins originally hail from North America, as does the Teenage Mutant Ninja Turtle cartoon series which made them popular as children's pets. At liberty, the terrapins pose a risk of unknown proportions to wildfowl and fish. Anyone considering letting loose a problematic pet reptile should seriously rethink this idea, and instead find the creature a new (indoor) home with someone willing to care for it for the rest of its days.

provide Common Frogs and Common Toads with safe places to wait out the day. At night, they come out to search for insects, snails, slugs, worms and other creepy-crawlies. Both hibernate when things get too chilly for them and their prey.

If you find a frog or toad and want to know which it is, there are several things to look for. Frogs are smaller and slighter, while toads are more heavy set. Frogs are smooth-skinned, while toads are covered in little bumps (these are not warts, and contrary to urban mythology you can touch a toad without fear of becoming infested with warts overnight). Frogs have pointier noses than toads, and usually more distinct markings,

including a dark face-mask, while toads have prominent elongated bulges behind their eyes (their parotid glands, if you want to know). And finally, if your amphibian leaps gracefully away from you, it's probably a frog, but if it ambles off at a more sedate pace, it's more likely to be a toad. If you're lucky enough to see frogs or toads spawning (this happens in early spring – warm days in March are probably your best bet), the appearance of the spawn is another clue to identification. Frogspawn forms dense clouds, while toad spawn comes in long strings, comprised of double rows of eggs.

Above: *Common Frog*

If you find frog or toad spawn, please resist the temptation to scoop some up in a receptacle and take it home for your garden pond. Frogs and toads travel surprising distances and are more than capable of finding suitable ponds for spawning on their own – if your pond is amphibian-free there's probably a good reason for it, and you may need to look at what you can do to make it more wildlife-friendly.

The third amphibian of the parks, the Smooth (or Common) Newt, spends more of its time in the water, although it too hibernates on dry (or, strictly speaking, damp) land. It lays 200 or so single eggs in the water in early spring and pursues a mainly aquatic lifestyle until midsummer, when it comes out on to land and switches to a nocturnal insect-hunting lifestyle until hibernation time in autumn. Adult newts need to come to the surface to breathe, and this is when you're most likely to spot them. Newts are quite unlike frogs and toads, being elongated rather than squat, and possessing long tails. In spring male Smooth Newts grow a resplendent wavy 'crest' or ridge along their backs and tails, for showing off to the females.

The fish of the parkland lakes provide lunch to grebes, Cormorants, Grey Herons and, in St James's Park, pelicans. It can't be much fun to be a park fish with all of these voracious hunters on your tail. The ones that are spared most of this unwelcome attention are the large Mirror Carp, which grow too big for even a heron to tackle. The biggest fish drift around close to the surface in plain view of the birds and us, secure perhaps in the knowledge that they're big enough to choke a Cormorant. There are Common Carp in the lakes too – these are covered with neat and obvious scales, while Mirrors have a scattering of large, uneven and shiny scales here and there on their otherwise leathery skin. Both carps enjoy sunbathing – next time you're crossing St James's Park bridge on a warm summer day see if you can spot any of them drifting along below. Smaller fish that gather in shoals and show reddish fins and tails are likely to be Roach. The Perch is a very handsome predatory fish with big fins and a pattern of broad, vertical stripes – mature Perch are usually solitary but young ones form shoals. Even smaller fish are present too – sticklebacks and Gudgeons – but they are much more difficult to spot.

From as early as February, you'll start to notice insects on the wing in the parks. Butterflies like Commas and Red Admirals, which spend winter hibernating in their adult forms, will be active as soon as the air temperature hits around 14°C – given that central London is often a touch warmer than surrounding countryside, that means the first butterfly of the year could easily be seen in the parks. Queen Buff-tailed Bumblebees will also be out and about, zooming at high speed along the avenues and gardens in search of a sustaining nectar feed before looking for a suitable spot to build their new nests.

Later on in spring more butterflies appear, such as Small Whites, Holly Blues and Speckled Woods, and dragonflies and damselflies start to emerge from the lakes to begin their brief but exciting adult lifestyle of sex and violence (both dragons and damsels are voracious predators as well as enthusiastic breeders). You may notice mating damselflies flitting around in connected pairs, the male holding the female firmly behind her head with a pair of special claspers at the tip of his abdomen. The act is completed when the female loops her abdomen forwards under her body to collect the male's sperm, and the two form a wheel

Miniature wildernesses

The reed bed by the north-eastern shore of St James's Park lake is tiny, so it was quite a surprise to hear a Reed Warbler singing enthusiastically from it one April morning. I am accustomed to hearing that chugging, chirping, endless song from quiet reed-fringed lakes and rivers in remote wetland areas – it sounded quite otherworldly against a backdrop of typical London commuting noises. I dutifully notified the local bird recorder, who told me that other birdwatchers had reported the same bird. It didn't stay very long, presumably moving on in search of a bigger expanse of reeds and the opportunity to attract a female. However, its stay is a testament to the potential for creating real, 'wild' habitats in the city parks, and Reed Warblers do now breed in the reed beds in nearby Regent's Park.

Regent's Park also has two wildlife gardens – one a fenced-off area of wild scrubby grassland which has been left much to its own devices, the other a new carefully planned community wildlife garden which you can explore. As ever when trying to encourage biodiversity, the key is to start from the ground and work up, by establishing a diverse community of native plants – Honeysuckle, Primrose, Foxglove, Hazel and Dog Rose to name but a few. The plants bring the plant-eating insects like bugs and aphids, and they in turn bring the predatory insects, the birds and the frogs and toads. Seeding flower heads are left in place through the winter to provide food for birds and shelter for insects. Both wildlife gardens are great places to see London's more elusive birds – Coal Tits, Goldfinches, Jays and woodpeckers. The community garden also has wet and boggy areas – great for amphibians, damselflies and dragonflies.

Wherever native flowers are encouraged and a natural meadow-like environment develops, you will find butterflies – far more butterflies, in fact, than visit the colourful formal gardens with their rows of showy but non-native flowers. By night, they are replaced by moths, which are hunted by bats. The overall variety of species may not be as impressive as you'd find in natural meadows in the countryside proper, but the Royal Parks' wild corners are probably the best and most exciting places to see 'real wildlife' in the heart of the city.

shape. The most striking and attractive damselfly you're likely to see in the parks is the Banded Demoiselle, the male of which has a deep blue body and dark patches in all four wings.

By mid-summer, the wilder grassy areas of Kensington Gardens, Hyde Park and Regent's Park have butterflies including Large, Small and Essex Skippers, Gatekeepers and Meadow Browns, along with an assortment of moths including the striking Ruby Tiger. The rare Twin-spotted

Above: Male Banded Demoiselles displaying

Wainscot moth lives in lakeside reeds, while flying over the lakes there are Black-tailed Skimmer and Common Darter dragonflies. If you are extremely lucky you could see a Stag Beetle, a massive insect with (in the male) a fearsome pair of antler-shaped mouthparts – this species is something of a London specialist but is much more likely to be found in the suburbs. It's just one of more than 100 beetle species that have been found in the parks.

Many Londoners use the tube or bus to get to work when they could easily walk part of the journey – if that walk would take you through a Royal Park or two, consider throwing away your Travelcard, or perhaps just keeping it in your wallet a couple of days a week, and allowing a bit of extra time for your journey. If not, it's still worth visiting the parks when you can. Find excuses – a team-building office picnic, a lunchtime run, whatever suits you, and really get to know these priceless green spaces.

Joining up the chain

One Saturday in March 2005 when I was training for the London Marathon, I had the dilemma of needing to do a long training run but also needing to be at London Bridge by lunchtime for a pub crawl. I decided to run from my home in Bounds Green (N11) down to London Bridge in the morning, a distance of 16 miles by the route I chose. Wanting to see as much greenery as possible on the way, I planned a somewhat circuitous route that took me through Alexandra Palace Park, Highgate Wood, Hampstead Heath, Primrose Hill, Regent's Park, Hyde Park, Green Park, St James's Park and along the Thames for the home straight. I packed a change of clothes in a rucksack and set off with a handful of pages prised out of my old spiral-bound London A-Z so I didn't get lost.

It was a lovely day, and a lovely run. There were some fierce hills to contend with, especially coming up through Highgate Woods with its carpet of Wood Anemones. Running down the rough grassy slopes of the incomparably wonderful Hampstead Heath with the whole of the city spread out before me, I felt genuinely privileged to be a Londoner. A hovering Kestrel pulsed away high overhead, while noisy green Ring-necked Parakeets tore past at breakneck speed as I crossed the heath and headed down for Primrose Hill.

The ducks on the Serpentine and St James's Park lake were in splendid breeding plumage, the Coots were as ever knocking seven bells out of each other in arguments over who knows what, and throngs of tourists were going all mushy over the squirrels. The tall trees shaded the paths and gave some relief from the warm sunshine. I took a sneaky short-cut through Charing Cross station, crossed the river via the Golden Jubilee Bridge and headed east along the Thames path, glancing at the gulls that dipped and bobbed over the water and checking overhead for the Tate Modern Peregrines.

Arriving at the pub, I was exhilarated by my trans-London run, and impressed by how much of it had taken me through interesting wildlife-watching habitat, and how little time I'd spent pounding actual city streets – it was a real revelation. Never again would I feel quite so lost in a concrete jungle.

The Thames

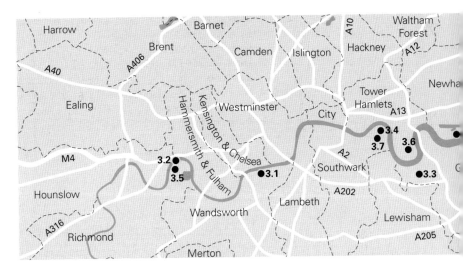

L ONDON'S GREAT river was once a key thoroughfare through the city. Now that most movement through the city is by road, rail or tube, the river is perhaps more significant as a barrier than as a route through the capital, with north and south connected by a selection of road-, rail- and foot-bridges and tunnels. Allegedly, crossing the Thames by road is completely prohibited by some mysterious law of physics if you happen to be travelling by cab late at night.

The Thames is England's longest river, and rises many miles from London, in Gloucestershire. Several towns and villages have been built around the upper Thames, including Oxford, Reading and Slough. As it heads seawards through the verdant Thames Valley, broadening all the while, its character and the wildlife it attracts change gradually, and it becomes tidal at Teddington Lock in south London. From here on in, the influence of seawater becomes increasingly important on the wildlife that uses the river. The wide, choppy Thames with its bridges, known and loved by many Londoners, is a world away from the peaceful freshwater stretches that wind along below the Chilterns.

It's easy to get intimately acquainted with London, and not just at ground level. Londoners are used to spending long segments of their day buried deep below the surface, waiting for the next train to Morden, Uxbridge or wherever. Above ground, the London Eye plus the many sky-scraping buildings in the City and Docklands lift us high into the London skies for a Peregrine's-eye view. The one place we cannot go, though, is into the river. Broad, deep and turbulent with strong currents and undertows, the Thames through central London is genuinely dangerous and if you overdo it on a boozy river cruise and jump in, you'll be very lucky to be pulled out again. It's a capricious channel of unknowable wilderness cutting right through our capital's heart.

While the closest we can get is to peer across the surface of the water from the deck of a boat, the Thames is not so hostile to all living things. Some of them you'll notice from the boat. Gulls float on the surface and scavenge around the boats. The gulls that breed along the lower reaches of the Thames are Lesser Black-backed and Herring Gulls – two big, mean-looking species which could almost be identical twins apart from

their wing and leg colours (dark grey/yellow in the former, light grey/pink in the latter). It's not known how many pairs there are as their nest sites are out of view, high up on flat rooftops.

In winter, more gulls arrive in central London to forage the Thames for discarded chips and other organic matter, and some young gulls spend their summers here too – the larger species are not ready to breed until they are three or four years old. On the railway bridge across the river just outside Victoria station, they line up in a convenient row each winter morning, exhibiting their key identification points – dainty Black-headed Gulls yet to develop their dark head plumage (silvery wings, red legs), gentle-faced Common Gulls (smoky grey wings, greenish legs), and now and then something different, perhaps a Yellow-legged Gull (mid-grey wings, and – you've guessed it! – yellow legs) or a Mediterranean Gull (the adults have distinctive pure white wing-tips), both of which are rare but regular visitors to central London.

Above: *Adult summer Mediterranean Gull*

Fishes of the Thames

The presence of Cormorants is as clear an indication as you could ask for that the Thames has a healthy fish population, for these birds eat little else. If you are neither a Cormorant nor a fisherman, you're unlikely to see any Thames fish, but over the years an impressive variety of species have been hoicked out of the London section of the river. They include freshwater and marine species, and among them are many familiar names such as Salmon, Rainbow Trout, two species of sticklebacks, Dace, Flounder, Minnow, Perch, Pike and Tench, as well as some more exotic creatures such as Short-snouted Seahorses and the venomous Greater Weever. Commercial fishermen working further downriver towards the mouth of the Thames haul in sizeable catches of Sprats as well as Mackerel, Dover Sole and Eels. The tidal creeks shelter masses of fish fry before they grow large enough to venture into the river proper.

Anglers in central London are more likely to be in pursuit of Roach, Bream and the like, although oddities turn up from time to time as well, some of them as a result of ill-advised liberations of pet fish. In 2009 an angler spotted an unfamiliar dead fish on the bank, which was later identified as a Walking Catfish *Clarias batrachus*. This fish, with its rudimentary lungs and weight-bearing pectoral fins, can exit the water and stroll about on land for short spells – an interesting beast indeed, but potentially bad news for the river's native fish as a potential competitor and carrier of disease.

Another alarming discovery was the Red-bellied Piranha which landed with a thud on the deck of a Thames boat in 2004 – piranhas are not known to fly in their native lands so presumably this one was dropped by a passing gull. The species cannot endure the low temperatures of the water in winter so we can at least be assured that the London Thames won't be adding 'piranha-infested' to its already long list of good reasons why you shouldn't swim in it.

The Thames fishes are just part of a rich and diverse ecosystem within the river. Molluscs like the unfortunately named Depressed River Mussel, various sea-snails, assorted crabs and other crustaceans (including the troublesome introduced Chinese Mitten Crab), insect larvae and aquatic plants are all there too, forging a living in the water or on the riverbed and sustaining each other. Yet the only visible sign you may ever see of this particular web of life is the occasional flash of squirming scales as a fish vanishes down a hungry Cormorant's gullet.

Above: Cormorant swallowing a Common Carp

The Thames through the city is not a great place for ducks – why would a duck bother with the rough water and constant passing boat traffic when it could make a short flight to one of the parks and live on an undisturbed lake with regular handouts of food? However, you will sometimes see small groups of Mallards on the Thames, usually keeping close to the shore and dabbling away at the unpromising-looking water.

Another common water bird you'll see on and around the river in central London is the Cormorant. This large, mostly black bird is inconspicuous when actually swimming as it floats so low in the water that it can appear to be just a protruding, reptilian head and neck – you're more likely to notice it in flight. Then, it looks a bit like a goose at first glance – long at the front end, short at the back, a pair of hard-working wings keeping its cigar-shaped body aloft. You might also notice Cormorants sitting on low floating structures in the water, standing very still and upright and often with wings spread wide, giving them the appearance of bizarre statues. They do this to dry off their plumage after a dip in the water – Cormorants are apparently not as waterproof as other swimming birds.

A boat trip to Greenwich

You can board an open sight-seeing boat to Greenwich from Westminster Pier – the trip will take an hour and will give you a great up-close-and-personal Thames experience, as well as a unique perspective on London. The guides on board will point out interesting sights – the commentary is often highly amusing.

As well as admiring the bridges and shoreline buildings, keep a lookout for wildlife. The bridge supports have many ledges and platforms on which Lesser Black-backed and Herring Gulls often stand. The boat will pass Cormorants close to eye-level as they swim and dive after fish.

As you pass Blackfriars Bridge, you might notice that carved on the pillars are representations of birds – freshwater birds on the upstream side and seabirds on the downstream side. Just beyond here you'll pass the Tate Modern on the south side of the river – scan the chimney for the Peregrines that often perch there.

There are two nature reserves close to Rotherhithe, attracting a variety of birds which may also be seen along the Thames here – they include Ringed Plovers and Great Crested Grebes. As you continue towards the sea, the chances of seeing sea- and shorebirds increase, especially in migration season – perhaps a passing Oystercatcher or, if you are very lucky, a Guillemot. A Ring-billed Gull from North America has since 1996 regularly spent the winter period (a long winter, from August until March!) on the Thames foreshore close to where you'll leave the boat, and other unusual gulls such as Glaucous, Iceland and Little turn up from time to time.

Greenwich Park is well worth a visit, if you're hungry for more birdwatching, with a good selection of typical parkland birds. The famous and fascinating Observatory is here too, and there are a few Red and Fallow Deer in the 'Wilderness'. The park also has a wildlife garden. There are plenty of other interesting things to do in the area before it's time to catch the boat back into town.

Heading eastwards away from the City, the Thames slowly broadens, and the chances of finding wading birds pottering about on the foreshore or seeing seabirds over the water increase. By the time you get as far as East India Docks, your chances of seeing a more interesting variety of birds have increased massively, especially during the spring and autumn migration period. The East India Dock Basin nature reserve, just past the Isle of Dogs, has breeding Common Terns on its tidal lagoon, as well as visiting Redshanks and Common Sandpipers. The buildings and rough ground along this stretch of the Thames are good for Black Redstarts in winter.

Opposite the Millennium Dome, the River Lee (or Lea – no-one seems to be able to decide) forks off from the Thames, winding its way north past a string of industrial parks and gas works. In due course its surroundings become more pleasant, and in fact the Lee Valley is one of the best areas in London for wildlife, with numerous reservoirs and wetland nature reserves along its course all the way to Hertfordshire and beyond. We look in detail at the Lee Valley in Chapter 6.

As you follow the river east out of central London, there are a few small nature reserves close to the river which are worth visiting. At Surrey Docks, the Trust for Urban Ecology manages two tiny reserves on the Rotherhithe peninsula. Lavender Pond Nature Park, created in 1981, covers just over 2 acres at the northern tip of the peninsula. It has an area of open water, fringed by reeds and alder trees. The other is Stave Hill Ecology Park, a little bigger and set further back from the river. This reserve has mainly deciduous woodland (including alder, birch and willow), scrub, grassland and a little wetland. These two unassuming nature reserves are batting well above their league in terms of the rare birds that birdwatchers have found over the years, with delights such as American Wigeon and Aquatic Warbler on the record books from before the redevelopment of the docks. More recently, a Firecrest was seen in the area in late 2008 and early 2009. The parks attract the usual variety of common breeding species.

The many pockets of greenery tucked between or behind riverside buildings, while not managed specifically for wildlife, can nevertheless be good places to look for common songbirds. The chances of finding a not-so-common migrant songbird go up the further east you head. Birdwatchers have found Firecrest and Chiffchaff lurking in shrubbery behind the Tate Modern, and various warblers around Mudchute Farm on the Isle of Dogs.

All the way along this stretch, there are small town parks not far inland from the river to both north and south, though they are not really worth a special trip for the limited wildlife they hold. Your best bet is to stay on the Thames Path and keep watching the river where you can (the path deviates from the river at some points, for example around Deptford). On the south shore by the Millennium Dome are the Meridian Gardens, while on the north shore by the Thames Barrier is the futuristic Thames Barrier Park. The park is an interesting place to visit with its strangely sculpted shrubs and impressive fountains, it is home to typical town-park wildlife. Opportunities to cross the river have been dwindling away since you left central London – the Woolwich Foot Tunnel is the last of them.

There is precious little interesting greenery immediately adjacent to the river for some distance beyond the barrier, but the river itself attracts ever more birdlife. At Crossness in Thamesmead on the south shore, a muddy foreshore attracts flocks of ducks and wading birds in winter, with Shelduck, Teal, Brent Goose, Dunlin, Redshank, Ringed Plover and several other species all possible. There is a new nature reserve here. A little further downriver on the north shore, the river frontage by the RSPB's Rainham Marshes reserve has even more birdwatching potential, though by now we are very much in the outer reaches of London.

Wrecked!

The morning after the Great Storm of October 1987, transport services were severely affected and many of us were grateful for the excuse to take the day off work or school and stay in bed. London-based birdwatchers, however, were up early and heading for the Thames or their local reservoirs by any means possible, knowing that the storm could have brought exciting new arrivals in from the sea.

Migrating seabirds will take refuge close to the shore when things get rough at sea, and when things get very rough, they can be pushed up major rivers like the Thames and carried well inland. When a seabird shows up far from the sea, it's described as having been 'wrecked'. The morning after the storm, there were confused Sabine's Gulls, Leach's Storm-petrels and Grey Phalaropes all across London, along with a few skuas, and the birdwatchers were having a field day ticking off these maritime wanderers.

Early on in the year before, there was an influx of some 40 Common Guillemots seen along the central London Thames with birds reaching as far upriver as Chelsea Reach. These auks, which look like mini-penguins and are great swimmers but less proficient flyers, otherwise appear singly in the Thames now and then but not on purpose. Other seabirds like Fulmar, Gannet and Manx Shearwater also appear along the Thames from time to time. The Shag, a smaller relative of the Cormorant, is slightly more common with a few records each year, both along the river and on the larger reservoirs.

We haven't seen a storm since to rival 1987 and hopefully we never will, but heavy weather does bring its compensations, especially for London birdwatchers.

Below: Leach's Storm-petrel by Tower Bridge

Before the construction of the Thames Barrier (completed in 1982), flooding was a serious risk to London, especially when stormy weather in the North Sea coincided with high spring tides. Now, when such conditions are imminent, the barrier is closed, its four gates holding back excess water until the threat has passed. Beyond the barrier, things get more exciting wildlife-wise, as undeveloped stretches of shoreline appear more frequently, and the river itself becomes ever wider and more attractive to birds. Seabirds you could see include Kittiwakes (a kind of particularly elegant sea-going gull), auks and terns.

Terns are gulls' prettier, smaller, more socially acceptable cousins, with graceful flight and dainty habits. The ones you're most likely to see on the Thames are Common Terns, which are silvery above, snow-white below, have a neat black cap and a black-tipped red bill. They have long, forked tails, and fly with graceful, elastic beats of their long, pointed wings – their elegance and daintiness is slightly spoiled by their discordant, screaming voices. They plunge dive to catch small fish from close to the water's surface, hanging in the air like hawks before dropping fast for a quick splash into the water. Although their feet are webbed, you seldom see them swim. Arctic, Black and Sandwich Terns are also sometimes seen on the lower Thames, more frequently the closer you get to the sea.

The Thames is generally better for mammals further upstream, where the margins become more vegetated and hospitable and Otters, Water Voles and Water Shrews may all occur. However, the closer you get to the sea, the better your chances of spotting a marine mammal. Both of our resident species of seals – the Grey and the Common – visit the outer Thames from time to time, and so do Harbour Porpoises. The latter superficially resemble mini-dolphins but are blunt-headed, podgier and more introverted in character – you're more likely to see one dozing on the surface with a fin poking in the air than showing off by performing any kind of acrobatics. Although both seals and porpoises have on occasion made it many miles upriver into central London, you're far more likely to see them on the lower reaches of the Thames as it nears the sea.

Above: *Grey Seal by the Thames Barrier*

The Thames Whale

In January 2006, a remarkable string of events began on Thursday 19th, when the Thames Barrier control team informed the British Divers Marine Life Rescue that a whale had come through the barrier and was headed upriver.

Through the morning on Friday 20th, more and more Londoners reported seeing the whale in the Thames. When footage of the animal appeared on TV, the collective imagination of London was captured, and thousands of workers based near the river headed out to see it as it travelled under Waterloo Bridge and on towards Battersea.

The BDMLR, who had been monitoring the animal since its discovery, had identified it as a Northern Bottlenose Whale, and had also observed signs of injury and worrying behaviour from the animal (of course, swimming up a river is in itself worrying behaviour from a whale). The rescuers feared the whale was most unlikely to manage to make its own way out of the river.

On Saturday, the banks and bridges were thronged with tourists, many of whom had made a special journey to see the animal which the tabloids had now nicknamed, appropriately and predictably enough,

'Wally'. The whale was found near Albert Bridge at 9.25am, looking much weakened, and it was decided that a rescue operation must be mounted – the whale would be deliberately stranded on a sandbank, then lifted onto a barge, transported back down the river and released at sea.

The crowds, now filled with anxiety rather than excitement, watched as the whale was captured, examined and finally carefully lifted onto the barge, which then set off downriver, reaching the barrier by 5pm and followed every step of the way by the TV cameras. Sadly, the whale suffered a series of convulsions and died on board the barge before release could be attempted. A post-mortem showed it to be a young female, with a number of serious injuries which could have been caused by collisions with boats or by scraping herself on the river bed.

Sadly, few tales of whale strandings have happy endings, and the moment 'Wally' turned upriver she probably sealed her own fate. However, in her short time in the Thames she captivated thousands of Londoners, and hopefully this has highlighted the plight of whales generally, as worldwide they struggle to contend with our increasingly polluted, noisy and dangerous seas.

The Thames narrows a little at the Port of Tilbury, but beyond here it is virtually open sea now, and soon widens into the huge and complex estuary that divides Kent and Essex. The Isle of Sheppey is separated from mainland Kent by a narrow channel called the Swale, while just west of here the Medway, a major Kent river, branches

off from the Thames via a large estuarine basin with numerous islands. To the north, Benfleet Creek and Vange Creek create a complex of wetland on either side of Canvey Island.

Although this is still a built-up area, there remain many wonderful wildlife-watching places along the shorelines of both counties around the mouth of the Thames. If you visit them, it will give you some idea of what things might have been like further upriver before heavy-duty industrialization came along. The estuary complex as a whole attracts hundreds of thousands of wintering wading birds and wildfowl, including internationally important numbers of 12 species, all feeding on the rich shallow waters and foreshore. These in turn attract birds of prey. The Isle of Sheppey (which includes RSPB's Elmley Marshes reserve) is one of the best places in the whole of Britain to see birds of prey – you could easily see Marsh and Hen Harriers, Common and Rough-legged Buzzards, Peregrine, Merlin, Kestrel, Sparrowhawk, Short-eared Owl and Barn Owl all on a single winter's day here.

Even now, despite this astonishing richness of wildlife, developmental pressure on the land is

Pollution

City rivers are notorious for becoming polluted. Flowing through such fast-growing concentrations of people and industry, it is no surprise that the Thames's history should include long spells of terrible water quality with its associated damaging effects upon wildlife.

As the city grew, the open drains that flowed into the river saw more and more action, and the river became filthier and more unpleasant with each passing year. By the mid 1800s, the Thames had another name – the 'Great Stink'. Parliament was abandoned because politicians could not stomach the smell, and people were dying of cholera from drinking river-water not taken from sufficiently far upstream. The construction of embankments to speed the river's flow, and underground sewage systems and filtration plants to keep the water cleaner, did much to improve the situation. However, the city continued to grow and the improvements of the 1800s soon proved to be insufficient – by the 1950s Londoners once again had a rancid-smelling river with virtually nothing alive in it at all.

Another round of intensive improvements to the sewage system began in 1964 and was completed in 1974. In the years that have followed, fish, birds and other river life has returned with a vengeance and, happily, remain to this day.

Battling pollution, however, is a fight that will never be over. Even now, when severe storms hit the city, the rainwater runoff is more than the drains can cope with and sewage is released into the Thames. This happened in August 2004 and tens of thousands of fish died as a result. Ambitious new plans for managing London's waste and keeping the river clean, including the construction of a 22-mile sewage tunnel under the river, are currently underway.

It's very difficult to keep such a big river, flowing through a heavily built-up area, clean and wildlife-friendly, but great strides have been made in the right direction. Unfortunately, unenlightened people who think the Thames is still the open sewer of centuries past continue carelessly to flush dangerous things down drains and throw rubbish into the water, and even a little piece of debris is a potential hazard to wildlife. It's your river, so look after it and do what you can to keep it healthy and junk-free.

intense. With London's existing airports desperately busy, the search has long been going on for a suitable place to build a new airport to serve the city, and one of the areas in the frame was Cliffe on the Isle of Grain in north Kent. The RSPB, which had only just acquired the Cliffe Marshes to protect and develop their amazing wildlife potential, had a huge battle on its hands to protect the land from the developers – a battle which was eventually won... for now. In autumn 2009 the Mayor of London was still urging politicians to 'look seriously' at the option of a Thames Estuary airport and dismissing the concerns of the RSPB and other conservation groups.

Heading west and following the river upstream from central London, you'll pass myriad bridges and lots of very built-up riverfront around the twistiest section of river, until you reach a bit of green relief in the form of Battersea Park on the south shore, just beyond the imposing power station (look out for Peregrines overhead). Battersea Park comes right up to the waterline, and also contains a decent-sized lake with many islands, so it is a good spot for some low-key urban wildlife-watching. Grey Herons breed here, as do Great Spotted Woodpeckers and (possibly) Tawny Owls among the commoner parkland species. A few rarities have been found, including Pied Flycatcher, Hobby (which is unusual in central London but more common in the suburbs) and (on the river shore) Rock Pipit. Assorted bats have been seen here, while the lake has the usual range

of species, including visiting Cormorants and breeding Great Crested Grebes. The park has some impressive specimen trees, but unfortunately at ground level it is mostly uninspiring close-cropped 'amenity grassland'.

The Thames is becoming appreciably narrower by this point, and pockets of greenery along the banks are getting more numerous. On the south shore is the small Wandsworth Park, with the larger Hurlingham Park directly opposite – the latter has a small pond. Beyond Putney Bridge, Bishops Gardens straggles along the north shore, while on the south side is the wonderful London Wetland Centre (which we cover in detail in Chapter 4). As you follow the river north then loop back around south, you'll see the first island – a longish vegetated strip known as Chiswick Eyot, which provides shelter for wildfowl, hosts a selection of rare water-snails and has recently been designated a Local Nature Reserve.

A little further around the loop on the southern shore is the Leg of Mutton nature reserve, centred on the vaguely mutton-leg-shaped Lonsdale Road Reservoir, which is separated from the river by a narrow, wooded strip of land. The variety of wildlife you could see on and around the reservoir is testament to how far behind you've left the city – four species of bats and four amphibians (including the rare Great Crested Newt) hunt over and in the reservoir respectively, while Pochards are among the birds breeding on the lake. Winter wildfowl is more varied, with Shoveler and Gadwall joining the commoner

Beyond London

You have probably walked along part of the Thames Path – perhaps on a visit to the London Eye or the Tate Modern. You may not realise that this path is actually 184 miles long and follows the course of the Thames from its source in the Cotswolds down to the Thames Barrier – if you have a spare two weeks and are feeling energetic you could walk the whole way. It is one of 15 National Trails – long-distance walking paths that explore iconic routes around England. At various points, you'll be crossing over to the opposite side of the river (and in some places you can choose between both).

From Teddington Lock, the Thames ceases to be tidal, completing a radical change in character from the river known and loved by all who spend time in central London. Its course is more complex and meandering, with numerous islands, extra channels and tributaries.

The Thames is a major feature of the beautiful town of Windsor, but first you must negotiate the not-quite-so-beautiful town of Staines, passing under the M25 between these towns. Things become progressively more rural beyond Windsor, as you make your way to Reading. Beyond Reading, the river passes through or close to several towns and villages like Dorchester, Tilehurst and Henley-on-Thames. Typical river wildlife should be easy to see, with swans and ducks cruising along the water and Kingfishers zipping past, while (in summer) warblers sing from the riverside reeds and willows. Water Voles and Water Shrews may be seen with patience and luck, while those endowed with superhuman patience and who are especially lucky could come eye to eye with a Thames Otter.

The next town along is the pretty market town of Abingdon. The river is still substantial enough to be navigable by boat, and there is a string of locks for them to use, as well as attractive arched footbridges for walkers. The beautiful Thames and its complexity of tributaries is busy with pleasure-boats between Abingdon and Oxford – the famous and pretty Iffley Lock is also in between these two towns. The last electric locks are found just beyond Oxford – beyond here they are operated manually. Many have lovely lock-keepers' cottages attached.

The dwindling Thames passes through or skirts past numerous villages and by now is little more than a stream, crossed by several simple plank footbridges as it wends through water-meadows. Its fringes are reedy and its waters weedy, with little sign of the impressive watercourse it will become. The source of the Thames, a mile north of the village of Kemble, is a remote spot marked with a stone monument. It is a fitting spot to end a pilgrimage, but by here the water itself has often dried out completely.

species. The rare Lesser Spotted Woodpecker may hang on in the wooded areas here.

Playing fields and small gardens surround the river much of the way from here to the next significant areas of greenery bordering the Thames, which are the Royal Botanic Gardens at Kew to the south and Syon Park to the north. The Grand Union Canal/River Brent branches off here, heading north and separating at Brentford, where the canal goes on to connect London with Birmingham and Leicester. By now, the river is quiet, and slow enough for shyer riverside breeding birds like Kingfisher and Moorhen to occur. There are more wooded islands on the way, offering nesting places for herons and wildfowl (with Canada Goose probably the most common species).

The Thames now winds south through leafy Richmond and Twickenham, with playing fields and gardens bordering its banks on both sides. Various yacht and rowing clubs attest to the prosperity of this area. You can reach one of the Thames's most famous islands – Eel Pie Island – via a footbridge. The island has a fair amount of wildlife-friendly greenery as well as an eclectic range of architectural styles to puzzle over.

The complex lock at Teddington marks the point where the Thames escapes the tidal influence and, pretty much, where it enters Greater London. By this point the water in the Thames has already completed three-quarters of its journey to the open sea. Every Londoner who thinks they know the Thames should visit it further upriver once in a while, or maybe even track it to its source.

Parks of the South-west

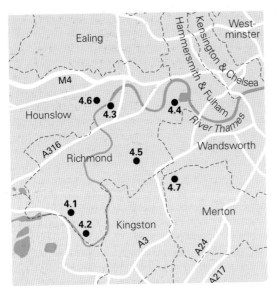

4.1 Bushy Park
4.2 Hampton Court Park
4.3 Kew Gardens
4.4 London Wetland Centre
4.5 Richmond Park
4.6 Syon Park
4.7 Wimbledon Common

BEYOND THE heart of central London, the south-west has more and larger blobs of green on the map than the other three corners of Greater London. The wildlife enthusiast based in this part of London is fortunate indeed, with many interesting wildlife-rich green spaces to explore and a wealth of plants and animals to enjoy. Luckily for the rest of us, all of these places are easy to reach by tube and bus.

In Richmond Park, the chaos of central London feels a very long way away. With rolling grassy meadows, giant old trees, herds of grazing deer and ducks drifting across misty, tranquil lakes, the sense of 'proper countryside' is palpable. The 2,500-acre Richmond Park is the wildest of the Royal Parks, and perhaps the most exciting place to visit in the prosperous south-western suburbs of London. The gates are locked at night, but between 7am and dusk it's all yours and, although it's popular with walkers, runners, picnickers and the like, it never feels as crowded as the central London Parks and often you'll feel like you have the place to yourself. Just as exciting as Richmond

Park but totally different in character is the fabulous Wildfowl and Wetlands Trust reserve at Barn Elms, now popularly known as the London Wetland Centre. With Bushy Park, Hampton Court, Kew, Syon Park and Wimbledon Common all adding to the mix, here you have a great chance of seeing wildlife that is otherwise rare or non-existent in London.

Although Bushy Park adjoins Hampton Court, it actually has more in common with Richmond Park in many ways. For example, both are Royal Parks, and both have deer. Richmond and Bushy Park's famous deer are a mixture of Reds and Fallows – about 300 of the former (Britain's largest deer) and 350 of the latter (smaller but still quite a hefty deer) in Richmond, about half that in Bushy. In summer they are very easy to tell apart – the Fallows are light tawny-brown with white spots, the Reds richer and darker with no spots. Beware the odd very dark Fallow though. Another way to tell them apart is by the males' antlers. The main part of a Fallow's antler is wide and flattened, known as 'palmate' (think of the palm of your hand) while the

Reds' are more conventionally antler-shaped. If you want to annoy/impress your friends, you could also drop into conversation that the male Reds are called stags but the male Fallows are bucks, while female Reds are hinds and female Fallows are does.

Both species drop their antlers once a year (in late winter or spring) and grow new ones. The new antlers are covered in soft, velvety skin, which dries up and peels off once the antler is fully grown and has hardened – you may see stags/bucks walking about with long strands of partly detached skin dangling from their antlers, or rubbing their heads against trees to try to remove this skin. By autumn, the antlers are bare, bony and ready to be brandished at other deer in the rutting season. The hinds and does have their babies in early summer, and you should see plenty of baby deer around by

Rutting season

Britain doesn't have very much in the way of potentially dangerous wildlife, not since our ancestors decided in their wisdom to hunt our wolves and bears to extinction. However, adult Red Deer stags are formidable beasts and, while they are unlikely to attack human beings, we can see just how fearsome they can be when they do battle among themselves during the rut.

Deer are polygamous maters. The females don't need a male's help caring for their babies, so are quite happy to share the most physically impressive boys between them when it's mating time (from September into October). Therefore, the 'best' stags may gather a harem of 20 or more hinds, while their weedier brothers go without. Stags compete to keep hold of their existing entourage of hinds, impress any new ones and warn off other males by roaring, posturing and, if things really get heated, engaging in antler-clashing battles. In between these shows of machismo, each stag mates with all of his hinds as much as he can. It's a punishing regime –

by the time it's over the average stag has lost some 14 per cent of his bodyweight. Once the rut finishes, hostilities are suspended for another year and the deer separate into same-sex groups – the females to gestate and bear their young, the males to get their breath back.

The smaller Fallow deer rut a little later than the Reds, but with as much racket and gusto as their larger relatives. Like the Reds, they must be treated with particular respect at this time – the combination of bulk, full-grown antlers and a bloodstream loaded with testosterone makes for as dangerous a British wild animal as you could want

Above: *Rutting Red Deer stags*

mid-summer. Unsurprisingly, the offspring of the two species have different names like their parents – the baby Reds are calves, the baby Fallows are fawns.

Although dogs are allowed in all of the Royal parks, it's especially important in Richmond and Bushy Parks that you keep them under close control. A dog-deer confrontation could end very badly for both parties.

The deer are no longer hunted in these parks, though in the absence of natural predators an annual cull weeds out the sickly and keeps numbers at a sustainable level for the amount of deer-fodder naturally available. As it is, the parkland vegetation is very much shaped by the deer population. Leaves and twigs on mature trees are universally munched away to a height of 1.5 metres (the 'browse line'), while all newly planted trees must be fenced off or they would be consumed in their entirety by the hungry deer. Though they're a bit of a scourge for the trees, the deer do help to keep the park's flower-rich acid grassland in a healthy state.

Richmond and Bushy Park have their share of other mammals too, including Rabbits, Foxes, several bats and various small rodents and insectivores. If you see a little furry critter and don't know what it is, pay attention to its eyes, ears and snout. Big eyes + big ears + smoothly tapered pointy snout = mouse; smallish eyes + smallish ears + short blunt snout = vole; tiny eyes + small ears + long, narrow 'pinched off' snout = shrew. The long grass provides ideal hunting ground for shrews – it is they who are responsible for the outbursts of shrill, frantic squeaking that you may hear close to your feet as you walk. Both Common and Pygmy Shrews may be seen if you're very fortunate – they normally stay hidden from view. If you do get a good view of one, the best way to tell them apart is to look at the tail length relative to body length (less than half in the Common, more than half in the Pygmy).

Shrews live fast-paced lifestyles, needing to scoff down insects and other small prey almost constantly to keep their tiny hearts beating at nearly 1,000 times a minute. As such, they are, much of the time, more or less oblivious to anything other than the next meal. If you hear them squeaking away, you might get to see them zooming about through the long grass if you sit down quietly and watch. They tend to shuttle along preferred runways, and will dash right across your hand if you happen to accidentally place it in their path.

Grey Squirrels are, as ever, ubiquitous and easy to see in Richmond and Bushy Parks. Much more retiring are the parks' Hedgehogs, though if you visit late on a summer evening you may find one – listen for snuffling and rustling noises from areas of undergrowth.

Richmond Park's speciality is bats, with nine species recorded including rarer ones like Nathusius's Pipistrelle, Serotine and Brown Long-eared Bat – the latter one of the easiest bats to identify with its huge, petal-shaped ears, almost as long as its body. The Pen Ponds is a good place to base yourself for some bat-watching – scanning along lines of mature trees can be good too. Bushy Park boasts a small population of Water Voles around the Longford River. These are large voles, easily told from Brown Rats if you get a decent view by their blunt noses, small eyes and ears and shortish tails. They're also shy – visit early or late in the day and keep quiet to give yourself the best chance.

These wild parks are excellent for birds. Richmond has 63 breeding species, with many more on the list as casual visitors. If you want to get the most out of a birdwatching trip to the park

Ratty revived

It's the animal behind one of the most beloved children's fiction characters ever, but how many children today have seen a Water Vole? Not so many, given that the species has declined by 95 per cent since *Wind in the Willows* was written in 1908. What's more, many supposed sightings of this swimming rodent turn out actually to be Brown Rats, with all their unsavoury connotations. It doesn't help that Water Voles used to be known as Water Rats, and that Brown Rats are adept and enthusiastic swimmers. You'll know the real thing when you see it though, whether you find one sitting munching bankside vegetation, or hear the distinctive 'plop' of vole hitting water and spot the culprit swimming briskly away– that blunt little face is quite unlike a rat's pointy muzzle.

Strange but true – London is one of the best places to catch up with a Water Vole. The species has been hit hard throughout the UK by a number of environmental changes. One of the most profound has been the relatively recent addition to our fauna of a new and fearsome predator, which specialises in just the kind of watery habitats that the voles require. American Minks, escapees from fur farms, have taken rather well to life this side of the pond, and have chomped their way through a distressingly large proportion of our Water Vole population. They apparently have taken advantage of our depleted Otter numbers and moved into vacant Otter niches on river systems across Britain.

Now that Otters are making a recovery, the minks seem to be on the decline – good news for Water Voles. River pollution and bankside development have also played their part in the vole decline, but reintroduction projects are helping the voles to recover their numbers. The London Wetland Centre is one place where reintroduced Water Voles are doing very well, and if you are or have a child who's yet to meet Ratty, this would be the perfect place to find him.

Above: *Water Vole*

you will definitely need binoculars – though many of the birds here are just as approachable as those in the central London parks, others are not and you'll need the 'bins' for a proper look.

One of the star birds of Richmond and Bushy Parks is the Skylark, which nests on the ground in long grass. There's nothing like watching someone work hard while you're relaxing, and many people enjoying a parkland picnic will be serenaded by a Skylark, fluttering furiously as it sings and eventually climbing so high that it disappears into a clear blue sky. Because of these and other ground-nesting birds, it's best to keep to the paths and keep dogs on the lead, especially during the

Lean green squawking machines

One of the first things Londoners used to say to me when they found out I'm interested in wildlife was: 'Oh, my friends think I'm mad but I'm sure I saw a green parrot-thing flying over my street the other day.' or some variation on that theme. It seems now that most of us are well aware that the 'green parrot-things' really exist and accusations of insanity are no longer made, but people are still understandably curious as to where these glamorous birds came from and what they are doing here.

These long-tailed, long-winged, squawkers are Ring-necked Parakeets, and they originally came from the Indian subcontinent. Like many other parrot species, they have long been popular pets and that is where our wild ones come from – cage and aviary escapees. Though we think of parrots as tropical birds, the Ring-necks' extensive native range includes the Himalayan foothills so they are quite able to cope with our winter temperatures. They are adaptable feeders, demolishing tree buds in spring and devouring wild fruits and seeds in autumn and winter – they also visit bird tables. For nest sites they use old woodpecker holes in trees, vigorously and successfully fending off competition for these scarce resources.

Rumours abound that the first parakeets escaped from the film set of the African Queen in Shepperton in 1951, or that Jimi Hendrix let some loose because he thought the UK's bird fauna needed a splash of green. It seems more likely to me that the main source of birds was carelessly secured garden aviaries – and this long-lived and adaptable species just happens to manage very well in the UK, unlike budgies, canaries and other popular cage-birds. The late, great jazz trumpeter and birdwatcher Humphrey Lyttelton regularly observed a family party of RNPs in his Surrey garden from November 1974 – traced from a pair that escaped from a Mill Hill aviary earlier that year and promptly nested locally, so these individuals at least wasted no time in setting about populating the local area.

While the south-west London parks have been a stronghold for these raucous and eye-catching birds for some years, they are spreading fast. They are now found right across London, even in the central parks, linking the south-west birds with another long-established population in the Hither Green area of south-east London. From here they are forging out into Kent, where there is another isolated (but not for long, at this rate) population on Thanet.

While many of us have welcomed this flamboyant addition to our birdlife, there are concerns that the Ring-necked Parakeet may spell trouble for some of our native birds such as Nuthatches, Starlings and Stock Doves, all of which also nest in holes. A Belgian study has recently found that the parakeets affected Nuthatch numbers. There is no strong evidence yet that Ring-necked Parakeets have had an impact on other species here in the UK, but this will be a growing area of research in the near future. Watching the vast flocks flying into their communal roosts on winter evenings, it's difficult to imagine what, if anything, can or should be done about them.

Above: *Ring-necked Parakeets at Syon House*

nesting season. Warning signs are put up by park staff next to known nesting sites – a measure which has helped Richmond Park's Skylark population grow to 20 pairs, from just two or three in 1992.

The Pen Ponds and the little ponds in the Isabella plantation are home to various water birds, including the outlandishly pretty Mandarin Duck. This species is native to China, where in fact it is declining, and escapees from wildfowl collections have established sizeable feral populations in parts of southern England. There are feral Red-crested Pochards here too, the males sporting puffy, bouffant orange hairdos. You'll also see other waterfowl – Canada and Greylag Geese, Mallards, Coots, Moorhens, Great Crested and Little Grebes. In winter, Pochards and Tufted Ducks become more numerous, and rarer (at least for London) ducks may arrive. Migrating waders drop in occasionally. In spring, Sand Martins are the first insect-catchers to appear, hoovering up the first flies to emerge from the water. They are brown with white chins and bellies. They are soon joined by Swallows (long-tailed, blue-back with orange chins and white bellies) and House Martins (black above, white below, white rumps). In May the unrelated but similar-looking Swifts arrive – bigger, faster and blacker than the other three.

Spring migration time can be exciting, with warblers arriving, some of them staying on to breed including Common Whitethroats and Reed Warblers. Wheatears and Whinchats stop off to forage the open grass and scrubby areas respectively, and migrating or wandering birds of prey drift overhead. Common Buzzards and Red Kites are seen pretty much every year, and Honey Buzzard, Osprey and Marsh Harrier have also been seen. Still, fine days in April are best for raptor-searching. Sparrowhawks and Kestrels may be seen at any time, with Hobbies often overhead through the summer.

If you're trying to learn your bird calls, Richmond Park is a good place to do it with a wide but not overwhelming variety of species and not too many distracting human noises in the background. Easy ones to learn include the full-throated 'yaffling' laughter of the Green Woodpecker, the abrupt and agitated '*kick*' of the Great Spotted Woodpecker, the pleasant yelping '*jack*' of the Jackdaw and the ubiquitous screeching of the Ring-necked Parakeet. More challenging are the pleasant warbles of Robin, Wren, Dunnock and Blackcap, and the near-identical '*tack*', '*chack*' and '*seeee*' alarm calls given by all sorts of small birds when something they think might be dangerous is around, whether it's a hunting Sparrowhawk, a sleepy Tawny Owl or a keen wildlife-watcher like you.

The open, tree-scattered habitat in Bushy and Richmond Parks is attractive to Little Owls, which relish the variety of insects that thrive in this environment. They are not strictly nocturnal so look out for them in the daytime – little squat Starling-sized birds that fly with a bouncing flight. When they land they tend to bob their heads furiously while glaring at you with piercing yellow eyes under a pair of mad-professor white brows. Little Owl is an introduced species too, unknown on these shores until the 19th century, but its impact on our native wildlife has apparently been barely noticeable – perhaps because it originates from nearby continental Europe and is used to co-existing with much the same species.

The trees hold all three species of woodpeckers, the Lesser Spotted being the new addition that you won't find in central London. This is a sparrow-sized bird, much quieter and more discreet than the Great Spotted and Green Woodpeckers. The best time to look for it is in early spring, when its explorations of treetop twigs are unobscured by leaves. Stock Doves – delicate cousins of the more hulking Woodpigeon – nest in tree holes and forage the deer-cropped grass. Cuckoos, those arch nest-parasites, used to breed here and may still be seen or heard occasionally in spring. A Cuckoo in flight looks distinctly raptorial, with its pointed, fast-swishing wings, and small birds often react to it with alarm, but they don't show the same perspicacity when their first-born chick hefts the remaining eggs from the nest while the adults' backs are turned, then proceeds to grow into a ravenous and gigantic monster.

Reptiles and amphibians are, as ever, not that easy to see, but both Richmond and Bushy Parks have a reasonable variety. Grass Snakes, which are plain green with a yellow collar, are the only snakes to occur in Richmond and Bushy Parks. A small something scuttling away near your feet on a summer day may well be a Common Lizard. The amphibians are best observed in or around the ponds in spring, at mating time.

The first butterflies appear on warm days in March or even February – colourful Peacocks, Red Admirals, Commas and Small Tortoiseshells, and bright yellow male Brimstones and their creamy-white mates. By midsummer, the number of species reaches its peak. On a July day, Purple Hairstreaks dance around the oak canopy, Speckled Woods bask and tussle under the trees, and the flowery grassland can swarm with a bewildering variety of species.

Many of the grassland-loving species are brown, and thus easily overlooked in favour of their more colourful cousins. Don't ignore them though, they have their own charm and subtle beauty. The Meadow Brown, Gatekeeper and Small Heath all have a distinct dark 'eye-spot' on the outside of the forewing. The Meadow Brown is the biggest species of the three, and varies from pale to fairly dark brown. The Gatekeeper is brightest, its dark brown wings adorned with large patches of orange. The little Small Heath is sandy-coloured and infuriatingly restless.

The skippers are small, tawny-orange butterflies with the habit of resting with their back wings fully spread but their front wings swept back. They also have a buzzing, moth-like flight, and if you watch them carefully you'll see that they fly actually within the sward, deftly slaloming around the grass stalks as they seek out flowers or see off rivals. Here you could see Large, Small and Essex Skippers – the last two almost identical apart from the underside antennae tips, which are brown in the Small Skipper and jet-black in the Essex. Male Common Blues are indeed blue, but the females belong to the 'brown butterfly' club. Their underwings are fawn with a pretty jumble of white-circled black spots.

On sunny summer days, butterflies are energized by the warmth and can be extremely restless. Later in the day, when the air temperature starts to fall and shadows draw across the grass, many species will assemble in the last pockets of sunlight to bask with wings outspread and make the most of the remaining warmth. This can be a good time to look for them – the fiery orange-brown skippers dotted on tufts of seeding grass, Common Blues balanced head-down on dry flower heads.

The parks' mixture of plants and trees ensures they attract good numbers of other insects. The flowers are patrolled by a wide variety of bees and wasps, including nectar-feeding solitary bees and fiercely predatory solitary wasps – a total of 150 species have been recorded in Bushy Park – while decaying wood provides lunch for the larvae of a multitude of beetles, including the spectacular Stag Beetle with its antler-shaped mandibles. Well over 500 species of moths are on the Richmond Park list, and more than 1,300 species of beetles. If flowers are your thing, you'll enjoy tracking down the acid grassland specialities in Richmond Park, like Harebell and Tormentil and, in Bushy Park, the uninspiring named but rather pretty and excitingly rare Mudwort.

The other parks in this area are not so large or wild as Richmond and Bushy Park, but still offer good London wildlife-watching. Syon Park and Kew Gardens lie on opposite sides of the Thames. Both are mostly quite manicured but the riverfront offers extra interest. All botanists will enjoy a visit to Kew Gardens, even though many of the plants

Butterflies on the edge

Want to see butterflies in London? It's sad but true that your best bet is to head for the butterfly house at London Zoo – our capital is not great for these most exacting of insects. In the city centre, apart from in the bigger parks, we tend only to see those species that are wanderers by nature, like Peacocks, Small Tortoiseshells, Large and Small Whites.

The problems facing butterflies in city centres are the same as those for many other insects. In most species, the bulk of the lifespan is spent in non-flying form – as egg, then caterpillar, then chrysalis. Even those which live for months as adults spend most of that time in hibernation, waiting for the spring. The butterfly is left with only a few weeks at most of active flying life, and in that time its priority is to find a mate and reproduce, not to travel and disperse. Many species live in colonies and are fairly useless at the pioneering stuff – this makes them very vulnerable to habitat destruction, and very bad at seizing new habitat opportunities. If you were to create an absolutely optimal patch of Black Hairstreak habitat in Hyde Park, you'd be waiting a very long time for Black Hairstreaks to move in, even though this species was once widespread across the whole of southern England. For them to spread from the nearest existing colony, there'd need to be a pretty much unbroken chain of optimum habitat between Hyde Park and the wilds of Bedfordshire.

Because the green spaces of London are so fragmented, and divided up by so much inhospitable concrete, butterflies in London parks are scarcer than in similar parks in smaller towns. The parks of the south-west fare better by virtue of their size and proximity to each other, having extensive enough suitable habitat, replete with native flowers for egg-laying. The more urban gardens there are that offer similar patches of wildish grassland with native flowers, the better the chances for butterflies to spread back into the city's parklands again.

Sugar rush

Question – what's grey, furry, unbearably cute and is rumoured to live on Wimbledon Common? Answer – not what you think. For a start, this animal can fly (well, glide) from tree to tree, an ability that the Wombles were never credited with, even in their most far-fetched adventures. Nonetheless, a 'flying womble' was one of the suggestions when a poster on the Wild About Britain internet forums described his encounter with the mystery animal in autumn 2007 – but the consensus was that he had found a feral Sugar Glider.

The plot proceeded to thicken at speed, as other forum posters claimed that the common actually holds not one but a small population of the furry fliers and has done for some years. However, this was all news to the park rangers.

The story seems to have gone quiet now, and no photos of the Wimbledon Sugar Gliders can be found. Were any there in the first place? If so, have they died out or are they just laying low? On a well-watched site such as the Common, it seems unlikely that a breeding population will have avoided the notice of park rangers and surveyors over a number of years.

Sugar Gliders look a bit squirrel-like (apart from the baggy skin-flaps between their fore- and hind-legs that become their gliding 'wings' when airborne) but are actually marsupials and originally hail from Australia. They have become quite popular exotic pets in recent years, and there's no doubt that the Wimbledon Common gang, if it exists, would be descended from escapees. Enchanting and fascinating though they are, like all exotics they carry an uncertain payload when it comes to their impact upon our native wildlife (just think of the Grey Squirrel) so maybe it's just as well that the Wimbledon population doesn't seem to harbour any immediate ambitions to go underground, over ground and womble their way across London and beyond.

Left: Sugar Glider

on view are not UK natives. Bird species are not always fussy about where the plants originate from provided they can find enough food, and a good variety of species can be seen – Robins have even moved inside some of the glasshouses, where they fool visitors into believing that recorded birdsong is being played. There are also some wildlife areas within the grounds, including a lovely bluebell wood. Hampton Court Park adjoins Bushy Park and is a more regimented space, though it has some interesting ponds. Wimbledon Common and the adjoining Putney Heath are wilder, closer to Richmond and Bushy Parks in character although covering a smaller area. Dedicated birdwatchers have found a good variety of species on Wimbledon Common, which was also one of the last places in London to have nesting Red-backed Shrikes before this lovely species became extinct in Britain.

So the south-west has many wonderful parks, and as if that weren't enough, it is also home to one of the real jewels in London's wildlife crown – the London Wetland Centre. This is one of the nine reserves across the UK that belong to the Wildfowl and Wetlands Trust, a conservation group whose aims are pretty clear from their name. Like some of the other WWT reserves, the London Wetland Centre has a collection of captive wildfowl, some of which are endangered species involved in captive breeding and reintroduction projects. There is also an impressive array of educational facilities, and the restaurant and shop provide sustenance and wildlife-related retail therapy. By far the larger part of the reserve is made up of 'wild' areas, though, including excellent birdwatching hides. The WWT proudly proclaim this reserve to be the 'best urban site in Europe to watch wildlife' – a claim which is hard to refute, given the variety of species here and the ease with which you can observe them.

The captive birds are separated from the wild parts of the reserve by gates and clear signage, so there is not much risk of confusion. The collection,

which is the first thing you'll see when you enter the main part of the reserve, is divided by the region the birds hail from originally, so you'll find species from Greenland, South America and so on, all enjoying themselves in suitably landscaped pens. From here you'll enter the lovely 'Wildside' area, stunning in summer with a show of native wetland plants, and then on to hides that overlook the lakes. There is another wild area which is reached by going back past the collection to the entrance buildings and through the 'Waterlife' zone. This has several more hides including the superb Peacock Tower hide which gives you panoramic views from three levels.

The reserve has a large lake and two smaller ones, all overlooked by the hides. There is also a section of reed beds and another of grazing marsh which is cut through with numerous ditches. The whole reserve has been carefully landscaped to provide optimum habitat for birds and other wetland wildlife – although the built-up skyline of Hammersmith and surrounding suburbs presses in on all sides, you could easily imagine yourself standing in a little piece of Norfolk Broadland, surgically transplanted into this south-west London scene.

Wetland birds provide the main interest here. On the lakes ducks breed, and many more come here to spend the winter, including species like Pintail which is otherwise very rare in London, as well as Gadwall, Shoveler, Teal and Wigeon. The rarest British dabbling duck and the only one that's a summer migrant, the Garganey, shows up most autumns on its way further south.

In winter you could see a Bittern here – look for a big heavy-set, streaky brown, vaguely heron-shaped bird lurking by the reeds or flapping ponderously overhead. Another streaky and skulking brown bird, the Water Rail, lives here all year but is easiest to see in winter. The reserve feeding stations are at their busiest at this time too, with the usual selection of tits and finches joined by Reed Buntings, Great Spotted Woodpeckers and Ring-necked Parakeets. Snipes, Redshanks and other waders overwinter here, feeding on the muddy margins of the lakes and ditches, and Water Pipit is a local speciality, as is Jack Snipe.

There are numerous Lapwings here in winter, and some stay on to breed, serenading you with their ludicrous toy-trumpet calls while performing extravagant aerobatics over the grazing marsh. Dainty Little Ringed Plovers arrive in early spring and scuttle along the island shores like clockwork toys, looking for food and places to nest. Another early arrival is the Sand Martin, which nests here in tunnels in an artificial bank designed to resemble its natural riverbank home. The Highland cattle that are used to graze the marsh area attract passing Yellow Wagtails in spring – these bright little birds specialize in catching insects disturbed by the slowly moving animals.

Little Grebes, with their distinctive 'fluffy-looking' rear ends, nest in the quieter corners of the reserve, while Common Terns are on the increase, establishing an island colony. There was great excitement in 2006 when a pair of Avocets arrived and nested – sadly their chicks didn't survive, but there's no reason why future attempts should not succeed. What a coup it would be for this urban reserve to have a breeding population of the UK's most graceful wader, which was extinct in England not so long ago. Hobbies can often be seen high over the lakes through summer, dashing after

The Transformation of Barn Elms

If your London A-Z is a little out of date, you may see a quartet of squarish reservoirs sitting on the site that is now home to the wobbly-edged, multi-islanded lakes and ditches of the London Wetland Centre. These are Barn Elms Reservoirs, built in the late 1800s to provide a water supply for local people. With the planning and construction of the Thames Water Ring Main (completed in 1996) the Barn Elms reservoirs became redundant, though they remained an important area for wildlife with many diving ducks visiting in winter.

The Wildfowl and Wetlands Trust (WWT) joined forces with Thames Water to breathe new life into the area, which had already been designated a Site of Special Scientific Interest. They came up with an ambitious plan to completely re-landscape the site and establish a rich and varied wetland reserve which would attract wildlife and visitors in equal abundance. Part of the land was sold off for housing, the profits helping to kick-start a fund for the redevelopment of the site.

There followed five years of serious reconstruction work. The original reservoirs were demolished and in their place the new lakes were dug. Islands with naturally sloping sides were constructed, ditches excavated and the area planted with reeds and other suitable wetland species. Visitor infrastructure included a network of trails, birdwatching hides and buildings to house an array of facilities.

Sir David Attenborough opened the site in 2000, welcoming in an exciting new era for London wildlife enthusiasts. The reserve now attracts about 170,000 visitors a year, and hosts frequent school visits, exhibitions and all kinds of events. It's no surprise that this wonderfully successful project has inspired similar ventures in other cities across Europe.

dragonflies and the occasional martin, though they don't breed here. Five species of warblers do though, including both Reed and Sedge Warblers – ensuring that the reserve is a riot of confusing birdsong throughout spring and into summer.

The reserve is a good place for keen gull-watchers, that specialized subset of birdwatchers who often end up spending their leisure time scanning the hills and valleys of their local rubbish dump. April and May are the best months, although Iceland and Glaucous Gulls have both been found in late winter.

The London Wetland Centre has already amassed an impressive list of rare birds, including Black Kite, White Stork, Ring Ouzel and Spoonbill. Not all of them have stayed around long enough to get onto the lists of all London twitchers, but this site is one of the best in London for seeing a good variety of birds at any time, with a good chance of something more unusual.

Water Voles on the reserve descend from an introduced population – no surprise given that the whole site was built from scratch less than 20 years ago. Hopefully, they will prosper and spread, eventually joining up with other local populations. You can see them anywhere on the reserve, even swimming across the ponds in the captive ducks' pens, though the ditches and quieter pools are probably best. Younger visitors can get a feel for Water Vole life by exploring the giant replica Water Vole tunnel – one of several playground attractions in the Discovery Centre. Another reintroduced species here is the Slow Worm, that shy legless lizard which looks like a mini-snake and may be seen sunbathing in quiet corners. Another cold-blooded creature that is much more noticeable on the reserve is the Marsh Frog – there are several colonies here, all prone to sudden mass outbursts of noisy croaking.

There is, of course, a great wealth of insect life here. Good numbers of native wild flowers means butterflies, moths, bees and wasps are numerous. Small Copper, Comma and Holly Blue are among the more striking butterflies you could see.

The pools are nurseries for all kinds of flying insects that spend their early days as swimming or bottom-dwelling nymphs. Pond-dipping is a great way to peer into their underwater world – you could catch dragonfly nymphs with their bizarre, *Alien*-esque jaws that fire forward to seize prey as they stalk along. That prey could include creatures as large as tadpoles – these nymphs really are the lions of the pond. Most caddisfly nymphs grow up inside self-made tunnel houses built from bits of stone, shell, leaves or twigs, while mayfly nymphs swim freely, aided by the long, two- or three-pronged tails that persist into adulthood. These nymphs leave the water in spring or summer when they are full-grown and split their skins to allow the winged adult to emerge from what is now a papery husk. You may see such husks, known as exuviae, still attached to waterside vegetation – a perfect nymph-shaped shell except for the rip down the back.

The adult wetland insects are on the wing through summer. Some are more noticeable than others – it's hard to miss the huge Emperor Dragonfly with its bright green (female) or blue (male) abdomen as it zooms past in pursuit of some hapless smaller insect. Damselflies are hunters too but less powerful in flight – you're more likely to see them fluttering close by the water, snacking on midges and chasing each other. Look out for demoiselles courting each other with wingflicks. In all, half of the UK's dragonfly and damselfly species are found at the London Wetland Centre, and for many people they provide the most exciting spectacle at this superb reserve.

Marshlands and Reservoirs

ONCE UPON a time, the land around the tidal Thames would have been a rich paradise of marshy meadows and wetlands, perhaps home to Black Terns and Large Copper butterflies and the like – species which now no longer breed in Britain but live in such habitats where they persist unmodified on the continent. Many a London naturalist will have wistfully speculated about what delights might have been on view here centuries ago, before the city of London grew and spread into the eastern marshlands. Today, there is little sign of what it was like then, but a few pockets of marshland do remain and they provide some of the most exciting wildlife-watching anywhere in London.

At the other end of the capital is another concentration of wetlands, but beyond sharing a basic watery theme these are quite different. They are not remnant wetland but are artificially constructed and in some ways very obviously unnatural in appearance. The Staines Reservoirs and other reservoirs in west London have rather unpromising suburban surroundings, but by virtue of the amount of space they occupy they have proved themselves to form a really worthwhile wildlife-watching area.

The best of the eastern marshland sites is also the newest thanks to recent habitat enhancement – the RSPB reserve at Rainham Marshes. This patch of land on the north side of the Thames was once used as a Ministry of Defence firing range, and has long been closed to the public. Despite this, it has had problems with what our tabloids call 'feral youths' for many years. It has also been fought over by many would-be land owners in the past, with plans including a Disney theme park, part of the cross-Channel rail link and a bypass section of the A13. The last of these has indeed come to pass, but the rest of the site is now under the care of the RSPB, who have already done much to restore it to its former glory. No longer do visitors have to dodge armies of trail-bikers and other wildlife-unfriendly land-users – there is a fabulous visitor centre and network of trails to enable you to explore the reserve in comfort and safety.

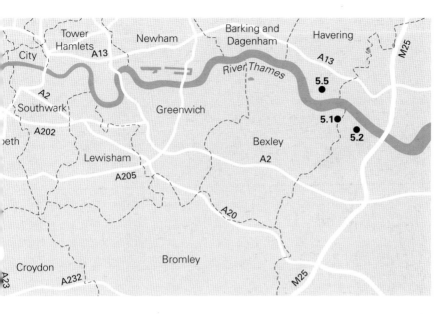

Rainham Marshes was attracting exceptionally rare birds well before it opened to the public – thankfully for London twitchers the RSPB arranged special public access to enable people to see the Collared Pratincole of July 2005 and the Sociable Plover that arrived later in the same year. The reserve opened the following year, and has continued to pull in the rarities, along with a supporting cast of other wetland birds. With the Thames foreshore thrown into the mix, it's no surprise the reserve has such a long list of species recorded.

5.1 Crayford Marshes
5.2 Dartford Marshes
5.3 King George VI Reservoir
5.4 Queen Mary Reservoir
5.5 Rainham Marshes
5.6 Staines Reservoirs
5.7 Walton Reservoirs

Above: *Sociable Plover (foreground) with Lapwing*

Building a Flagship

It probably came as a surprise to many that the Royal Society for the Protection of Birds chose to get involved with this unremarkable-looking strip of land in a rough-and-ready part of east London, with all its problems and issues. The RSPB is the largest conservation body in Britain, and most of its famous nature reserves are in beautiful and unspoilt countryside – wild Caledonian pinewoods, East Anglian coastal wetlands, towering cliffs packed with noisy seabirds.

However, take a look at the RSPB website and you'll see quite a few urban reserves. They may not have the same variety of species nor sense of wilderness as the rural sites, but what they do have is a large potential pool of visitors and so they present an opportunity to preach the worth of conservation to the masses – many of whom may know next to nothing about wildlife. Here is an area where the RSPB really excels, providing world-class visitor facilities to help educate and enchant people of all ages.

The transformation of Rainham Marshes from an over-drained wasteland dotted with munitions, into a major nature reserve of thriving marsh, wet meadow and open water is not yet complete. The site has been cleaned up and landscaping carried out, but work will continue to improve the mosaic of grassland habitats and ditches. The reserve's lagoons must be managed in synch with the silt dredgers who still use some of them – the RSPB ensures dredging operations won't disturb nesting birds.

It is perhaps the visitor facilities that are most important of all though, especially in the early years of the reserve's life. The remarkable visitor centre is worth the visit on its own, with its environmentally friendly features and wonderful views across the reserve. Creating an experience for visitors that's not only engaging and exciting but also welcoming and secure has been no mean feat in what was until recently a slightly scary place to visit, but the RSPB has managed it.

Throughout the year, Little Egrets stalk the ditches. If you imagine a somewhat scaled-down Grey Heron with pure white plumage, you have the basic idea of the Little Egret, a bird which has recently colonized southern England and seems to be intent on taking over the whole country. Like other herons, Little Egrets catch fish, frogs, small mammals, big insects – anything that doesn't run or jump away quickly enough. They are distinctive in flight, broad-winged and snowy-white, holding their necks tucked in and legs outstretched behind – when you see one flying you may notice that it has black legs with, curiously, bright yellow feet.

Also on view throughout the year are a quartet of wader species – Oystercatcher, Lapwing, Ringed Plover and Redshank. A lot of newcomers to birdwatching find identifying waders very difficult, but these four are all very distinctive. The Oystercatcher is the biggest, a sturdy black bird with a white belly, pink legs and a long orange carrot of a bill. The Lapwing looks black and white at first glance but has shiny green and purple iridescence and an orange-brown undertail. It has a dainty bill and a showy long upswept crest. Smallest of the group is the Ringed Plover, fawn and white with bold black bands across its chest and face (in summer it can be confused with the similar Little Ringed Plover). Redshanks are the most difficult to identify, being brown like so many other waders, but have eye-catching orange-red legs and broad white trailing edges to the wings.

A number of duck species are on the reserve's pools throughout the year, including Shelduck – large and elegant with white plumage relieved by black and chestnut markings. Gadwall, Mallard, Teal, Shoveler and Tufted Duck can also be seen year-round. Menacing these birds are Peregrine Falcons, while Kestrels hover over the grassland in search of voles and other small mammals.

Short-eared Owls and Merlins may be seen in winter, with Hen Harrier also recorded occasionally. As with all birds of prey, it's hard to predict just when one might appear, and often your view when it does is frustratingly brief. Merlins are especially speedy, dashing past after pipits and other little birds and leaving you with an impression of a vaguely raptorial blur. The harrier and the owl are more leisurely hunters, so if you find one you'll hopefully be able to watch it for more than a split second. Hen Harrier males are frosty grey-blue with black wingtips, the more frequently seen females and juveniles are brown with white rumps. Both are long-tailed, long-winged, elegant and graceful in flight and hold their wings in what the field guides invariably describe as a 'shallow V'. Short-eared Owls are the most diurnal of our owls. Their ear-tufts are so short as to be invisible most of the time, but they

make up for their lack of headgear by a pair of extraordinarily fearsome glaring yellow eyes.

Besides the usual suspects, little birds at Rainham in winter include Rock Pipit, Water Pipit, sometimes Firecrest, Brambling and, most excitingly, Penduline Tit. If this last species is missing from your field guide, that's because it is, normally, a very rare visitor to our shores. However, there's something about the reserve that clearly appeals to this very charming and amusingly named little bird (just so you know, it's their nests that are pendulous). They've shown up in small numbers in four out of five winters since December 2004. If you visit in hope of seeing one, check at the visitor centre to find out whether any have been seen and where the best place to look is. You will probably need be patient as they may not show immediately.

Come spring, migrating terns visit, breeding-plumaged waders refuel at the lagoons on their way up to northerly nesting grounds and Swallows and martins arrive (escorted by Hobbies, that migrate with them and eat a few of them on the way). Overhead, a migrating Red Kite or Osprey may cruise purposefully by. Little Ringed Plovers nest on the reserve, so do Redshanks, Snipes, both species of whitethroat and Cetti's, Sedge and Reed Warblers. The list may before long include Avocets, following a breeding attempt in 2008.

A summer visit can be quiet for birds, if you visit in the small window between the departure of spring passage migrants and the arrival of autumn passage migrants – 'passage migrant' just means a migrating bird that's visiting some intermediate point on its migratory journey. Although there are still the breeding birds to enjoy, this is a good time to look for other wildlife at Rainham – dragonflies, butterflies, Water Voles and more. The pretty Scarce Emerald damselfly flits among its more common relatives by the ditches. Foxes lead their heartbreakingly sweet cubs out into the open from late spring and you may find them snoozing or gambolling in the sunshine. Marsh Frogs croak

Above: Firecrest

away in the ditches, and grasshoppers and crickets thrum in the long grass.

Come autumn, the migrant waders are back. The handsome adult birds of the spring are now losing their breeding plumage and looking rather dishevelled following a hectic summer of chick-rearing. In a second wave come the youngsters themselves, pristine in their very first set of feathers and ready to begin their careers as birdwatcher-confusers. Some of the species you could meet are Little Stint, Curlew Sandpiper, Dunlin, Ruff, Spotted Redshank and Greenshank. If you're up for the challenge, a good way to get to grips with them is to join a guided walk with the warden, who'll help you with the subtle ID points while the birds are right there in front of you.

Mega-birds

If you've ever shown the slightest propensity for birdwatching, you have probably been called a 'twitcher' at least once. The public at large tend not to know that twitcher has a very specific meaning and covers only a minority of birdwatchers. The twitcher is a bird-logger, interesting primarily in adding as many names as possible to one or many 'birds I've seen' lists. Many twitchers keep regional lists – Britain, London, local patch, etc – and year-lists as well as their 'everything anywhere' or 'life' list. For these people, the arrival of a bird that's not on one of their lists triggers a mad dash to see it before it flies off (or, occasionally, dies).

Twitchers who keep a London list have a lot to aspire to, as 361 species have been recorded in the area (defined as everything within 20 miles of St Paul's Cathedral). They include some extreme rarities – hopelessly lost migrants which have strayed from as far away as Siberia and North America – such as Pied-billed Grebe, Naumann's Thrush, Brown Shrike, Lesser Kestrel, American Robin, Hume's Warbler, Solitary Sandpiper, Cream-coloured Courser and of course the Sociable Plover at Rainham Marshes in 2005. With phone and pager services and the internet, news of rarities spreads fast.

Going on a twitch is, in many ways, the opposite of how many of us imagine birdwatching to be. Rather than searching for peace, quiet and solitude, you're looking for a big crowd – the people who arrived before you and know where 'The Bird' is. Rather than actively searching and exploring, you're often stuck in one spot, staring for hours at the one small shrub into which 'The Bird' disappeared two minutes before you arrived. And sometimes, rather than being in beautiful wild surroundings, you're at a sewage farm, a rubbish dump or somewhere equally unprepossessing – lost migrant birds are often not that discriminatory about where they stop for a rest.

The closer you are to the sea, the better your chances of finding your own rare birds. Wandering vagrant land birds must have made an unanticipated and unplanned sea crossing to have ended up in Britain, and so often tend to collapse gratefully down onto the first dry land they see. If that dry land is at all suitable for that species' foraging requirements, so much the better. Rainham may not be on the coast but it's close to the mouth of the Thames. It is probably the biggest migrant trap in London overall, as it has something to offer for land birds and water birds alike.

Terns and gulls are also on their travels in autumn. Besides the common species you could see Yellow-legged and Little Gulls, and Black and Arctic Terns. The Swallows and martins swarm in huge feeding binges over Rainham's pools, hoovering up the last of the midges and mozzies to put on as much weight as they can before migrating. In a matter of days they'll be living off those fat reserves as they traverse the bleak immensity of the Sahara. As the summer birds move on, the winter visitors start to return and the circle is complete.

On the other side of the river, Dartford Marshes is a similar area of rough (in all senses of the word – it is ill advised to venture here alone), damp pastureland, sitting in the shadow of the massive M25 suspension bridge across the Thames. Lacking the injection of cash and manpower that Rainham has enjoyed, the area has less good habitat and is certainly less visitor-friendly than the RSPB reserve, but despite this (and numerous developments that have encroached onto the land) it's still worth a visit for the dedicated wildlife-watcher. You can expect to see a range of crows, finches, gulls and waders. High tide pushes waders off the river shore and into the fields. Littlebrook Lake, by Littlebrook Power Station, attracts diving ducks and sometimes grebes and divers, which are less likely on Rainham's shallow pools, as well as a large concentration of gulls to delight the larophiles. There are no pleasant strolls along purpose-built nature trails though, so you'll have to make do with walking the minor roads and scanning the marshes from the roadside.

Also on the south of the Thames but across from the River Darent are Crayford Marshes, which are similar to Dartford Marshes – rough grazing pasture with some ditches and scattered scrubland. Viewing is even trickier than it is at Dartford, though.

Over on the north shore of the Thames, and east of Rainham, there are more grazing marshes among the industrialized landscape of Barking and Dagenham. There is also a small but charming nature reserve here – The Ripple – which is managed by the London Wildlife Trust. Here there are groves of Silver Birch trees leading you to a new wild flower meadow, sprouting out of what used to be a dumping ground for industrial waste. Orchids are rumoured to relish 'disturbed' landscapes, and this would seem to be borne out by the scene at The Ripple in summer, as hundreds of Southern Marsh and Common Spotted Orchids flower, attracting butterflies and a host of bees, wasps and sawflies, many of them too obscure to warrant their own English names.

On the opposite side of London, the reservoirs around Staines are up there with Rainham Marshes as exceptional places in our area to watch birds. Set inland, well beyond the tidal limit of the Thames, they offer a tremendous contrast with the open, sea-scented environs of the eastern marshlands.

Since they were built in 1902, the original Staines Reservoirs (North Basin and South Basin – guess which one's which) have been joined by the larger King George VI Reservoir immediately to their west, which was built during World War II. The trio of water bodies has proved very attractive to birds and to birdwatchers. The basins are concrete-banked, with little vegetation around the edges, and at first glance rather austere in character. However, to an overflying water bird looking for somewhere to stop off, the expanse of water must look appealing. For birdwatchers, the causeway that divides the two Staines basins is a good place to scan over both of them. You may well meet other birders doing the same thing, whilst trying to stop their telescopes and tripods being blown over. This is not the cosy and friendly wildlife-watching experience you'll enjoy at sites like the London Wetland Centre, but the unusual birds that show up now and then make it worthwhile, if your interest is keen enough.

Winter brings birds from the north, many of them specialist fish-catchers that prefer deep water. Flocks of Great Crested Grebes gather, looking a lot less impressive in their winter plumage – the orange ruff and long head tufts are discarded for the non-breeding season in favour of a much more utilitarian grey-and-white look. The much rarer Black-necked Grebe visits in small numbers most years, usually in late autumn or early spring. The other two unusual grebes – Red-necked and Slavonian – show up in some years. They too are in their nondescript winter plumage, but if they hang around long enough into spring they'll begin to moult, and this is when you may get the chance to admire their lovely summer outfits – all three are more colourful than Great Cresteds.

Divers, equally as aquatic as the grebes, also visit the reservoirs from time to time between autumn and spring. Great Northern is the heftiest, Red-throated the slightest and Black-throated occupying the middle ground. All three are sturdy, dagger-billed birds, larger and bulkier than Great Crested Grebes and even more capable of vanishing underwater in dives so long that you start to worry about their lungs. Like grebes they look grey and uninteresting in winter, and acquire much more attractive plumage in spring – which incidentally makes them much easier to tell apart.

Young Cormorants, browner than their parents, are confusable with divers. Check the way the bird sits in the water – Cormorants sit very low, divers a little higher, and Cormorants tend to hold their heads more uptilted. A close view will show you that the Cormorant's bill ends with a down-curved tip, rather than a dagger-like point like the grebes and divers. The Cormorant really gives itself away when it dives, though, often doing a flashy little pre-dive jump to help it plunge more deeply.

The reservoirs also occasionally attract diving ducks, including some species that are more at home out at sea, like Common and Velvet Scoter and Long-tailed Duck. Very bad weather at sea could drive other seabirds this far inland and on a few occasions after big storms birdwatchers have found such maritime species as Sabine's Gull and Leach's Storm-petrel here. Some other seabirds,

like Kittiwakes and Little Gulls, are more regular and probably are here on purpose as part of a breakaway overland-migrating faction, rather than being storm-driven.

At migration times, many other interesting birds may call in at the reservoirs but often they don't stick around at these rather austere water bodies, especially the waders who find little to eat on the concrete shores. Therefore, the twitchers who want to see them have to be prepared to drop everything and dash to the reservoir quickly if they want to tick them off on their list. Every few years, however, one or other of the basins is drained, and the muddy, puddle-scattered, slushy mess left behind is highly attractive to waders. Over the years, the drained basins have drawn in some very unusual species, including this little haul of vagrant waders – Baird's, Buff-breasted and Pectoral Sandpipers, Long-billed Dowitcher, two Wilson's Phalaropes and three Lesser Yellowlegs. Most of these will have set out from somewhere in North America, intending to travel somewhere in southern North America or even South America. Something went badly wrong – dodgy navigation, inclement weather, or both... and they ended up here. We can only guess how many others perished over the Atlantic. Staines might not be as pleasant as the Florida Keys but it's better than a watery grave.

The reservoirs are quiet in summer. The odd wandering Hobby may drift overhead, looking for some big dragonflies to catch. A few ducks of the commoner species spend the summer on the reservoirs. Later in summer, Swallows, martins and Swifts come to dash and dart low over the water, and it's not long before it's migration time again.

What about other wildlife around the reservoir? There isn't a lot of it to see. Common freshwater fish live in the water, as evidenced by the fish-eating birds that catch them. Staines has a rather unfortunate wild mammal-related claim to fame in that a bat suffering from rabies was found in the town in 2004, not far from the reservoir. It was a Daubenton's Bat, a species

Reservoir-watching

If you ever want to read an evocative account of how utterly soul-destroying it can be to base all your birding hopes, dreams and time around a reservoir, I recommend you get a copy of *Gone Birding* by Bill Oddie. In the early part of the book, he recounts his long years of hard service birdwatching at Bartley Reservoir near Birmingham – essentially, day after day of staring through barbed wire at a bleak, concrete-edged bowl of water and seeing perhaps one gull a week as reward for his patience. It's amusing stuff but not likely to inspire the budding birder to head for their local reservoir to recreate the magic.

Staines Reservoirs and their neighbours never seem to be quite as lifeless as Bartley sounded, but there's no denying that this isn't always fun and exciting birdwatching. There is usually not very much to see apart from whatever's on the water, and that may well be so far out on the water that even with a good telescope it's difficult to tell what it is. Other wildlife is around but not particularly noticeable. At the best times of year for birds, the causeway can be windswept and freezing.

If you're the kind of frontier-loving person who relishes a bit of graft for your birds, you'll enjoy reservoir-watching a lot more. As with most things, the more time you invest, the richer your rewards will be. With a clear view of skies overhead, you can enjoy the wonders of 'viz mig' – visible migration – when pipits, thrushes and other land birds stream overhead early on autumn mornings on their way to... somewhere else. On winter days you can count Pochards and rejoice when you beat your personal best. You can visit your reservoir every day for 20 years and dramatically raise your odds of being the lucky finder of a seriously rare and impressive bird, like the people who found the Roller at Staines in 1959.

If you love beautiful scenery and don't mind whether you see bunnies, butterflies or Bullfinches, you will probably not get that much out of a birdwatching trip to a place like this. However, if you are on your way to becoming a more fanatical type of birdwatcher, if you own warm and windproof clothing, and if you have plenty of patience, you could do a lot worse than adopting a reservoir as your local patch.

Above: *Meadow Pipits migrating over Staines Reservoir*

particularly associated with water, and you can see lots of non-rabid Daubenton's and other bats catching insects over the reservoir on summer evenings. The few scattered trees and the ground around them provide homes for insects and rodents.

Staines Reservoirs are but a small part of a large complex of water bodies around the valley of the River Colne. The larger King George VI Reservoir, which attracts a similar mix of species as the Staines basins, has no public access. A few wildfowl surveyors are allowed in, but that is all. Upriver, there is a string of smaller lakes and gravel pits, running from Uxbridge up to Rickmansworth. Some of these are used for sports like windsurfing and so are not popular with birds. Those that are worth a visit include Broadwater Gravel Pit, Stocker's Lake (which is a local nature reserve), and Springwell Lake, which is part of another nature reserve called Maple Lodge. Some of these lakes have more vegetated margins and surrounding trees, which means that while they lack the size, and therefore rarity pulling-power, of the Staines basins, they have a more interesting mix of other species, both bird and non-bird.

Close by are several other reservoirs. The largest is Queen Mary Reservoir, not far from Staines. This very deep and almost circular reservoir is a typical concrete-banked basin which attracts diving birds such as divers and grebes, although after years of gravel extraction it is too deep in many places for bottom-feeding diving ducks. Access is covered by the same Thames Water birdwatching permit that will get you into King George V and Walthamstow Reservoirs and several others. There are more reservoirs south-east of Queen Mary – the Walton Reservoir group – which are similar deep, concrete-banked basins. Island Barn Reservoir does have vegetated banks, as do the decommissioned Molesey Reservoirs in the same group, and these are more hospitable to wildlife. Queen Elizabeth II Reservoir hosts a large gull roost, and all attract assorted winter wildfowl.

Just the other side of the M25 and therefore strictly speaking beyond the scope of this book (but not necessarily beyond your reach) are the reservoirs and gravel pits around Wraysbury, which offer more good birdwatching.

If you're fed up with all that open water, head for Staines Moor, an area of marshy meadows by the River Colne. It's not a moor in the conventional sense but it is a pleasant place (though not a quiet one, by virtue of its proximity to Heathrow airport) and is a Site of Special Scientific Interest because of its interesting plant communities. Here, botanists can search out the Brown Galingale, a species of sedge with delicate blades and chunky brown flowers, which occurs at only two other sites in the UK. A whole host of other interesting grasses and sedges grow here, while more eye-catching to many are colourful flowers like the Southern Marsh Orchid and Yellow Flag Iris.

The presence of bumpy anthills made by nearly 200 years of Yellow Meadow Ant activity testifies that here are some ancient meadowlands indeed. In fact, these are the oldest such anthills in the UK. More discreet but no less fascinating is the moor's mollusc population – more than 60 species of snails and slugs have been found here. In summer, butterflies flit between flowers and dragonflies and damselflies menace the smaller insects.

A few pairs of Redshank and Lapwing nest in the damper areas, with Skylarks in the drier grassland. Sedge and Reed Warblers breed too, giving you the opportunity to learn how to separate their somewhat similar songs. One rule of thumb is that if you can see the bird easily, it's more likely to be a Sedge Warbler. 'Sedgies' are the more extrovert, males often singing from clearly visible perches and also performing elegant little song flights from time to time. You'll see no such exhibitionism from the Reed Warbler – it often picks the exact centre of its clump of reeds, stays low down and from there churns out its 'song' – an endless chuntering stream of squeaky churring. The Sedge Warbler's song has a similar relentless quality but is more varied, with some warbling phrases and also toneless grinding rattles.

In winter, heavy rain floods the fields and various birds are attracted by this. Among the Lapwings may be a few Golden Plovers and Ruffs – the former plumper and spangly-backed, the latter long-necked and scaly-looking with their pale feather fringes. Wigeons, which enjoy the combination of shallow water and soggy exposed grassland, are among the ducks that visit in winter. Wild geese, unusual in London (those parkland armies of feral Canadas and Greylags don't count), are sometimes found here, especially White-fronted Geese with their blotchy black bellies and white bands at the bill base. Short-eared Owls have been almost guaranteed here in winter lately, while other predators like Hen Harrier and Merlin have both been recorded.

Whose land is it anyway?

[Anti-]Airport activists are up in arms at the time of writing because BAA is planning to build a new rail link – 'Airtrack' – across the Staines Moor SSSI for Heathrow that will link it more directly to the south-western rail network, serving such places as Guildford, Dorking and Reading.

Staines Moor is a common (a place where villagers are allowed by the landowners to freely graze their livestock) and has been so since medieval times. Each registered 'commoner' has the right to graze one horse or two cows on the moor, and everyone may use the land for 'air and exercise'. This isn't just a courtesy, the rights described are legal ones, although the laws involved are a convoluted mixture of ancient and modern. Crucially, though, common land may only be used for another purpose if equally advantageous land is provided in exchange, and this may be where the BAA plans fall down.

The encroachment of development upon green spaces in London is a problem that won't go away, and even when a strong case exists against a planned development, as is the case with Staines Moor, it's hard to avoid a sense of impending doom. After all, the rail link must, BAA will argue, go *somewhere*. Back when London was founded, there can have been few voices protesting the destruction of this wetland or that woodland to make space for more homes and industry – free land would have seemed limitless. Now, a look at the London street map shows a space crammed to capacity with roads, shopping areas, transport hubs, industrial buildings and all the other stuff we need, with wild spaces squeezed in amongst all that concrete.

Every battle over a place like Staines Moor is unique and must be fought on its own merits. Not every battle can be won, and a victory here often just means there will be a defeat somewhere over there. It's easy to feel disheartened. But the stronger stance is to feel happy that we still have what we have, and to make the very most of it all. Not only will you have a better time, but you'll be more inspired to sign that petition, write that letter to Parliament, and generally do what you can to stand up and be counted when it matters.

In and around the Lee Valley

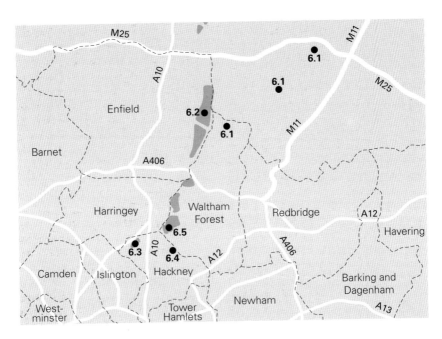

THE RIVER Lee (or Lea) journeys south from its source at Leagrave in Bedfordshire to join the Thames at Woolwich. Its valley provides a flyway for migrating birds. Along its course, it passes numerous reservoirs, marshes and other interesting places, and the Lee Valley Walk enables you to explore them all, both within and beyond the M25. It is probably worth mentioning right from the start that the words Lea and Lee are often used interchangeably, particularly south of Hertford, with Lea the more frequent spelling for the upper part of the river. As pronunciation is the same, this only affects those of us trying to read (or write) about them. The park is managed by the Lee Valley Regional Park Authority, which uses the word Lee in its publicity and so we will adopt this spelling rather than Lea.

The most northerly of the Lee Valley reservoirs is King George V Reservoir, a very large and roughly oblong water body with a causeway slicing it in half east to west (so, strictly speaking,

6.1 Epping Forest
6.2 King George V Reservoir
6.3 Stoke Newington Reservoirs
6.4 Walthamstow Marsh
6.5 Walthamstow Reservoirs

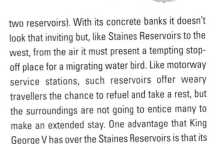

two reservoirs). With its concrete banks it doesn't look that inviting but, like Staines Reservoirs to the west, from the air it must present a tempting stop-off place for a migrating water bird. Like motorway service stations, such reservoirs offer weary travellers the chance to refuel and take a rest, but the surroundings are not going to entice many to make an extended stay. One advantage that King George V has over the Staines Reservoirs is that its surroundings are more rural, with woodlands and extensive open pasture on the eastern side.

The north basin is less disturbed and seems to be better for birdwatching but both are worth a look. You have to buy a permit to watch birds here, from Thames Water who owns the site. At £10 for a year it's not a huge outlay, especially if you're keen and local – it will also give you access to certain other London reservoirs, including Walthamstow Reservoirs. Birds often commute between here and the next reservoir immediately to the south, William Girling Reservoir ('The Girling'). The reservoirs are known collectively as Chingford Reservoirs. Unfortunately, there is no public access to William Girling Reservoir and only a few wildfowl counters are allowed in. Therefore if an unusual bird does visit, birdwatchers can only hope that it gets bored with the Girling and takes at least a day trip up to King George V. A speciality of the Girling is Black-necked Grebe, with up to 30 being recorded here in winter. If you're determined to see them you can view the reservoir from Mansfield Park to the east, but you need a good telescope and a good eye as the birds are distant dots on the water. If you want a decent view of the species but don't have a scope, you'll need to wait for one to turn up elsewhere.

Grebes and ducks may visit between autumn and spring. Among the commoner species, look out for Goosander, which are large, graceful, 'saw-billed' ducks. Though no living bird species has actual teeth (one of many weight-saving adaptations to a flying life), the sawbills have the closest thing to teeth you'll find in the bird world – the insides of the mandibles are lined with little points, like the teeth of a saw. This tells you just what these birds are good at – grabbing and holding onto slippery fish. Most diving ducks eat plant matter or molluscs and other invertebrates they find on the lake or sea bed. Only the sawbills are fish-eaters, and these sleek, long-bodied birds have a distinct air of the predator about them. Male Goosanders have black, green-glossed heads and pied wings, females are brown-headed and grey-backed, but both sexes have a peachy wash on their white chests and bellies.

Arguably one of the more attractive diving ducks is the Goldeneye, and you should be able to see this for yourself in winter as there are usually 40 or more present here on any given day. They are compact, round-headed, short-billed ducks with staring yellow eyes and impressive diving skills. You can often get an idea of how adept a swimming bird is at surface-diving by observing how high it sits in the water. Gulls, which don't surface-dive at all, are very buoyant with their long wings standing well clear of the water. Dabbling ducks, which immerse their heads, sometimes tip forward to upend but only surface-dive in dire emergencies, are quite high-floating too, the line of their backs staying much the same or angling up towards the tail end and the tail itself comfortably clear of the surface. Diving ducks like Goldeneyes have much lower profiles and slope downwards towards the tail end, with the actual tail often sitting on or just under the surface.

In spring, Common Sandpipers en route to northern rivers and lonely lochs stop off here to glean what they can from the unpromising banks. If you disturb one it will fly off on stiff arched wings with a volley of panicked piping calls, showing off its broad white wing-bars. It probably won't go that far, and when it settles again you can get a proper look at it – a smallish, sandy-and-white wader with an engaging habit of frantically bobbing its back end up and down.

Another migrant that may call in at these reservoirs, especially in autumn but sometimes also in spring, is the Osprey. This wonderful, big, fish-eating raptor spends its winters in Africa, as in northerly latitudes its fish prey spends less time near the surface in winter, making hunting problematic. Migration often involves lengthy stopovers at good fishing places up and down the UK, especially those that lie on a straightish line in between the Osprey's breeding grounds in

Rings, tags and sat nav

We have long been fascinated by bird migration. Back in the 18th century, many naturalists believed that Swallows spent their winter hibernating, buried out of sight in mud at the bottoms of ponds! This sounds bizarre to us now, but perhaps when our own powers of travel were so much more limited, it was inconceivable that a bird you could fit in your hand could make it unaided across the Channel, let alone further afield. Now we know where most migrating birds spend their summers and winters, and the routes they take between them – much of this knowledge has come through ringing studies.

Uniquely marking individual wild birds – usually with numbered leg rings but occasionally with a wing or neck tag – gives us a way of finding out what they do, where they go and how long they live. Birds can be ringed in the nest as chicks, or as adults which ringers trap in mist nets that do not harm the birds. Many trapping sites are located at good migration places to catch birds whilst they are on the move. The ring fits loosely around the leg but isn't big enough to trap the toes, and doesn't seem to cause the bird much concern. Of course, most birds will live and die without ever being seen closely enough for a human to read a numbered ring on its leg, but if you ring enough birds you will eventually get some recoveries, whether a dead bird or a living one that is seen or trapped again.

Ringing in the UK is governed by the British Trust for Ornithology, who trains ringers, issues rings and collates ringing recovery data. Ringing began more than a century ago in 1909, and today some 800,000 birds are ringed each year, of which somewhere between one in 50 and one in 100 are recovered in some way. That amounts to a very large volume of data. To get some idea of what this means, take a look at the *Migration Atlas*, produced by the BTO, in which ringing recovery data is plotted on maps to show how detailed a picture we've built of the migratory habits of lots of familiar and not so familiar UK birds.

Because Osprey nests are large and relatively easy to find, a large proportion of UK Ospreys are fitted with coloured rings as chicks, and it's often possible to read the rings on such large birds from a distance, so we already know a great deal about Osprey travels. At the start of the 21st century, researchers have been taking this a step further and fitting a few Ospreys – chicks and adults – with small satellite transmitters. Now, for the first time, we can follow the migration of an individual Osprey every step of the way – the results yielded so far have been extremely interesting. If you see an Osprey with an aerial poking out of its back feathers when you visit King George V Reservoir, get online and you may be able to find out exactly where it's been, as well as follow where it goes next.

Scotland and good points to cross the English Channel. Most Ospreys seen in London pass straight overhead, and so you should consider yourself fortunate if you see one at all. However, if you're very lucky you may get the opportunity to see one fishing or perched in a tree around one of the reservoirs.

One of the big features of birdlife at the Chingford Reservoirs is a winter gull roost of truly epic proportions. There can be many thousands of birds using the two reservoirs in winter, about two-thirds using William Girling Reservoir and the remainder King George V (around 40,000 were counted one evening in January 2004). Almost all of the birds involved are (in descending order of size) Great Black-backed, Herring, Lesser Black-backed, Common and Black-headed Gulls. They start to arrive in the afternoon, often travelling in strings or Vs as if impersonating geese, and they make an impressive spectacle, whether you are a gull fan or not. Dedicated gull-watchers will be trying to pick out the handful of individuals that don't belong to the five common species from this bewildering throng of gull-kind.

Three of the rarer species share a common feature – white primaries. These are the long wing feathers that poke out furthest when the bird is at rest, and in adults of all five of the regular species they are black–tipped with white spots or edges, so if you find a gull with solid white primaries you've found something special. The largest white-winged gull is the Glaucous Gull, which is similar to a big Herring Gull with a pale grey back and wings and those white wing-tips. Its smaller, more delicate cousin is the Iceland Gull, closer to Common Gull in shape with long wings and a gentle-looking, rounded head. These two hail from the far north, breeding in Iceland, Greenland and other Arctic lands, and only a few bother to fly this far south each year.

The third white-winged gull is the Mediterranean Gull, a recent UK colonist from southern Europe, which is more along the lines of a Black-headed Gull in size and pattern. It is slightly larger, has a hefty scarlet bill and, when it acquires its breeding plumage in late winter, a coal-black hood which reaches well down its nape, unlike the Black-headed whose hood is chocolate-brown (it was presumably named before we knew there was a blacker-headed gull out there) and only reaches the back of its head.

Adult gulls of the five most common species are relatively easy, it's identifying the young ones that causes birdwatchers the worst headaches. Big gulls take four years to reach adult plumage, and pass through a baffling array of moult stages on the way. Size and shape can help but size can vary considerably and shape is often dependent on posture. Add to that a good measure of taxonomic uncertainty – biologists are forever reclassifying species but it seems to be particularly rampant with gulls. Gull ID is an evolving science and modern field guides may include some newly-defined species that look similar to Herring Gull, but are identified by features such as shape and wing-pattern. Beware of becoming too interested in gull identification – it can become an obsession, and before you know it your ideal Sunday afternoon is one spent on a rubbish dump with only a telescope for company.

The river itself – both the navigation section on the west of the reservoirs and the diversion on the east – is worth a look for some light relief in the form of small birds. Kingfishers zip up and down over the water, and if you're lucky you'll see one paused on a riverside branch, ready to dive headfirst after some unlucky minnow or stickleback. Grey Wagtails frequent the watercourses too, showing off their brilliant yellow bums as they strut about wagging their long tails. The surrounding fields attract Pied and (on passage) Yellow Wagtails and once a Citrine Wagtail, a rare vagrant from the east.

Heading south, the Walthamstow Reservoirs are smaller and, with their vegetated islands, somewhat friendlier-looking water bodies.

Although most of them also have the dreaded concrete margins, the islands provide shelter for birds and their edges offer aquatic vegetation which encourages insects. There are 11 reservoirs here if you include Banbury Reservoir, all packed neatly together like jigsaw pieces with the narrowest of causeways in between. Some have 'proper' names but the cluster of four smallish reservoirs in the south-east of the area have numbers instead (note that one of them has a narrow waist halfway across its length and is therefore treated as both Reservoir 2 and Reservoir 3!). Different sections of the River Lee – the navigation, the diversion and the flood relief channel – pass on either side of the complex of reservoirs. Footpaths run around and in some cases between all of them. You can obtain a day permit or an annual permit to visit the reservoirs at the office by the gate.

As with the bigger reservoirs, these attract plenty of ducks in winter, the most numerous being Mallard, Teal, Shoveler, Pochard and Tufted Duck. Some stay through summer, as do the masses of Canada and Greylag Geese that graze the banks and accost visitors for food. The island trees provide winter roosting places for Starlings and Woodpigeons, and suitable nest sites for Grey Herons and Cormorants. A recent addition as a breeding bird in London is the Little Egret, which has bred in the heronry since 2006. In spring and autumn, a few waders will call in, though they rarely stick around.

The lakes are popular with anglers, who periodically haul colossal Common or Mirror Carp from the depths. On sunny days, you could see these leviathans basking just below the surface. Some of them top 13kg – too large even for the notoriously capacious-throated Cormorant to gulp down. Other common fish include Rudd, Roach, Perch and Bream.

From mid-spring dragonflies and damselflies start to appear. Red-eyed Damselflies, Banded Demoiselles, Black-tailed Skimmers, Emperor Dragonflies and Brown Hawkers are among the species found here, but the scene is dominated by masses of Common Blue and Azure Damselflies. The males look like electric-blue needles bobbing gently on an invisible blur of wings, scouring vegetation for food and females. Identifying blue damselflies can be tricky (especially the females). If you visit later in the day the damsels will be spending more time resting, which will allow you to scrutinize them more carefully.

Immediately south of Walthamstow Reservoirs is Walthamstow Marshes Nature Reserve, a block of fairly unspoilt marshland sliced in half by a railway line. How marshy the place is depends on recent rainfall, but there are always damp patches as well as some reed bed and drier, scrubby areas. This place is most interesting in spring and summer, when its diverse flora is on show, insects are on the wing and hosts of warblers have arrived and are singing furiously in the race to attract a mate and breed.

The marshy parts of the site hold both Reed and Sedge Warblers in summer. The scrubby areas are more attractive to Blackcaps, Whitethroats and Lesser Whitethroats – the last two can be told apart by the rusty-brown wings of the Whitethroat and the grey-and-white look of the Lesser Whitethroat. The warblers feast through the summer on a rich supply of insects and other invertebrates, encouraged by the well-managed wild plant communities here. Little Owls visit the marshes from time to time and cause distress among the small songbirds, but these owls are mostly insect-eaters themselves.

Walthamstow Marshes have plenty of Wood Mice and Field Voles, which in turn attract Kestrels. With their extraordinarily acute eyesight, these falcons can actually see where voles have urinated in the grass on their travels – and given that voles dribble pee practically constantly, the ability to spot the pee-trails helps a hovering Kestrel to easily locate a hapless vole. The Kestrel hangs, body steady between pulsing wings as it

Above: *Little Owls are superbly camouflaged*

scans the ground. It falls a few feet for another scan then finally drops fast into the grass to secure the furry prize.

All those tasty rodents attract other predators too. With a bit of luck, you could bump into a Stoat or a Weasel here. Both are brown, elongated rippling creatures with shortish furry tails, neat round ears and a perky expression. Stoats are larger, with black tail tips and more neatly divided brown upperparts and white underparts, though often all you'll get is a fleeting glimpse. If you do spot one of these little livewires racing past, try squeaking at it – you can make a good squeak by kissing the back of your hand with tightly pursed lips. Both Stoats and Weasels are very curious by nature and it may decide to come back and investigate you in case you turn out to be a giant mouse. It's not unknown for shoelaces to be attacked. Watching a Stoat fearlessly taking down a Rabbit four times its size is enough to convince anyone that we are very lucky we're relatively big

animals, with such swift and audacious predators at large in our country.

In years gone by, Hackney Marshes was probably a wonderful wildlife place, much like Walthamstow Marshes to the north (but bigger). The land has been drained now and the turf is kept cropped short, forming a vast 'green space' but one that is pretty unattractive to wildlife, especially as most of it is football pitches. However, all this cropped grass does (when free of footballers – dawn is good) provide a good foraging place for thrushes and gulls in winter – both find it easy to dig up worms, leatherjackets (daddy-longlegs pupae) and other soil creatures in the short turf. Redwings, which with their strong face pattern look like Song Thrushes having a bad day, arrive as early as September, although they tend to begin their winter stay in our country by eating all the berries they can find before moving onto the fields. There will undoubtedly be Mistle Thrushes here too, big, sandy-pale and heavily spotted below.

Olympic impact

In 2005 London won the contest to host the 2012 summer Olympics, and the city rejoiced. Then it was time to get on with the hard work of creating suitable facilities for so many athletes and events – in just seven years and in a city where free space is already at an absolute premium.

There was much consternation among nature-lovers when it was announced that the main Olympic Park would be built in the Lower Lea Valley, just south of Hackney Marshes. There will be other developments elsewhere in the area. Inevitably, wildlife habitat will be destroyed, but the Olympic Delivery Authority is taking steps to minimize the impact, including arranging extensive surveys to assess just what wildlife is living in the area already.

Fish from the small Pudding Mill River have been caught and moved to the River Lee. Some 2,000 newts and hundreds of frogs have also been relocated. It's not possible to round up all the wildlife but to compensate for habitats that will be lost, a new nature area is planned for the Olympic Park. It is to be called the Waterworks Park and will include a Sand Martin nesting bank. Stretches of river that are at present polluted and full of rubbish will be cleaned up and remodelled to be better for wildlife. The accommodation in the Olympic Village, which will become housing for ordinary people after the event, will be designed to be wildlife-friendly as well as environmentally sound. They will hopefully include green and brown roofs to provide extra habitat, and boxes or 'ways in' for birds that like to nest in buildings, such as Swifts.

It is encouraging to see the efforts being taken to minimize the impact of this development on the wildlife of the Lee Valley. Although it will bring major change and not all of it positive, most Londoners still see the Olympics coming to their city as a generally good thing – if the whole project brings any long-term benefits for London wildlife, that can only help.

Above: Sand Martins

Thrushes obtain their prey with a straightforward search/listen/pounce system. Gulls, which are of course not specialized invertebrate hunters like the thrushes, have a neat trick for catching worms. Look out for them doing it here – they seem to jog on the spot, pattering their big webbed feet rapidly on the ground for a few seconds. Then they wait. It may be a trick learned from watching footballers warming up… but more likely the gulls' drumming feet creates sound and vibrations that mimic the falling of heavy rain. Earthworms surface when it rains, as the wet ground makes it easy for them to move about, but of course there's no rain this time, just a hungry gull.

How did this behaviour develop? It seems to be an extension of a behaviour they practise in more traditional seaside environments, called 'puddling'. Here, the gulls do their Riverdance impressions in shallow rock pools, creating a disturbance which alarms tiny fish and other rock pool creatures, making them dash for shelter and thus reveal themselves to the sharp-eyed and quick-billed gulls. The same trick works on land, albeit for different reasons. As avian intelligence goes, gulls are close to the top of the scale, showing adaptive and inventive abilities in common with such bird brainboxes as crows and parrots.

A little way from the Lee Valley proper are Stoke Newington Reservoirs, a pair of rather small reservoirs just south-west of the Walthamstow Reservoirs group. Though they look on the map pretty unpromising, these reservoirs have yielded some remarkable records for those who've watched them – and the skies over them – consistently. In a concerted effort to get a clear picture of how many raptors overfly the area in the course of one spring, watchers logged nine Common Buzzards and eight Red Kites going over in April and May 2009, along with a Marsh Harrier and a Black Kite – the latter a real rarity for anywhere in Britain, let alone London. In between raptors, the birdwatchers have also observed

several species of butterflies including Holly Blues and Green-veined Whites using the scraps of vegetated land around the reservoirs. A few ducks and other water birds use the reservoirs as well.

Beyond the M25, the Lea Valley heading northwards has more great wildlife habitat. For an interesting wildlife-themed day trip out of London, you could do much worse than visit the woodland and extensive jumble of lakes just north of Waltham Abbey. The River Lee Country Park at Fishers Green has birdwatching hides and other facilities and is a great place for wetland wildlife, most famously for wintering Bitterns. With Bitterns now regularly found at the London Wetland Centre, Fishers Green has lost one of its unique selling points, but is still a great place to see wetland wildlife in a lovely, peaceful setting that's just a stone's throw from London. Just to the south, adjoining Waltham Abbey, is Cornmill Meadows, a haven for butterflies, dragonflies and other insects.

Another speciality at Fishers Green is the Nightingale, a rarity in London but prospering here. You don't have to come at night to hear one – they sing through the day. They are, however, summer visitors and won't be around until mid-April at the earliest. A nearby Nightingale singing is pretty much unmistakable, even if you've never heard one before – the notes have a remarkable full, rich and almost emotional quality. If the Nightingale is a bit further away its special song may become lost among the general avian hubbub. The song is very varied but perhaps the most distinctive part of it is a series of long, drawn-out, soft and very high-pitched 'seeeeee' sounds, which precede a tumble of deeper, almost throbbing liquid notes. Like so many skilled singers the Nightingale usually hides in deep cover and lets its voice do the talking – it is an unremarkable-looking bird anyway, like an oversized Robin that's mislaid its red breast

Back inside the M25, a street or two east of King George V Reservoir are Yardley Hill and Pole Hill, which make up the westerly tip of Epping Forest, the largest and probably the most important

Woodland watching

There is an art and a craft to wildlife watching. Luckily, you can still see plenty of wildlife without having the first clue about that art and craft, especially in places like central London where the animals are quite accustomed to people and therefore pretty fearless. You can also see plenty of birds on a reservoir if you have a telescope, because the scope reaches well beyond the sort of distance that would cause the bird to decide you're too close and it's time to fly away.

In the woods, it's all different. The trees hide the wildlife from you and vice versa, but you can be sure that 9 times out of 10 a deer will hear you coming before you hear it, and a woodpecker will see you and deftly sidle out of view while you're busy scanning the wrong tree. It's very easy to spend hours in the wood and go home feeling you didn't really see anything.

To get the most out of a woodland visit you do need to pay a little attention to fieldcraft. That doesn't mean you must dress in camouflage gear and smear yourself with fox dung, but it does mean keeping the noise down, moving a little more slowly than you might otherwise, and paying close attention to what your senses are telling you. Noise means heavy footfalls, so tread softly, but also make sure you talk in a low voice if you're out with others and beware of clothes-noise. Many a jacket that looks great for country walks makes a complete swishy racket when you walk about in it. Not only does noise tell the wildlife where you are, but it can make you miss sounds made by nearby animals.

Time of day is another factor. It really is worth rising early, when you'll have the wood more or less to yourself. Birds are particularly active in the early morning, eager to do some singing to remind their neighbours whose territory it is, and to have some breakfast after the long night. Also, an early visit means you may catch nocturnal mammals on their way back to bed.

Mammals mostly have a powerful sense of smell, so if you spot some distant deer and want to get closer, circle round until any breeze is blowing from them towards you and not the other way round – that way they shouldn't pick up your aroma (there really is no point trying to mask your human smell – even if all you can detect from your armpit is a pleasant whiff of neutral-scented deodorant, the woodland mammals will be able to pick up a whole lot more).

It's also well worth pausing now and then and just seeing what you can see around you. Not only will this force you to be really quiet and to look more carefully, but animals can get used to the presence of a non-moving human very quickly, and may even come quite close to you.

Left: *Male Purple Hairstreak butterfly on an oak leaf*

area of woodland in London and very much on the radar of wildlife-watchers based around this part of the Lee Valley. The forest covers 6,000 acres, extending north-eastwards to Theydon Bois and Epping, and although it is cut through with numerous roads it remains a really valuable area of wildlife habitat.

Most of the forest comprises mixed deciduous trees, mainly Beech, oaks, Hornbeam and birches. Some of the trees are very mature and each one has its own thriving ecosystem of invertebrate life. The forest is a popular area for walkers and there are numerous clear 'rides' – these are convenient for people but good for wildlife as well, especially flowers and butterflies – and also some open meadowland areas and a number of ponds, some of them large enough to attract wildfowl.

The woodland birds include all three of the UK's breeding woodpeckers, other tree-climbers in the form of Nuthatches and Treecreepers, Tawny Owl, several species of tits, finches and warblers, and a few real specialities. One such bird is the Woodcock, a long-billed brown wader which performs its 'roding' display flight at dusk over the forest in spring, circling and calling. It can be viewed flying above some of the forest clearings, though you should take care when visiting the forest in the late evening as the car parks are sadly used for various unsociable activities.

On the edges of the open patches live a few Tree Pipits which, like Meadow Pipits, look like mini-thrushes with spotty underparts and brown upperparts. 'Tripits' are summer visitors to Britain, whereas 'Mipits' are resident and can also be seen in winter on the marshes. There are several subtle plumage and structure points that distinguish them from each other and can be learned with practice. Both pipits sing in flight, but the Meadow Pipit often takes off and lands on the ground, while the Tree Pipit's song flight begins and ends in a tree. Be careful, though, as this behaviour quirk does not always hold true and 'Mipits' may sing from trees or shrubs. The best way to tell them apart is to learn the song – that of the 'Tripit' is a bit more interesting and varied.

Another Epping Forest speciality is the Marsh Tit. The forest also used to have a few pairs of the near identical Willow Tit but they now appear to have disappeared, which is very sad although it makes things easier for you – if it's a small brown tit with no white wing-bar or nape and a neat black cap and bib, it's almost certainly going to be a Marsh Tit. With good views, you should see the slight two-tone pattern on the cheek (white towards the bill, transitioning abruptly to a very pale fawn towards the neck) that is one of the most reliable ways of telling Marsh Tits from Willows. Call is another quite good clue – the Marsh Tit's usual call is a distinctive sneezing *'pitchou'* while the Willow gives an equally distinctive nasal, sneering *'jiiiir'*. Sadly the Marsh Tit itself is now rare in the forest and may be going the same way as its relative.

Winter can be quiet in the woods, though finches such as Siskins and Lesser Redpolls may visit. This is the time to check the larger ponds – Connaught Water in the south of the forest is probably best and attracts a variety of wildfowl.

Fungal feasts

Woodlands are better than any other habitat in this country for fungi, or at least for the visible parts of fungi – the fruiting bodies which we call (without meaningful discrimination) mushrooms or toadstools. These structures are the fungal kingdom's version of flowers – they exist solely to produce and release spores. The main growing part of the fungus is a mass of threadlike mycelia that is usually out of sight, in the soil or within the decaying wood out of which the fruiting body appears.

Epping Forest has about 1,200 species of fungi. Londoners, ever enterprising, have turned in increasing numbers to the practice of gathering wild fungi to eat, and it is to woods like these that they head, cotton bag in hand and field guide in pocket to ensure they don't accidentally pick a Death Cap, Destroying Angel or other similarly lethal species by mistake. Unfortunately, a mushroom picked before it matures and lets loose its spores (and they mostly have to be if you want them to taste nice) is a mushroom that makes no contribution to its parent fungus's reproductive success. Also, it deprives specialist mushroom-eating insects of their food source. Once the restaurateurs started getting involved, the annual mushroom harvest became unsustainable and ecologically damaging.

The Epping Forest Conservators have done their bit to safeguard the more delicious wild fungus species by introducing a licensing scheme. Only licence-holders may pick mushrooms in the forest, and only in limited quantities. Collection for commercial purposes is strictly forbidden.

If you want to pick mushrooms here, first you must apply for a licence. Next, learn your mushrooms – the ones to avoid as well as the ones to go for. There are helpful field guides on the market, but there's no substitute for a guided, expert-led fungus foray to introduce you to the goodies and the baddies face to face.

Below: *White-lipped Snails on Fly Agaric toadstools*

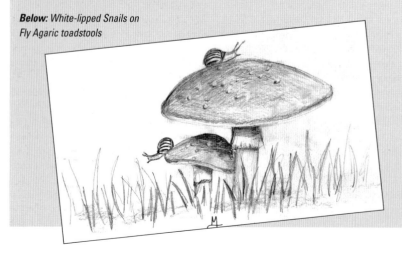

Mandarin Ducks are present all year round, although they are most numerous in winter. The males are at their ludicrously bright best in winter and early spring, when the lavish crest, big orange wing 'sails' and riot of clashing colours are freshly grown and ready to be paraded before the more modest greyish females.

Wild mammals in the forest include Fallow and Muntjac Deer, the former rather shyer than their Richmond Park counterparts. Muntjacs are, like Fallows, non-natives that have settled in and prospered. They are native to south-east Asia and our population apparently descends from escapees from Whipsnade and Twycross Zoos. Muntjacs are tiny deer, the size of an average dog, with solitary habits, so are not easy to see. Visiting early, walking stealthily and keeping the breeze blowing in your face are all going to improve your chances. Muntjacs sometimes sit back on their haunches like a cat or dog, which along with their hunched backs and the male's little tusks gives them a peculiar appearance unlike a deer. The woods also have Rabbits and the usual selection of small rodents, shrews and bats. Hedgehogs and Moles are here but hard to see, the latter especially due to its subterranean ways.

Grass Snakes, Adders and the common amphibians all live in the forest. Adders are distinctive with a zig-zag patterned back, and favour drier and sunnier areas while the Grass Snake rarely strays far from water, like the amphibians that are its favourite prey. If you stray off the path and get too close to an Adder, it may warn you off with a throaty, cat-like hiss. If you actually tread on one (which probably won't happen as they are sensitive to the vibrations produced by stomping human feet nearby) it may bite you so wear walking boots and stay on the paths. Trampling vegetation is not wildlife-friendly, and you could tread on something much less able to defend itself than an Adder.

Epping Forest is a common and until the second half of the 20th century people still grazed their livestock on the meadows and glades here. The animals occasionally wandered from the forest and, as recently as the 1980s, cows could be seen from time to time grazing on roundabouts in Chingford, or feeding in the front gardens of unfortunate homeowners who had forgotten to close their gates. The practice of grazing livestock declined sharply through the 1970s and 1980s and by the mid 1990s had ceased entirely. As a result, landscape and flora of the forest began to change, to the detriment of a wildlife community that had co-existed with the grazers for more than 1,000 years. Now, there are cows grazing in the forest once again, but they are not commoners' animals – they're a herd of pedigree English Longhorns provided by the Epping Forest Conservators. Many grassland flowers need well-grazed turf to flourish, and they in turn have their entourages of dependent insect species. So the cows are helping to conserve the grassland wildlife, and the scheme in turn is helping to conserve the cows, for they are a rare breed that has in the past almost become extinct.

Hidden Gems

ALTHOUGH THIS book is concerned with observing animals and plants that are generally at large in London, on the streets and along the river, there are also plenty of specific sites you can go to see wildlife. Previous chapters have looked at areas of London that form reasonably natural geographical groupings, but there are, of course, plenty more good sites that are rather isolated and so are often somewhat neglected. This chapter deals with a mixed bag of great wildlife-watching places in all parts of London.

Hampstead Heath is one of London's real jewels, and it is no surprise that the surrounding suburbs command such astronomical property prices – having the heath on your doorstep is worth big bucks. This is, famously, where Bill Oddie does his birdwatching these days, and he is just one of several committed heath-watchers who put in the hours exploring the grassland, trees, scrub and ponds on this wonderful rolling green space just on the edge of central London. One of the most notable features of the heath is how high the land rises. The views from Parliament Hill are famously far-reaching, and this is a great place to observe visible migration. Some of the heath's most surprising records – birds like Red-throated Diver, Whimbrel and Brent Goose – were all seen from this watchpoint, flying over en route to somewhere less urban.

Ring-necked Parakeets streak overhead in squawking gangs. The scrubby areas and reed beds attract warblers, and Green Woodpeckers lick up armies of ants from the grassland anthills. The usual common mammals live in the park. Watching pipistrelles and Daubenton's Bats hunting over the ponds is a very pleasant way to pass a warm summer evening. Later on, you may hear or even see one of the heath's Tawny Owls. The Highgate ponds are a chain of smallish lakes that run down the eastern edge of the heath. Three of them are used by intrepid outdoor swimmers of the human variety. On the other side of the heath are more ponds – there are 25 in total on the heath,

attracting common water birds. The woods close to Kenwood House hold Jackdaws, which is about as close as they get to central London.

A short distance to the north, **Highgate Wood** holds a surprisingly fine array of woodland birds and flowers, the former including woodpeckers and Nuthatch and the latter including Bluebells and Wood Anenomes.

7.1 Alexandra Park
7.2 Beckenham Place Park
7.3 Beddington Farm
7.4 Brent Reservoir
7.5 Camley Street Natural Park
7.6 The Chase Nature Reserve

7.7 Esher Commons
7.8 Hampstead Heath
7.9 Highgate Wood
7.10 Hounslow Heath
7.11 Trent Country Park
7.12 Wormwood Scrubs

Proving that you don't need lots of space to make a worthwhile place for wildlife, **Camley Street Natural Park** was created from an old coal yard in a tiny sliver of land around the Regent's Canal, behind King's Cross Station. It covers just 2 acres, but is a lush little oasis with reed beds around the canal and rows of Silver Birches sheltering you from the urban frenzy all around. The park opened in 1985 and has become much loved as a little refuge from city life in one of the most built-up parts of London. The reed beds attract Reed Warblers and Reed Buntings, and even Kingfishers sometimes fish the canal. A local speciality is the beautiful Earthstar fungus, which looks like a round ball set atop a star.

The spectacular Alexandra Palace, in north London near Wood Green, is surrounded by the pleasant **Alexandra Park** with its amenity grassland, patches of quiet woodland and lines of scrub, as well as an adjoining reservoir. While the park doesn't have much resident wildlife that's out of the ordinary, it is another of north London's high points and so is a good place to watch for migrating birds, as well as to enjoy spectacular views across London. Pied and Spotted Flycatchers, Stonechats, Whinchats and other scarce-for-London songbirds pass through in ones and twos each autumn. Regular watchers have found delights such as Red Kite, Wood Warbler, Ring Ouzel, Firecrest, Turtle Dove and Jack Snipe.

This park has a good variety of insects, including a population of White-letter Hairstreaks. These rare butterflies depend on elm trees, their caterpillars feeding on nothing else, and their numbers have taken a big hit in the wake of Dutch Elm Disease. The disease kills most elms in their infancy, and the young saplings are all that's left for the butterflies.

Further north still, in the borough of Barnet, is **Trent Country Park**. It is the reward for those who travel the Piccadilly line to its northern conclusion at Cockfosters, and has a 'real-countryside' feel, away from noisy roads and human hubbub. The park was once part of Henry IV's favourite hunting ground, and the mansion in it has undergone many changes of use, including being a prison for captured enemy officers during the Second World War. Today the estate is home to Middlesex University.

There are areas of farmland around the woodland and rough grassland, which is probably what gives the area its strong rural vibe – that and its popularity with horse riders and mud-spattered cross-country runners. Farmland birds you might see in the fields include Red-legged Partridges, dumpy colourful birds which you may have seen (but probably didn't recognize) in the supermarket – they were introduced from the continent to be hunted and eaten, as they are bigger and meatier than our native Grey Partridges. The fields may also attract flocks of Rooks, country cousins to the Carrion Crows that happily live in the city centre. Rooks look longer-billed than Carrion Crows, because they have bald faces. They also have a somewhat dishevelled, baggy-trousered look alongside the sleeker crows. Another farmland bird here is the Yellowhammer, a colourful relative of the Reed Bunting.

Trent Park has a couple of lakes, which attract Mandarin Ducks as well as the usual common water birds – Moorhens, Coots, Mallards and random feral geese. The woodlands have Lesser Spotted Woodpeckers, Nuthatches and Treecreepers as well as commoner species. Sadly, Spotted Flycatcher no longer breeds here. Woodland mammals like Badgers, Foxes, Hedgehogs and Wood Mice are all present, though shy and elusive. Butterflies seen here include the Ringlet, an attractive medium-sized species with dark-chocolate wings marked with a row of cream-ringed spots. This grassland butterfly is generally common throughout the UK but its distribution map shows a large hole over the London area – it is really only in outlying sites like this that you're likely to see one and even here it is uncommon.

If you're not worried about escaped convicts, **Wormwood Scrubs** in west London is worth a look, especially for migrating songbirds in spring and autumn. Although well known for its prison, 'The Scrubs' also has a nature reserve, established in 2002, where you can see common parkland birds year-round and, most years, scarcer species passing through. These may include Whinchats, Nightingales, Wheatears and Redstarts. The newest celebrity in the birding world, David Lindo (aka 'The Urban Birder'), is a Scrubs birder and has done much to entice Londoners to visit.

As well as the birds, the nature reserve has some interesting insects, including the spectacular Stag Beetle. This massive burly insect, a real London speciality, is most often encountered in flight, as males zoom about on warm summer evenings, hoping to sniff out a female. A flying male presents an alarming spectacle, to say the least, with its spread wing cases and fearsome mandibles extended like weapons systems. It is, however, quite harmless. That great size is achieved from between three and seven years spent as a growing larva, steadily munching through vast quantities of rotting wood. This long maturation period means Stag Beetles need ample supplies of undisturbed dead wood, which site managers in London nature reserves now ensure they have.

Close to the start of the M1 in the Hendon/Neasden area of west London, **Brent Reservoir** or 'The Welsh Harp' is a fairly large reservoir set in surroundings which include patches of recreation ground as well as residential streets and business parks. Unlike so many London reservoirs, Brent has natural banks and so is more hospitable to wildlife. A long list of rare and unusual birds have been found here, from the Little Bittern and Pallas's Sandgrouse that were 'collected' (i.e. shot) in Victorian times to the Blue-winged Teal that was captured in a less invasive way (on camera) in 1996.

The south-eastern corner of the reservoir is known as the Eastern Marsh and is the best part for wildfowl – accordingly, it is overlooked by a pair of birdwatching hides (you need a key, obtainable for a small fee from the Welsh Harp Conservation Group, to use them). An arm of the reservoir extends northwards to form the Northern Marsh, another good birdwatching area. Great Crested and Little Grebes nest in these marshy corners, Common Terns breed on purpose-built rafts out in the deeper water, flocks of dabbling ducks spend the winter here and a few waders visit at migration times. These include Green Sandpipers and Greenshanks, neither of which are obviously green. A close view in good light may show a vaguely greenish tint to the sandpiper's dark back, or enable you to see the greyish-green

***Above:** Male Stag Beetle*

legs that give the Greenshank its name.

As well as almost 250 species of birds, the reservoir has a long list of butterflies thanks to its relatively wild surroundings. In 1999 Marbled Whites were seen here for the first time, and have now established a colony – visit in July to see them as they visit thistles, knapweeds and other nectar-rich flowers. These most attractive butterflies have boldly patterned black-and-white wings but are actually members of the group known as 'browns', which includes less exciting-looking species like Meadow Browns and Small Heaths. You can amaze your friends by asking them to count the legs of a resting Marbled White – if they know a

Above: *Marbled White butterfly on Knapweed*

little about insects they'll be expecting to see six but in fact there are only four. All of the 'browns' and several other groups of butterflies are, functionally speaking at least, quadrupeds. The front pair of legs is still there, but they are tiny stubs, held against the head and only noticeable if you look very closely.

The reservoir's moth list, just shy of 200, includes some species that are very rare in London. There are, of course, many more that are very common and some of them, like the stunning Swallow-tailed Moth, are beautiful enough to be worth a second look any time.

The sandy soils from north-west London down into Surrey provides a foundation for several areas of light woodland and heathland, both within and outside of the M25, which attract an ensemble of wildlife that you're unlikely to find anywhere else in London. The best heaths are on the wrong side of the M25, such as the wonderful Thursley Common which is a National Nature Reserve. The heaths within London have been historically rather neglected and mismanaged, with the result that the expanses of open heather are lost or much reduced. Nevertheless, they remain worthy of exploration. **Esher Commons** (an SSSI) is one of the larger expanses, as are the nearby Prince's Coverts and Epsom Common – all three sites are mostly wooded although there are efforts underway to restore heathland at Esher Commons at least. Heathland restoration schemes elsewhere in the UK have proved to be very successful, with specialist heathland birds like Woodlarks and Nightjars quick to move into the new habitat, so hopefully the scheme at Esher will bring these birds back to their old haunts. A mature heathland is a wonderful thing, especially in summertime when dragonflies skim over the heather, lizards skitter off from their basking spots as you approach, male Silver-studded Blue butterflies gather to mob the females, and, after sunset, Nightjars begin their astonishing, hypnotic churring song and flit like huge, weightless moths

through the darkening sky. It's well worth taking the hop over the M25 to visit Thursley on a sunny July day and fantasize about having a similar experience within the London limits one day.

If you read birdwatching reports for London you're bound to see the name **Beddington Farm** (or Beddington Sewage Farm) cropping up again and again. The farm lies south of Mitcham Common, and with some 250 species of birds seen here over the years, is one of the most important birdwatching places in London. While few of us can get excited about visiting a former sewage farm, this site of wetlands, grassland and scrub can offer sights you won't find anywhere else in the city, most notably a huge breeding colony of Tree Sparrows, a species that is rare and declining across Britain. Here they are encouraged by the provision of nest boxes and feeders. The farm remains a working site with gravel extraction and landfill ongoing, and so only keyholders are allowed in to watch birds. Keys are notoriously difficult to come by (almost a case of 'dead birdwatcher's shoes'), but there are regular guided walks here and also you can view some of the site from surrounding footpaths.

Hounslow Heath, two miles south-east of Heathrow airport, is a former Royal hunting ground and has also had stints as a military training ground. Up until 1973 it was used for gravel extraction and waste dumping. Now, like many other such sites, it has been reinvented as a nature reserve. Unlike other so-called heaths in London this one has remnants of genuine heathland with actual heather – work is ongoing to extend these areas – as well as flower-rich acid grassland. One of the most attractive species of flowers you'll see here is the Bee Orchid, an extraordinary flower which looks like a bee, having evolved to entice real bees to come over and attempt to copulate with it, thereby unwittingly pollinating the flower. The bee in question doesn't live in this country, so most British Bee Orchids are self-pollinated. Cowslips also grow on the acid grassland, while the heath has Bell Heather and Dwarf Gorse. Hounslow Heath is important for its plant and insect communities – it is also probably London's best place for reptiles with Adders, Grass Snakes, Common Lizards and Slow-worms all present.

The sites of the gravel extraction are now wetlands with reed beds which hold a small selection of water birds and, of course, plenty of aquatic plants and insects. Although there is free access across the rest of the heath, you need the warden's permission to access this part, The scrubland is busy with singing warblers in summer, with flocks of Siskins and Lesser Redpolls present in winter. Plenty of rare birds have shown up over the years, including oddballs like White Stork and Red-backed Shrike.

South-east London is probably the most impoverished corner of the capital for wildlife, with no sizeable reservoirs and mainly small to tiny green spaces that have no more wildlife than you can expect to see in the city centre parks. One of the larger and more interesting parks is **Beckenham Place Park**, in between Beckenham and Bromley. The little River Ravensbourne, which flows through underground channels along much of its journey, is here a clear and pretty tree-lined stream, providing some extra interest to this park of amenity grassland, rough meadowland and woodland. Kingfishers occasionally shoot past, though the river is a little too shallow for them. It's ideal for Grey Wagtails, though, and is also a good place to see Banded Demoiselle damselflies in summer. The west side of the park is more undisturbed and has more woodland, so is best for birds, butterflies and the occasional woodland mammal. South-east London has a huge urban Fox population but in this park you could see other mammals too – perhaps Hedgehogs, bats, shrews and rodents.

The **Chase Nature Reserve** between Dagenham and Romford is one of the best places for wildlife in east London. Over 50 years of birdwatching has produced a list of more than 190 species, including such twitcher-enticing 'megas' as Pine Bunting and Great Snipe. The nature reserve's mix of shallow lakes, grassland, woodland and river makes for a good mix of breeding birds and other wildlife too, including the very rare Black Poplar tree. This tree has male and female forms, of which the females are by far the rarer, so The Chase's six female trees are cared for with great devotion. The wetlands are home to our rarest and most glamorous species of newt – the Great Crested. Breeding birds include Lapwings, Little Ringed Plovers and Skylarks.

There are, of course, many other places in London where you can enjoy watching wildlife. Every green space, however small, will attract common birds and insects, and there is always the chance of something out of the ordinary. This book can only cover a selection of places – there is almost certainly somewhere not far from where you live or work that will provide you with interesting wildlife sightings. Hopefully, though, you'll also feel inspired to venture further afield and visit some of the places you've never been to before.

Many wildlife-watchers will choose to adopt a 'local patch' that they can visit easily and frequently, and watch and record everything there over a long period. Such extended periods of observation can be incredibly rewarding if you have the patience, and the willingness to sometimes turn your attention away from your 'favourite' kinds of wildlife and learn about something else. No birds around in the park? See whether you can identify some the different kinds of bees and wasps visiting the flowers. Wrong time of year for flowers? Have a go at moss identification. One day you may find something quite remarkable, like the scientists who discovered a new-for-the-UK bug in the Natural History Museum garden, or the birdwatcher who found London's first Grey-cheeked Thrush in an unassuming woodland just north of the M25. Wildlife-watching really is a hobby for all times and

Below: *Grey-cheeked Thrush*

all places – nearly all of the most exciting discoveries of London wildlife have been made by local patch-watchers putting in yet another day of patient study.

Whether you invest several hours a day or a few minutes a year in your wildlife-watching, be sure of one thing; the city of London is not a lifeless concrete desert – far from it. Every day we learn more about the astounding variety of life that shares our capital with us and understand more how important it is to take care of that life as carefully as we look after ourselves. The more people who enjoy and appreciate London's wildlife, the better for us all.

Websites and Books

To FIND out more about London, wildlife and the conservation schemes discussed in this book, here are some handy websites and further reading material.

Websites

The internet has been an absolute godsend for wildlife enthusiasts – it's now possible to disseminate information more quickly and easily than ever before. The links below range from those of government organizations to blogs by enthusiastic individuals.

London wildlife websites

A wiki for London Birders – information on local patches, recent reports, the London bird list and more: http://editthis.info/londonbirders/Main_Page

The website of the London Natural History Society: www.lnhs.org.uk

East London Birders' Forum events, recent sightings and photos: www.elbf.co.uk

Lee Valley Park: www.leevalleypark.org

Rainham Marshes: www.rspb.org.uk/reserves/guide/r/rainhammarshes/index.asp

London Biodiversity Partnership: www.lbp.org.uk/index.htm

An organization dedicated to conserving one of London's best-known species, the Black Redstart: www.blackredstarts.org.uk

Birding in London (especially Wormwood Scrubs) and beyond with David Lindo: www.theurbanbirder.com

What's in My Backyard? Find out which species have been found on your local patch: www.gigl.org.uk/WIMBY/tabid/57/Default.aspx

The London Wildlife Trust: www.wildlondon.org.uk

Wildlife in and around the Hackney area: www.hackneywildlife.org.uk

Wildlife and conservation in Epping Forest: www.cityoflondon.gov.uk/Corporation/LGNL_Services/Environment_and_planning/Parks_and_open_spaces/Epping_Forest/EF_wildlife.htm

Welsh Harp Conservation Group: www.brentres.com

Bird sightings and access information for Beddington Farm: www.diporglory.co.uk/

Buying a permit for Thames Water reservoirs: www.thameswater.co.uk/cps/rde/xchg/SID-0950FB2F-97CE90D7/corp/hs.xsl/6206.htm

General wildlife websites

The Wildlife Trusts' website, with details of more than 2,200 reserves: www.wildlifetrusts.org

Amphibian and Reptile Conservation: www.arc-trust.org

Bat Conservation Trust: www.bats.org.uk

Buglife: www.buglife.org.uk

Butterfly Conservation – protecting our butterflies and moths: www.butterfly-conservation.org

Plantlife: www.plantlife.org.uk

Other websites

Transport for London's journey planner – work out how to get anywhere by tube, bus, boat and train: http://journeyplanner.tfl.gov.uk

All you need to know about congestion charges: www.tfl.gov.uk/roadusers/congestioncharging/

Overland rail travel into and out of London: www.nationalrail.co.uk

Online street maps: www.streetmap.co.uk

Plotting routes on foot around London: www.walkit.com/cities/london

Books

Field guides are books designed to help you identify the animal or plant you've seen. There is a bewildering variety on the market, and they vary greatly in quality and quantity of information. The ones recommended below mainly stick to British wildlife, but you'll find many that cover Britain and mainland Europe as well. Also listed are some books specifically on London wildlife, and a handful of the huge number of other wildlife-themed books on the market, some already mentioned in the text.

Field guides

New Holland European Bird Guide by Barthel, P; and Dougalis, P. New Holland, London, 2008.

Bill Oddie's Birds of Britain and Ireland by Oddie, B. New Holland, London, 2001.

New Holland Concise Bird Guide. New Holland, London, 2010.

Nature by Night. by Albouy, V; and Chevalier, J. New Holland, London, 2008.

New Holland Concise Butterfly and Moth Guide. New Holland, London, 2010.

New Holland Concise Wild Flower Guide. New Holland, London, 2010.

Wildlife Trusts Guide to Insects by Hammond, N; Doyle, S; and Carter, S. New Holland, London, 2002.

Wildlife Trusts Guide to Trees by Hammond, N; and Doyle, S. New Holland, London, 2002.

Mammals of Britain and Europe by MacDonald, D W; and Barrett, P. Collins, London, 1993.

Field Guide to Mushrooms and Other Fungi of Britain and Europe by Eppinger, M. New Holland, London, 2006.

London wildlife books

Where to Watch Birds in London by Mitchell, D. Christopher Helm, London, 1997.

Wild London by Green, I. Tiger Books, London, 2005.

London's Natural History by Fitter, R. Collins (New Naturalists series), London. (2006) 1945.

The Breeding Birds of the London Area, by Hewlett, J. (Eds). LNHS, London, 2002.

General wildlife books

The Naturalized Animals of Britain and Ireland by Lever, C. New Holland, London, 2009.

Gone Birding by Oddie, B. Methuen, London, 1983.

Millennium Atlas of Butterflies in Britain and Ireland by Asher, J. *et al.* Oxford University Press, Oxford, 2001.

Photographing Garden Wildlife by Taylor, M; and Young, S. New Holland, London, 2006.

The Complete Garden Wildlife Book by Golley, M. New Holland, London, 2006.

Where to Go

Getting about in London

The most popular means of travel in London is probably the extensive and (mostly) swift and efficient underground train (tube) network. The 11 colour-coded lines cover, between them, vast swathes of London suburbia, and in central London you are rarely more than five minutes' walk from a station. At many stations, especially in the centre, you can connect with one or more other tube lines and in the suburbs there are frequent connections with overland trains. All the main London rail terminal stations connect with multiple tube lines. Stations display maps of the full network which are easy to follow (note that you cannot extrapolate actual distances from the space between the stations on the map). Tube coverage is rather thin in south-east London, though overland rail is good.

Tube fares work on a nested 'zone' system, with the central area of London comprising Zone 1, a ring around this forming Zone 2, the next 'layer' outwards being Zone 3 and so on until Zone 6. Travel within outlying zones is generally cheaper, as are journeys that stay within a single zone. Many London commuters will have travelcards covering a month or more, which give them cheaper tube (and bus, and train) journeys. For day trips into London from outlying towns, a day travelcard covering all the zones is often the cheapest option, especially if you are visiting two or more places, but for casual travel within London it's worth investing in an Oyster card. You can top these up with money and they will give you big discounts on the London transport network, compared to the cost of buying single or return tickets. The cost of your journey is calculated when you touch the card against the yellow Oyster readers as you arrive at and leave stations, and when you board buses. A day of many journeys will be capped at the cost of a day travelcard. Note that many outlying overland rail routes don't yet accept payment by Oyster, though.

London buses are a cheaper but, regrettably, often slower option for getting around. However, if you are not pressed for time and prefer to have some clue what your surroundings look like, taking the bus is a more pleasant option, and they do go to more places. Many central London bus stops display digital details of which buses are expected and when, though they don't have quite the same level of accuracy as similar displays at tube stations. Using buses to reach the outlying parts of the city can take a very long time and involve several changes, but buses are often a good option for completing your journey once you've taken a tube or train to get within striking distance of your destination.

Local overland trains cover London suburbs on all sides of the city, departing from the main terminals at Charing Cross, Cannon Street, Blackfriars, Victoria, Paddington, Euston, Kings Cross, St Pancras, Marylebone and Liverpool Street. There are also the Thameslink trains which traverse the city north to south, going via London Bridge and St Pancras. For many of the non-central sites, the overland rail option is as good a bet, if not better than heading for the nearest tube station. The Docklands Light Railway (DLR) is a small overland (mostly) network of rather charming little window-fronted trains that serves the Docklands area in east London.

For those with mobility problems, London transport is generally good. Most modern buses and trains can accommodate wheelchairs and have doors level with the street or platform. Many tube stations have no easy step-free access, though, so check the tube map which gives details of which stations are and are not accessible.

If you have nerves of steel, cycling is a quick way to negotiate the streets of London. Cycle lanes exist here and there (and you can use bus lanes). Many London cyclists jump traffic lights, hop up on pavements, go the wrong way down one-way streets, nip down 'no cycling' paths in the parks and do other naughty things, none of which can be condoned – if that's your style, prepare to be sworn at now and then and perhaps arrested. Bike theft in London is a huge problem – if you can't stash your bike in your office or somewhere else that's safe, a combination of a sturdy lock and a bike which at least *looks* very cheap should help deter the thieves.

Driving in central London is slow, costly and expensive, as is parking. The congestion charge zone covers most of central London and it will cost you £8 to enter it (£10 if you don't pay on the day) between 7am and 6pm Mondays to Fridays. Parking places are typically difficult to find and very expensive once you do. Visiting the outlying parks and other interesting wildlife places by car is often not much better. Taxis give you the option of enjoying car rides through town without worrying about congestion charges or parking, but fares can be steep – share taxis with friends whenever you can. Black cabs accommodate five passengers – hail them with the usual display of shouting and waving, but only if they're empty and the orange light is lit. Using unlicensed taxis is risky and best avoided.

If it suits your journey, you can also travel along the Thames by boat. The boats call at 20 piers along the river, from Woolwich Arsenal pier in the east to Putney pier in the west. Fares are reasonable, and in fact nonexistent in the case of the Woolwich Free Ferry, which takes passengers across the Thames beyond the Thames Barrier for nothing. There is an Oyster card discount on some services.

The cheapest option of all is walking. For every Londoner who's allergic to walking there's another who walks daily to and from work rather than taking the tube and makes their colleagues feel bad for being so lazy. Walking in London can certainly be dull, stressful (on busy streets), scary (at some road crossings) and confusing. However, for every nightmarish route along a packed shopping street with multiple intersections there is probably a back-street way that's more relaxing and also more interesting – if you're a walking kind of person, take your A-Z and do some exploring. It's amazing how much of the city you can traverse via parkland or riverside paths. The streets of central London are generally pretty safe to explore at all times, but certain suburbs are downright dangerous to walk around in after dark, so use local knowledge and common sense.

The sites

The significant wildlife-watching sites discussed in this book are arranged alphabetically below. For each site, there is a grid reference, postal district and details of how to get there by public transport.

Alexandra Park
Map 7.1, page 90
Grid reference TQ302900
• By tube: The nearest station is Wood Green on the Piccadilly line. Cross the Broadway and follow Station Road to Alexandra Palace station, cross the rail bridge and the entrance to the park is ahead on your left.
• By rail: Trains from Moorgate (King's Cross on weekends) to Hertford North or Welwyn Garden City call at Alexandra Palace station. The journey takes about 20 minutes from Moorgate, 10 from King's Cross. Leave the station via the far exit (i.e. not via the ticket hall) and the park is ahead of you on the other side of the rail bridge.
• By bus: Buses on route W3 from Finsbury Park serve Alexandra Park. Many others, including route 29 from central London, serve Wood Green. Route 134 is among several that serve Muswell Hill on the other side of the park.

Battersea Park
Map 3.1, page 51
Grid reference TQ282772
• By tube: There are no nearby tube stations.
• By rail: Battersea Park rail station is at the south-eastern corner of the park. Trains between London Bridge and Victoria call there.
• By bus: Many routes serve the area including 137, 156, 344.

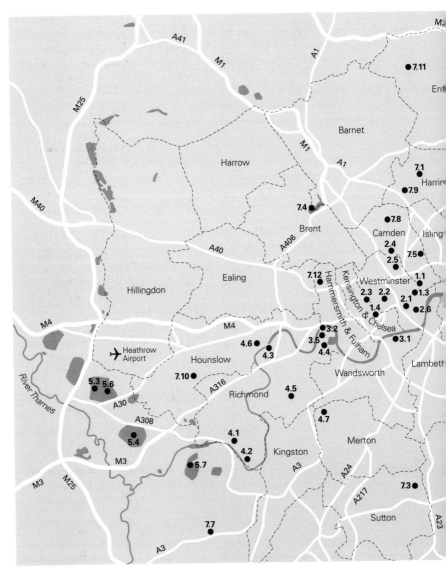

Streets of London
1.1 Centre Point
1.2 Tate Modern
1.3 Soho Square
1.4 Natural History Museum

Royal Parks of Central London
2.1 The Green Park
2.2 Hyde Park
2.3 Kensington Gardens

The Thames
3.1 Battersea Park
3.2 Chiswick Eyot
3.3 Greenwich Park
3.4 Lavender Pond Nature Park
3.5 Lonsdale Road Reservoir
3.6 Mudchute Farm
3.7 Stave Hill Ecology Park
3.8 Thames Barrier Park
3.9 Thamesmead

Parks of the South-west
4.1 Bushy Park
4.2 Hampton Court Park
4.3 Kew Gardens
4.4 London Wetland Centre
4.5 Richmond Park
4.6 Syon Park
4.7 Wimbledon Common

Marshlands and Reservoirs
5.1 Crayford Marshes
5.2 Dartford Marshes
5.3 King George VI Reservoir
5.4 Queen Mary Reservoir
5.5 Rainham Marshes
5.6 Staines Reservoirs
5.7 Walton Reservoirs

In and Around the Lee Valley
6.1 Epping Forest
6.2 King George V Reservoir
6.3 Stoke Newington Reservoirs
6.4 Walthamstow Marsh
6.5 Walthamstow Reservoirs

Hidden Gems
7.1 Alexandra Park
7.2 Beckenham Place Park
7.3 Beddington Farm
7.4 Brent Reservoir
7.5 Camley Street Natural Park
7.6 The Chase Nature Reserve
7.7 Esher Commons
7.8 Hampstead Heath
7.9 Highgate Wood
7.10 Hounslow Heath
7.11 Trent Country Park
7.12 Wormwood Scrubs

2.4 Primrose Hill
2.5 The Regent's Park
2.6 St James's Park

Beckenham Place Park
Map 7.2, page 94
Grid reference TQ383708
• By tube: There are no nearby tube stations.
• By rail: Ravensbourne and Beckenham Hill rail stations are on the edge of the park in the south and north respectively. Trains from Blackfriars take about 25 minutes to reach Beckenham Hill, a little longer from Ravensbourne. Footpaths lead straight into the park from both stations.
• By bus: Route 54 from Catford stops on Beckenham Hill Road, on the western edge of the park. Route 208 stops on Bromley Hill on the opposite side.

Beddington Farm
Map 7.3, page 93
Grid reference TQ290662
• By tube: The nearest tube station is Tooting Broadway on the Northern Line, from here you'll need to take a bus.
• By rail: Hackbridge rail station is adjacent to the western edge of the farm. It is served by trains from Victoria, which take about 30 minutes.
• By bus: Buses 127 and S1 stop at Hackbridge station.

Brent Reservoir
Map 7.4, pages 91-92
Grid reference TQ215870
• By tube: The easiest way is to go to Brent Cross on the Edgware branch of the Northern Line, and from there take a bus.
• By rail: Hendon station is served by trains from St Pancras (the journey takes about 13 minutes). From the station take Station Road west (i.e. not crossing the motorway flyover), turn left onto the Broadway and then right into Cool Oak Lane which will lead you to the reservoir.
• By bus: From Brent Cross tube station bus 142 goes to Cool Oak Lane on its way to Watford. Routes 182, 245, 297 and 302 stop on Neasden Lane near the western end of the reservoir.

Bushy Park
Map 4.1, pages 54-61
Grid reference TQ160690
• By tube: There is no near tube station. The nearest is Richmond on the District Line but from here it is a long bus journey with a change at Kingston.
• By rail: Teddington station, served by trains from Waterloo (journey time just over 30 minutes), is nearby – from the station head south along Park Road and turn into Chestnut Avenue to enter the park. Hampton Court station (35 minutes from Waterloo) is also close to the southern side of the park.
• By bus: Numerous buses serve the vicinity of the park, including routes 111, 131, 216, 415,440, 572 and 726. From central London you will have to change buses several times, typically at Hammersmith, Richmond and Kingston.

Camley Street Natural Park
Map 7.4, page 90
Grid reference TQ298836
• By tube: The park is a short walk from King's Cross St Pancras tube station (Victoria, Piccadilly, Northern, Circle, Metropolitan and Hammersmith and City lines) – head up St Pancras Road between the two overland rail stations of St Pancras and King's Cross and the Park is opposite the far end of St Pancras station.
• By rail: St Pancras and King's Cross rail stations are very close – see above for directions.
• By bus: Many buses stop along Euston Road and Pentonville Road, including routes 10, 18, 30, 76, 91, 203, 390 and 476. -

The Chase Nature Reserve
Map 7.6, page 94
Grid reference TQ514858
• By tube: Dagenham East on the District line is the nearest tube station. From here head north up Rainham Road South, then turn right into Dagenham Road and follow this road to the information centre.
• By rail: The nearest station is Romford, which is served by trains from Liverpool Street. The journey takes about 25 minutes.
• By bus: Route 174 stops nearby on the west side at the Farmhouse Tavern (request stop). The 252 stops in Upper Rainham Road on the east side.

Chiswick Eyot
Map 3.2, page 51
Grid reference TQ218779
• By tube: Turnham Green and Stamford Brook, both on the District line, are nearby. Make your way south to the Thames via Turnham Grinter, Chiswick High Road and Chiswick Lane from Turnham Green station, go via Goldhawk Road from Stamford Brook station.
• By rail: There is no nearby rail station.
• By bus: Many buses serve the area, including H91 and 120.

Crayford Marshes
Map 5.1, page 71
Grid reference TQ532775
• By tube: There are no nearby tube stations.
• By rail: Train services from London Cannon Street call at Erith and Slade Green stations (journey time about 30 minutes) en route to Dartford and also on a looped route via Sidcup. Ray Lamb Way crosses the marshes and can be reached from either of these stations.
• By bus: Several buses serve Erith, including the 99, 229 and 602. Buses 89 and B13 stop by Slade Green station. It is a long and complex bus journey from central London.

Dartford Marshes
Map 5.2, page 71
Grid reference TQ544774
• By tube: There are no nearby tube stations.
• By rail: The nearest station is Dartford, which is served by various trains from Cannon Street, Charing Cross, London Bridge and Victoria (journey time between 40 minutes and an hour, depending on the route). From Dartford station head north through a residential area (a long walk of at least a mile) for Joyce Green Lane, taking the footbridge over the A206. Beyond the footbridge, footpaths head north across the marshes.
• By bus: Many buses serve Dartford, with routes 476 and 477 going closest to the marshes.

Epping Forest
Map 6.1, pages 83-87
Grid reference TQ420985
• By tube: From south to north, Buckhurst Hill, Loughton, Theydon Bois and Epping on the north-eastern end of the Central line (Epping branch) all pass close to the eastern edge of the forest.
• By rail: Chingford station adjoins the forest in the south. It is served by trains from Liverpool Street. From the station take Bury Road north into the forest or Ranger's Road north-east into the forest (via Connaught Water).
• By bus: Bus 179 serves Chingford Station, from Barking via Gants Hill and Woodford Green. A bus journey here from central London involves several changes and may take a couple of hours.

Esher Commons
Map 7.7, pages 92-93
Grid reference, TQ135624
• By tube: There are no nearby tube stations.
• By rail: Oxshott station is adjacent to Oxshott Heath, part of the Esher Commons area. Stopping trains to Guildford from Waterloo (South West Trains) stop at Oxshott.
• By bus: Routes 218, 415, 427, 437, 513 and 527 all stop close to the area.

The Green Park
Map 2.1, pages 21 and 25
Grid reference TQ290799
• By tube: Green Park tube station, on the Piccadilly, Jubilee and Victoria lines, adjoins the park at its northern corner.
• By rail: Victoria is the nearest train station. From here it is a 10-minute walk to the park via Buckingham Palace Road/Buckingham Gate.
• By bus: Many buses stop on Piccadilly, which runs along the north-western edge of the park, including 8 and 38 from Victoria station. More than 50 different routes stop nearby.

Greenwich Park
Map 3.3, page 45
Grid reference TQ390775
• By tube: There are no nearby tube stations.
• By rail: Greenwich station is a short walk from the park, east along Greenwich High Road then right up Stock Street. Trains call at Greenwich from Charing Cross and London Bridge – there is also a DLR stop there.
• By bus: Many buses serve Greenwich, including routes 177, 180 and 199.

Hampstead Heath
Map 7.8, page 88
Grid reference TQ273866
• By tube: Hampstead tube station, on the Edgware branch of the Northern Line, is a short walk from the southern edge of the heath. Going via Flask Walk and Well Walk is probably the most direct way. Tufnell Park and Archway tube stations on the High Barnet branch of the Northern Line allow you to access the eastern edge of the heath via a slightly longer walk.
• By rail: Hampstead Heath rail station is served by London Overground trains, change at Highbury and Islington (overland rail or tube). From the station head up Parliament Hill. Gospel Oak station is also close, to the south-east of the heath.
• By bus: Many buses serve the area. Route 24 goes all the way from central London to Pond Street near Hampstead Heath station with no changes, though it does take nearly an hour.

Hampton Court Park
Map 4.2, pages 54-55 and 63
Grid reference TQ166676
• By tube: There is no near tube station. The nearest is Richmond on the District Line but from here it is a long bus journey.
• By rail: Hampton Wick station, served by trains from Waterloo (journey time about 30 minutes), is nearby. From the station take High Street South and Park Road to reach the park. Hampton Court station (35 minutes from Waterloo) is an alternative option.
• By bus: Numerous buses serve the Hampton Court/Bushy Park area; see Bushy Park for more details.

Highgate Wood
Map 7.9, page 88
Grid reference TQ283887
• By tube: Highgate tube station is nearby, on the High Barnet branch of the Northern Line. Head north up Archway Road then turn right up Muswell Hill Road – the wood is on your left.
• By rail: There is no nearby rail station.
• By bus: Numerous buses serve Archway Road, including routes 4, 17, 41, 143, 390, C11 and W5.

Hounslow Heath
Map 7.10, pages 93-94
Grid reference TQ123745
• By tube: Hounslow Central on the Piccadilly line is about a mile or so east of the heath, follow Lampton Road south then Staines Road west.
• By rail: Hounslow rail station is less than a mile from the heath. Services from Waterloo take about 16 minutes. From the station go up Station Road, left onto Hanworth road then right up Simpson Road to reach the south-eastern corner of the heath.
• By bus: Routes 116, 117, 237, 417 and H23 call along Staines Road by the main entrance to the heath.

Hyde Park
Map 2.2, pages 25-41
Grid reference TQ275803
• By tube: Hyde Park Corner tube station, on the Piccadilly line, adjoins the south-eastern corner of the park, while Marble Arch and Lancaster Gate tube station on the Central line adjoins the north-eastern and the north-western corners respectively. Knightsbridge (Piccadilly line) is near to the southern edge. Follow exit signs when leaving whichever station you use to ensure you emerge by the park and not on the wrong side of the road.
• By rail: Paddington is the nearest station – from here head down Spring Street and Lancaster Terrace to the north-western corner of Hyde Park.

• By bus: A great many buses serve the area from all directions – take any bus heading for Marble Arch, Hyde Park Corner or Knightsbridge.

Kensington Gardens
Map 2.3, pages 25-41
Grid reference TQ265803
• By tube: Lancaster Gate tube station on the Central line adjoins the north-eastern corner of the gardens, while Queensway on the same line adjoins the north-western corner. On the south, High St Kensington (District and Circle lines) and South Kensington (Piccadilly, District and Circle lines) are nearby.
• By rail: Paddington is the nearest station – from here head down Spring Street and Lancaster Terrace to reach the north-eastern corner of Kensington Gardens.
• By bus: A great many buses serve the area from all directions – take any bus heading for Bayswater, Kensington High Street or Knightsbridge.

Kew Gardens (entry charge)
Map 4.3, pages 61-63
Grid reference TQ182769
• By tube: Kew Gardens tube station on the District line is very close – from the station take Station Parade then Lichfield Road.
• By rail: There is an overland rail connection on the same line as the tube station – trains go from Richmond and take 3 minutes (trains from Waterloo to Richmond take about 20 minutes).
• By bus: Routes 7, 65 and 391 stop close to the main entrance.

King George V Reservoir (permit required)
Map 6.2, pages 76-79
Grid reference TQ374964
• By tube: There is no nearby tube station.
• By rail: The entrance to the reservoir is at the south-eastern corner of the south basin. Ponders End station is nearby to the south-west

of the reservoir. Trains from Liverpool Street to Hertford North call here – journeys take around 20 minutes. Chingford station is west of the reservoirs – a longish walk away. It is also served by trains from Liverpool Street, and Chingford is the final stop on the branch.
• By bus: Bus route 313 goes from Chingford station to Enfield and stops at the bottom of Kings Head Hill.

King George VI Reservoir
Map 5.3, page 74
Grid reference TQ041732
• By tube: There is no nearby tube station.
• By rail: Staines station is less than a mile away.
• By bus: several bus routes serve the area, with routes 116, 203, 216, 417, 419, 436 and 572 calling nearby along the south edge of Staines Reservoirs' south basin.

Lavender Pond Nature Park
Map 3.4, page 46
Grid reference TQ362803
Follow the directions for Stave Hill Ecology Park (see page 108) – the site is just a little further north on the Rotherhithe peninsula.

London Wetland Centre (entry charge)
Map 4.4, pages 57 and 63-65
Grid reference TQ228770
• By tube: The nearest tube station is Hammersmith, on the Piccadilly, District and Hammersmith and City lines. From here take a bus or walk (about 2 miles) along Hammersmith Bridge Road, which becomes Castelnau, and turn left up Queen Elizabeth Walk for the centre entrance.
• By rail: The nearest rail station is Barnes, which is a 20-minute journey from Waterloo. From here, go north up Rocks Lane, turning right when you reach Queen Elizabeth Walk (about a mile's walk).
• By bus: The 'Duck Bus' (route 283) runs from Hammersmith station to the centre entrance. Routes 33, 72 and 209 from Hammersmith stop nearby at the Red Lion stop, a short walk from the centre.

Lonsdale Road Reservoir
Map 3.5, pages 51-52
Grid reference TQ218775
• By tube: The nearest tube station is Hammersmith, on the Piccadilly, District and Hammersmith and City lines. From here take a bus or walk (about 2 miles) along Hammersmith Bridge Road, which becomes Castelnau, and turn right down Lonsdale Road.
• By rail: The nearest rail station is Barnes Bridge, which is a 20-minute train journey from Waterloo. From Barnes Bridge station, walk north along The Terrace and Lonsdale Road to reach the reservoir.
• By bus: Route 419 from Hammersmith to Richmond serves Lonsdale Road, several others stop nearby.

Mudchute Farm
Map 3.6, page 46
Grid reference TQ382787
• By tube: There is no nearby tube station.
• By rail: DLR station Mudchute is adjacent to the western edge of the farm, the next station down (Island Gardens) adjoins the south-western corner.
• By bus: Routes D1, D6 and D7 call nearby.

Natural History Museum
Map 1.4, page 19
Grid reference TQ267790
• By tube: The museum is clearly signposted from South Kensington tube station (Circle, District and Piccadilly Lines). The main entrance is on Cromwell Road.
• By rail: Victoria is the nearest rail station, but is the best part of two miles' walk away.
• By bus: Routes 14, 49, 70, 74, 345, 360, 414 and C1 stop nearby.

Queen Mary Reservoir (Permit required)
Map 5.4, page 74
Grid reference TQ070695
• By tube: The nearest tube station is Heathrow Terminal 4 on the Piccadilly line, but walking from there really isn't an option.
• By rail: Ashford station (not to be confused with Ashford in Kent), served by trains from Waterloo, is about 1.5 miles away from the main entrance to the reservoir.
• By bus: Route 592 will take you from Ashford station to the reservoir. Routes 440, 555 and 557 are among those that stop along Staines Road West by the reservoir.

Primrose Hill
Map 2.4, pages 24 and 41
Grid reference TQ276839
• By tube: Chalk Farm on the Edgware branch of the Northern line is the nearest tube station. Reach the hill via Regent's Park Road.
• By rail: South Hampstead station is north-west

of the hill, some 20 minutes' walk away. Trains from Euston (London Overground) call there.
• By bus: Routes 27, 168 and 274 are among the many that pass near the hill.

Rainham Marshes (entry charge)
Map 5.5, pages 66-71
Grid reference TQ535800
• By tube: There is no tube station nearby.
• By rail: The nearest station is Purfleet, which is served by trains from Fenchurch street. From Purfleet Station, turn right, follow London Road/ High Street to 'The Royal' pub. From here head down to the Thames and join the riverside path (a joint foot and cycle path). Follow this path over the bridge and turn left to reach the reserve, or continue along the path to view the foreshore (access to which is free).
• By bus: Route 44 runs daily between Grays and Lakeside shopping centre via Purfleet. Other routes serving Purfleet include the 11, 103 and 372.

The Regent's Park
Map 2.5, pages 24-41
Grid reference TQ281828
• By tube: You are spoiled for choice. Regent's Park tube station on the Bakerloo line is on the south side of the park, a couple of streets away. Cross Marylebone Road and take one of the side streets heading north to reach the Outer Circle road that runs around the park's perimeter. On the south-eastern corner is Great Portland Street tube station on the Metropolitan, Hammersmith and City and Circle lines – again, just a couple of streets away. Baker Street tube station on the Bakerloo, Metropolitan, Hammersmith and City and Circle lines is at the south-western corner of the park, while Camden Town tube station on the Northern line (at the point where the two branches briefly converge) is a little further out at the north-eastern corner and is the preferred stop for those visiting London Zoo.

• By rail: Euston station is the nearest. From here go west along Euston Road until it becomes Marylebone Road, then take one of the side streets heading north to reach the Outer Circle.
• By bus: Many buses serve the roads around the park, including routes 88 and 453 from Oxford Street.

Richmond Park
Map 4.5, pages 54-63
Grid reference TQ200730
• By tube: The park is about 1.5 miles from Richmond tube station, on the District line. You'll need to traverse Richmond town centre, then head up Richmond Hill to Richmond Gate.
• By rail: Richmond station has an overground component as well as the tube train part. Trains from Waterloo take from 15-25 minutes depending on the number of other stops made. North Sheen station is about 1.5 miles north of the north-western corner of the park – again served by trains from Waterloo, which take about 25 minutes. Go south down Manor Road, turn left onto Upper Richmond Gate then second right down Kings Ride Gate for a path to access the park via East Sheen Common.
• By bus: Richmond is well served by buses. Route 85 stops close to the southern entrance to the park on Kingston Vale.

St James's Park
Map 2.6, pages 24-41
Grid reference TQ294798
• By tube: The nearest tube station is St James's Park on the Circle and District lines. From here go north up Queen Anne Gate and cross Birdcage walk to reach the southern side of the park. Charing Cross tube station on the Bakerloo and Northern lines is also nearby.
• By rail: Charing Cross station is closest. From here head south-west along The Strand, cross Trafalgar Square onto The Mall (through the large gate). The park is on your left.

• By bus: Many routes pass nearby. Routes 3, 11, 12, 24, 88, 453 are among those that stop nearby at Trafalgar Square or Haymarket (from Haymarket go south, turn right onto Pall Mall then left down the steps to reach The Mall.

Staines Reservoirs
Map 5.6, pages 71-74
Grid reference TQ051731
• By tube: There is no nearby tube station.
• By rail: Ashford station, served by trains from Waterloo (and not to be confused with Ashford in Kent), is about a mile away. Turn left out of the station and follow Church Road, Stanwell Road and Town Lane north.
• By bus: several bus routes serve the area, with routes 116, 203, 216, 417, 419, 436 and 572 calling nearby along the south edge of Staines Reservoirs' south basin.

Stave Hill Ecology Park
Map 3.7, page 42
Grid reference TQ361797
• By tube: Canada Water tube station, on the Jubilee line, is west of the park, about 15 minutes' walk away through residential streets.
• By rail: There is no nearby rail station.
• By bus: Routes 225, 381 and 395 call nearby.

Stoke Newington Reservoirs
Map 6.3, page 83
Grid reference TQ326876
•By tube: Manor House tube station on the Piccadilly line is nearby. Walk east along Woodbury Down, then turn right along Woodberry Grove/Lordship Road to reach the reservoirs.
• By rail: Stoke Newington and Stamford Hill stations are both about a 15-minute walk away. They are served by trains from Liverpool Street, which take 10-15 minutes.
• By bus: Many routes serve the nearby thoroughfares of Seven Sisters Road or Green Lanes. They include routes 29, 141 and 253 and 259.

Syon Park
Map 4.6, pages 61-63
Grid reference TQ171766
- By tube: There is no nearby tube station.
- By rail: Syon Lane is the nearest railway station. Trains from Waterloo call there, taking about half an hour. From the station, head south down Spur Road then north-east along London Road to reach the park entrance on your right.
- By bus: Routes that call nearby include the 237, 267, E2 and E8.

Thames Barrier Park
Map 3.8, page 46
Grid reference TQ412799
- By tube: There are no nearby tube stations.
- By rail: Pontoon Dock station on the DLR is next to the north-western corner of the park.
- By bus: Routes serving the area include the 474.

Thamesmead
Map 3.9, page 46
Grid reference TQ474811
- By tube: There is no nearby tube station.
- By rail: Abbey Wood is the nearest rail station. It is served by trains out of Charing Cross and London Bridge, which take 25–35 minutes. It is a long walk north to the shore, but there are

buses connecting with this and other nearby rail stations.
- By bus: Routes 178, 244, 401, 472 and X53 serve the area.

Trent Country Park
Map 7.11, page 90
Grid reference TQ290970
- By tube: Cockfosters, the northern terminus of the Piccadilly line, is adjacent to the park. You could also leave the tube one stop earlier at Oakwood to walk through a narrow south-eastern extension of the park.
- By rail: The nearest rail station is Hadley Wood, a two-mile walk away. Trains from Moorgate call there, taking about 30 minutes. It is west of the park – head east along Lancaster Avenue and then turn right into Cockfosters road.
- By bus: Route 298 goes to Cockfosters from Southgate, passing the park entrance. Routes 298 and 384 also serve Cockfosters.

Walthamstow Marsh
Map 6.4, pages 80-83
Grid reference TQ350878
- By tube: There is no nearby tube station.
- By rail: The nearest rail station is Clapton, less than a mile south-east of the reserve, and served

by trains from Liverpool Street. From Clapton station, go east down Southwold Road onto the riverside path, and cross the footbridge over the river to reach the reserve.
• By bus: Buses on routes 253, 38, 48, 56 and 333 all stop nearby.

Walthamstow Reservoirs (Permit required; day permit can be bought on arrival)
Map 6.5, pages 79-80
Grid reference TQ353890
• By tube: Tottenham Hale tube station (Victoria line) is west of the reservoir group, a five-minute walk away. East of the reservoirs is Blackhorse Road tube station, also on the Victoria line and taking just over five minutes to walk.
• By rail: Both stations are also served by overground trains. Trains from Liverpool Street to Tottenham Hale take 10 minutes. Blackhorse Road is on the Barking to Gospel Oak line.
• By bus: Buses 123 and 230 from Wood Green serve Tottenham Hale, as does route 41 from Archway.

Walton Reservoirs (Permit required)
Map 5.7, page 74
Grid reference TQ122685
• By tube: There is no nearby tube station.
• By rail: Hersham station is nearest, served by trains from Waterloo to Guildford. From here head north up Molesey Road for Queen Elizabeth II and Island Barn reservoirs.

• By bus: Bus service 501 goes from Hersham station up Molesey Road. Other routes serving Molesey Road include 131 and 451.

Wimbledon Common
Map 4.7, pages 62-63
Grid reference TQ247723
• By tube: Southfields, Wimbledon Park and Wimbledon tube stations, all on the District Line, are all east of the common and a mile or more away.
• By rail: Wimbledon rail station is served by trains from Waterloo. The common is about a mile's walk north through residential streets.
• By bus: Buses serving the area include routes 57, 85, 200 and 718.

Wormwood Scrubs
Map 7.12, page 91
Grid reference TQ221818
• By tube: East Acton, on the Central line, is the nearest tube station. From here, go north-west up Erconwald Street to reach the Scrubs.
• By rail: Willesden Junction is the nearest railway station, around a mile north of the eastern corner of the Scrubs. Trains (London Overground) call there from Euston. To reach the Scrubs from this station, make your way down Scrubs Lane via Tubbs Road and the High Street.
• By bus: Route 220 goes down Scrubs Lane, while on the other side route 72 goes down Old Oak Common Lane.

Species Guide

Species Guide

THERE HAVE been more than 350 bird species recorded in London, and many times that number of plants, insects and some other groups. Therefore, any attempt to illustrate everything you could conceivably see in London would have resulted in a book the size of a breeze block. However, a large proportion of those species are a) rare; b) small or difficult to see; c) gone altogether, i.e. no longer found in London; or d) all three.

In the interests of portability, this section is limited to the commoner and more noticeable species, along with the odd scarcity added to inspire you. Hopefully, there's a better than 80 per cent chance you'll find what you're looking for in here. If you do find something which isn't covered in these pages, please refer to one of the field guides recommended in the 'Websites and Books' section (page 96-97).

TREES

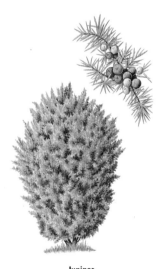 

Juniper
Juniperis communis
6m. Small conical evergreen tree or shrub, female plants with clusters of dark purple berries. Widespread though not especially common.

European Larch
Larix decidua
40m. Deciduous conifer. Male flowers yellow, female flowers red. Cones oval, tight scales. Common ornamental tree.

Norway Spruce
Picea albies
20-40m. The archetypal Christmas tree; prickly needles and long narrow cones. Planted widely for commercial purposes.

Scots Pine
Pinus sylvestris
35m. Conifer with flat, spreading crown. Needles long, cones rounded with large scales. Native to Scotland, widely planted as ornamental tree throughout UK.

Yew
Taxus baccata
10-25m. Long-lived conifer, also planted as hedge. Fruits red, berry-like. Planted ornamentally, also in woodlands.

London Plane
Platanus x hispanica
20-40m. Deciduous tree with variegated bark, large lobed leaves and spherical fruit. Common ornamental tree in city centre.

Alder
Alnus glutinosa
15-25m. Deciduous, leaves oval, produces catkins in spring, fruit small red-brown cones. Commonest in damp habitats such as river banks.

Silver Birch
Betula pendula
15-30m. Deciduous; whiteish bark, diamond-shaped toothed leaves, catkins in spring. Common and widespread, favours light dry soil.

Downy Birch
Betula pubescens
8-14m. Deciduous, like Silver Birch but bark brown and leaves hairy on underside. Prefers wetter soils than Silver Birch.

Hornbeam
Carpinus betulus
15-25m. Deciduous, forms broad round crown. Catkins becoming winged seeds. Leaves oval. Woodlands with heavy soils.

Hazel
Corylus avellana
8-10m. Trunk branches near base. Deciduous.
Leaves oval, catkins in spring, then hazelnuts.
Woodlands, forming understorey.

Beech
Fagus sylvatica
20-35m. Graceful, smooth-barked deciduous tree.
Leaves oval, fruit small nuts in bristly case. Mixed
woodland, also planted ornamentally (including
violet-leaved 'copper' form).

Sweet Chestnut
Castanea sativa
20-30m. Deciduous, leaves long and toothed,
catkins in spring, fruit edible chestnuts in spiny
case. Woodlands, prefers acidic soils.

Turkey Oak
Quercus cerris
20-40m. Broad-crowned, deciduous. Leaves long,
lobed; fruit squat acorn in bristly cup. Widely
planted ornamentally and in woodlands.

Holm Oak
Quercus ilex
30m. Like Turkey Oak but leaves smooth, acorns
elongated in scaly cup. Prefers dry soils.

Sessile Oak
Quercus petraea
20-40m. Tall oak with smoothly lobed leaves and
oval acorns in scaly cup. Prefers light, acidic soils.

English Oak
Quercus robur
15-40m. Wide-domed oak. Deeply lobed leaves,
long oval acorns in scaly cup. Woodland (often
dominant species) and more open situations.

Large-leafed Lime
Tilia platyphyllos
20-40m. Deciduous, large hairy heart-shaped
leaves, small spherical pendant fruit. Woodland
and widely planted ornamentally.

Common Lime
Tilia x europaea
20-45m. Similar to Large-leaved Lime, fruit grows in clusters, leaves flatter at base. Woodland and widely planted ornamentally.

Small-leafed Lime
Tilia cordata
20-25m. Similar to Large-leaved Lime, leaves rounder, fruit more elongated and in clusters. Woodland and widely planted ornamentally and commercially.

Wych Elm
Ulmus glabra
20-30m. Deciduous, broad-domed. Leaves toothed ovals, fruit flattened wing with central seed. Woodland and hedgerows.

English Elm
Ulmus minor
30m. Similar to Wych Elm, narrower shape. Mature trees rare due to Dutch Elm Disease. Most often found as sapling-like 'suckers' in hedges.

Tamarisk
Tamarix gallica
8m. Shrub-like, deciduous. Leaves delicate fronds,
flowers pinkish small elongated clusters.
Planted ornamentally in gardens and parks.

Goat Willow
Salix caprea
8-12m. Round-crowned, deciduous. Oval leaves,
catkins (including grey 'pussy willow').
Widespread in woods and more open situations.

Crack Willow
Salix fragilis
10-20m. Similar to Goat Willow. Leaves long
and narrow, bark deeply fissured. Often in damp
situations – boggy woodland and riversides.

White Willow
Salix alba
10-30m. Taller than Crack Willow, with narrower
shape. Leaves have white underside.
Lowland, often near rivers.

Grey Willow
Salix cinerea
10-30m. Deciduous. Leaves oval with pointed tips. Catkins green (male) or yellow (female). Damp situations, hedgerows.

Weeping Willow
Salix x sepulchralis
10-18m. Deciduous. Branches grow downwards. Leaves long and narrow, yellowish. Damp areas, widely planted in ornamental gardens.

Common Osier
Salix viminalis
10m. Deciduous. Branches quite erect. Narrow willow-like leaves, silvery on underside. Damp habitats.

Grey Poplar
Populus canescens
25-40m. Deciduous. Leaves toothed, vaguely diamond-shaped. Bark becomes blackish with age. Damp habitats.

Black Poplar
Populus nigra
15-25m. Similar to Grey Poplar, leaves smoother and triangular, bark darker. Damp habitats, also widely planted as a windbreak.

White Poplar
Populus alba
25m. Rounder than other poplars, leaves lobed (five points) and toothed. Bark grey-white. Wet areas, but generally quite tolerant of other conditions.

Aspen
Populus tremula
15-25m. Deciduous, round-crowned, bears catkins. Leaves round, rustle in slightest breeze. Prefers damper habitats, including hillsides and woodlands.

Rhododendron
Rhododendron ponticum
10m. Evergreen, leaves long ovals, shiny, flowers large loose pink blossoms. Invasive in woodlands, widespread and often planted ornamentally.

Wild Pear
Pyrus pyraster
12-25m. Round-crowned, deciduous.
Leaves oval, blossom whitish, fruit small pears.
Hedgerows and woodlands.

Crab Apple
Malus sylvestris
2-9m. Similar to Wild Pear, blossom pinker,
fruits small sour apples. Widespread in mature
woodland and hedgerows.

Medlar
Mespilus germanica
5-7m. Deciduous, squat low crown, oval leaves,
white blossom, small pear-shaped fruit.
Woodlands.

Rowan
Sorbus aucuparia
5-20m. Deciduous, delicate. Leaves small,
pinnate. Blossom white, then clusters of red berries.
Woodlands, widely planted as ornamental including
in city streets.

Whitebeam
Sorbus aria
5-20m. Deciduous, broad crown. Leaves oval,
shiny. White flower clusters become red berries.
Dry woodlands, especially on limey or chalky soils.

Wild Service Tree
Sorbus torminalis
15-25m. Deciduous, round-crowned.
Leaves lobed, white blossom becoming
round brown fruit. Mixed woodlands.

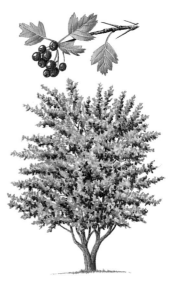

Hawthorn
Crataegus monogyna
10-16m. Deciduous, thorny. Leaves deeply lobed,
white blossom becomes red berries.
Common hedgerow shrub, also woodlands
and scrubby countryside.

Midland Hawthorn
Crataegus laevigata
12m. Similar to Hawthorn, leaves shallow-lobed.
Widely planted in cities, also found in woodlands.

Blackthorn
Prunus spinosa
5m. Deciduous, leaves oval, very thorny.
White blossom becoming dark round fruit (sloes).
Hedgerows and scrubland.

Wild Plum
Prunus domestica
6-10m. Deciduous, oval toothed leaves, creamy-white
flowers mature into dark purple plums. Planted in
orchards and gardens, naturalized elsewhere.

Myrobalan Plum
Prunus cerasifera
8-12m. Similar to Wild Plum, fruit rounder
and redder. Hedgerows and field edges.

Wild Cherry
Prunus avium
25m. Deciduous. Leaves long, oval with
pointed tip, toothed. Fruit small red cherry.
Mixed woodlands.

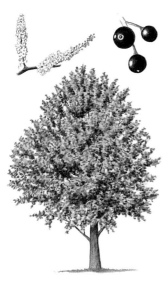

Bird Cherry
Prunus padus
10-20m. Similar to Wild Cherry.
White flowers, fruit a small black cherry.
Woodlands on lime soil.

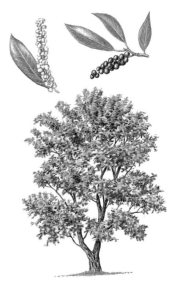

Cherry Laurel
Prunus laurocerasus
15m. Deciduous, loose spreading crown,
smooth-edged shiny leaves, long clusters of berries.
Common ornamental shrub, also in woodlands.

Dogwood
Cornus sanguinea
6m. Deciduous, leaves oval. Fragrant white
flower clusters become small blackish berries.
Forms understorey in woodlands.

Spindle
Euonymus europaeas
6-10m. Deciduous, round-crowned. Leaves shiny.
Sparse greenish flowers become red berries.
Prefers limey or chalk soils in woodland
or scrubland.

Holly
Ilex aquifolium
6m. Evergreen, leaves spiny and shiny, clusters of
red berries on female plants. Ornamental tree or
shrub, also in hedgerows and woodlands.

Box
Buxus sempervirens
6m. Evergreen, leaves oval, shiny, fruit round
and blue-green. Ornamental hedging shrub, also
woodlands, tolerant of shade.

Purging Buckthorn
Rhamnus catharticus
6m. Deciduous, small round crown; leaves oval,
pointed tips; berries black in small clusters.
Sandy or chalky soil.

Alder Buckthorn
Frangula alnus
6m. Similar to Purging Blackthorn, squatter with
rounder leaves. Damp woodland and
in hedgerows.

Horse Chestnut
Aesculus hippocastanum
20-35m. Deciduous. Leaves palmate, flower spikes
whitish, fruit large shiny conker in spiky case.
Woodlands, widely planted ornamentally
(including pink-flowered forms).

Field Maple
Acer campestre
10-12m. Deciduous. Leaves 5-lobed, seeds round
with paired wings. Woodlands, tolerates varied
soil conditions.

Sycamore
Acer pseudoplatanus
15-35m. Deciduous, spreading. Leaves toothed,
5-lobed, flowers green and pendant, seeds winged.
Widespread in woods and parkland.

Norway Maple
Acer platanoides
15-25m. Similar to Sycamore, more conical,
flowers upright yellowish clusters. Woodland and
widely planted ornamental tree.

Ash
Fraxinus excelsior
20-30m. Deciduous. Leaves pinnate, fruit small
catkins, fruit long winged 'keys'.
Woodland and hedgerows.

Privet
Ligustrum vulgare
5m. Evergreen, leaves long, pointed, shiny, fruit
purple-black berries. Common in garden hedgerows.
Prefers limey or chalky soil.

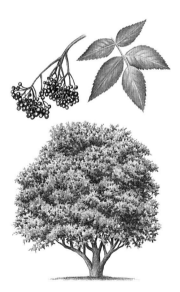

Elder
Sambucus nigra
10m. Deciduous, leaves pinnate. Flowers broad
umbrella-shaped white clusters, berries black.
Common in woodlands and scrubland.

Guelder Rose
Viburnum opulus
6m. Deciduous, spreading. Leaves lobed.
Dense white flower clusters become red berries.
Hedgerows and woodlands.

WILD FLOWERS

Mistletoe
Viscum album
Up to 1m in diameter. Flowers are tiny and green, berries white. Flowers Nov-Feb. Found on branches of mature trees.

Hop
Humulus lupulus
Up to 6m tall. Male flowers small, in branched clusters; female flowers (on separate plants) cone-like. Flowers Aug-Sep. Hedges and scrub.

Common Nettle
Urtica dioica
Up to 1.5m tall. Covered with stinging hairs, flowers small with four greenish petals. Flowers Jun-Aug. Hedges, woods and waste ground.

Redshank
Persicaria maculosa
Up to 80cm tall. Leaves show a dark central spot or smudge. Pinkish-red flowers in dense spikes. Flowers May-Oct. Favours disturbed damp soils.

Common Sorrel
Rumex acetosa
Up to 60cm tall. Upright perennial. Leaves are dark green, arrow-shaped; flower spikes reddish. Flowers May-Jul. Grassy habitats, from meadows and woodland rides.

Water-Dock
Rumex hydrolapathum
Up to 2m tall. Tall perennial, long narrow oval leaves. Flowers Jul-Sep. Wetland areas, typically growing beside rivers and lakes.

Broad-leaved Dock
Rumex obtusifolius
Up to 1m tall. Upright perennial. Stalked leaves oval; small greenish flowers on spikes. Flowers Jun-Oct. Disturbed ground such as field margins, tracks and waste ground.

Good-King-Henry
Chenopodium bonus-henricus
Up to 50cm tall. Red-tinged plant. Leaves triangular, small, reddish flowers on spikes. Flowers May-Aug. Waste places and cultivated ground; often common on arable land.

Fat-hen
Chenopodium album
Up to 1.5mm tall. Upright annual. Has powdery white covering. Leaves narrow, flower spikes whitish. Flowers Jun-Oct. Waste ground and disturbed arable land.

Three-nerved Sandwort
Moehringia trinervia
Up to 5cm tall. Delicate, downy annual. Leaves oval, pointed; stalked white flowers 5-petalled. Flowers May-Jun. Rich, damp soils in relatively undisturbed woodland.

Common Chickweed
Stellaria media
Up to 90cm tall. Straggly annual. Leaves oval, tiny white flowers 5-petalled. Flowers mainly Jul-Nov. Disturbed ground and cultivated soils.

Lesser Stitchwort
Stellaria graminea
Up to 50cm tall. Straggly perennial, often among grasses. Leaves long, narrow, white flowers 5-petalled. Flowers May-Aug. Grassy places like meadows and woodland rides with acid soils.

Sticky Mouse-ear
Cerastium glomeratum
Up to 40cm tall. Stickily hairy
annual. Leaves are oval, pointed;
5-petalled white flowers in
clusters. Flowers Apr-Oct.
Dry, bare ground.

White Campion
Silene latifolia
Up to 1m tall. Stickily hairy
perennial. Leaves oval; 5-petalled
white flowers in small clusters.
Flowers May-Oct. Hedgerows,
grassy verges, recently disturbed
and cultivated ground.

Red Campion
Silene dioica
Up to 1m tall. Downy, upright
biennial or perennial. Leaves oval,
hairy; flowers 5-petalled,
deep pink. Flowers mainly Mar-Nov.
Wide variety of grassy habitats.

Ragged-Robin
Lychnis flos-cuculi
Up to 80cm tall. Upright perennial.
Flowers pinkish-red and ragged-
looking, 5-petalled. Flowers
May-Aug. Damp habitats –
water meadows and damp
woodland rides.

Marsh-marigold
Caltha palustris
Up to 60cm tall. Creeping perennial.
Leaves kidney-shaped or round,
Flowers large and yellow.
Flowers Mar-Jul. Marshes,
wet woodlands and fens.

Wood Anemone
Anemone nemorosa
Up to 30cm tall. Perennial. Leaves
three-lobed. Flowers have 5-10
white or pink petal-like sepals.
Flowers Mar-May. Open woodlands,
often forming extensive carpets.

Meadow Buttercup
Ranunculus acris
Up to 1m tall. Downy hairy perennial. Leaves are divided into 3-7 segments, flowers yellow. Flowers Apr-Oct. Grassy meadows and verges. Often abundant.

Traveller's-joy
Clematis vitalba
Up to 30m long. Woody climber, smothers shrubs. Leaves pinnate. Fruits reddish, feathery. Flowers Jul-Sep. Hedgerows, woodland margins and scrub; lime-rich soils.

Common Water-crowfoot
Ranunculus aquatilis
Up to 1m long. Annual or perennial; grows on water. Five white petals, leaves round. Flowers Apr-Aug. Slow-flowing streams and rivers, and still waters.

Common Meadow-rue
Thalictrum flavum
Up to 1m tall. Upright perennial. Fern-like leaves; flowers white, 4-petalled, many yellow stamens. Flowers Jun-Jul. Damp lowlands on alkaline soils.

Lesser Celandine
Ranunculus ficaria
Up to 30cm tall. Perennial. Dark green heart- or kidney-shaped leaves; flowers yellow, 8-12 petals. Flowers Mar-May. Open woodland and hedgerows.

Common Poppy
Papaver rhoeas
Up to 70cm tall. Hairy annual. Leaves much divided. Large bright red papery flowers. Flowers Apr-Aug. Disturbed soil including wheat fields.

Garlic Mustard
Alliaria petiolata
Up to 1.2m tall. Upright biennial.
Leaves heart-shaped, smell
garlicky; flowers white, 4-petalled.
Flowers Apr-Jul. Hedgerows,
woodland rides and scrub
habitats, on limey soils.

Shepherd's-purse
Capsella bursa-pastoris
Up to 40cm tall. Annual or biennial.
Leaves close to stem. White
4-petalled flowers. Fruits heart-
shaped. Flowers mainly Apr-Oct.
Disturbed ground in gardens, and
on tracks and arable land.

Lady's Smock
Cardamine pratensis
Up to 55cm tall. Perennial.
Pinnate leaves at base. Flowers
pale pink, 4-petalled, in clusters.
Flowers Apr-Jul. Permanently damp
ground in grassy habitats.

Charlock
Sinapis arvensis
Up to 2m tall. Upright annual.
Dark toothed leaves. Flowers
yellow, 4-petalled. Fruits are long
pods. Flowers Apr-Oct. Arable land
and disturbed waste ground.

Meadow Saxifrage
Saxifraga granulata
Up to 50cm tall. Hairy perennial.
Leaves kidney-shaped, hairy; white
flowers 5-petalled. Flowers May-Jul.
Very scarce in grassy meadows on
neutral or alkaline soils.

Meadowsweet
Filipendula ulmaria
Up to 2m tall. Upright perennial.
Leaves much divided. Small white 6-
petalled flowers on sprays. Flowers
Jun-Sep. Damp soils in meadows,
marshes and stream margins.

Field-rose
Rosa arvensis
Up to 1m tall. Clumping shrub.
Leaves pinnate. Flowers white,
5-petalled. Fruit red rosehip.
Flowers Jul-Aug. Woodland
margins, hedgerows and
scrub habitats.

Dog-rose
Rosa canina
Up to 5m long. Scrambling thorny
shrub. Leaves pinnate. Flowers pink
or white, 5-petalled. Flowers Jun-
Jul. Hedgerows, woodland margins
and scrub habitats.

Wood Avens
Geum urbanum
Up to 60cm tall. Hairy perennial.
Lobed leaves, 5-petalled yellow
flowers, fruits with hooked hairs.
Flowers Jun-Aug. Shady woodland
and hedgerows.

Tormentil
Potentilla erecta
Up to 30cm tall. Delicate perennial.
Leaves appear 5-lobed. Flowers
4-petalled, bright yellow. Flowers
May-Sep. Grassy habitats
including meadows and heaths.

Silverweed
Potentilla anserina
Up to 80cm long. Creeping perennial.
Leaves silvery-green. Flowers
yellow, 5-petalled. Flowers Jun-Sep.
Open habitats including roadside
verges, waste ground.

Common Gorse
Ulex europeaus
Up to 2m tall. Spiny evergreen
shrub. Flowers yellow, coconut-
scented; fruit furry grey pod.
Flowers Apr-May. Heaths and
rough grassland on acid soils.

Broom
Cytisus scoparius
Up to 2m tall. Deciduous shrub.
Green stems, leaves tiny, flowers
like Common Gorse. Flowers
Apr-Jun. Open woodland and
heaths on dry, acid soils.

Tufted Vetch
Vicia cracca
Up to 2m tall. Scrambling perennial.
Pinnate leaves, tendrils, bluish-
purple flowers. Flowers Jun-Aug.
Grassy and scrub habitats including
meadows and hedgerows.

Common Vetch
Vicia sativa
Up to 75cm tall. Downy,
scrambling annual. Pinnate leaves,
tendrils, pinkish or purple flowers.
Flowers Apr-Sep. All sorts of
grassy habitats.

Common Restharrow
Ononis repens
Up to 70cm tall. Hairy perennial.
Flowers pink and white, borne in
clusters. Fruits are small pods.
Flowers Jul-Sep. Dry, grassy
places on calcareous soils.

Common Bird's-foot-trefoil
Lotus corniculatus
Up to 35cm tall. Variable perennial.
Leaves in 3 parts. Flowers red-
tinged yellow, fruits green pods.
Flowers Apr-Sep. Grassy habitats;
tolerates a wide range of soils.

Black Medick
Medicago lupulina
Up to 20cm tall. Annual or
perennial. Similar to Common
Bird's-foot Trefoil; pods black.
Flowers Apr-Oct. Dry, grassy
places and disturbed ground.

White Clover
Trifolium repens
Up to 20cm tall. Prostrate perennial. Leaves in three parts. Small white flowers borne in round heads. Flowers Apr-Oct. Grassy habitats.

Kidney Vetch
Anthyllis vulneraria
Up to 90cm tall. Annual, biennial or perennial. Leaves pinnate, yellow flowers in kidney-shaped heads. Flowers Apr-Sep. Grassy and rocky habitats on calcareous soils.

Wood-sorrel
Oxalis acetosella
Up to 10cm tall. Downy creeping perennial. Leaves clover-like; flowers single and whitish. Flowers Apr-May. Undisturbed woods and hedgerows. Common under oaks and Beech.

Meadow Crane's-bill
Geranium pratense
Up to 80cm tall. Hairy perennial. Leaves deeply lobed. Flowers bluish-violet, 5-petalled, in clusters. Flowers Jun-Sep. Meadows and roadside verges, usually on base-rich soils.

Herb-Robert
Geranium robertianum
Up to 30cm tall. Straggling, delicate annual. Leaves deeply lobed. Flowers pink, 5-petalled. Flowers Apr-Oct. Shady places such as rocky banks, hedgerows and woodlands.

Fairy Flax
Linum catharticum
Up to 15cm tall. Delicate annual. Leaves long, narrow. Flowers 5-petalled, white, on long slim stalks. Flowers May-Sep. Grassy habitats both wet and dry, but almost always on calcareous soils.

Dog's Mercury
Mercurialis perennis
Up to 50cm tall. Upright hairy
perennial. Flowers insignificant,
leaves shiny, dark green, long ovals.
Flowers Mar-May. Woodlands,
especially under oaks or Beech;
sometimes abundant.

Sun Spurge
Euphorbia helioscopia
Up to 50cm tall. Upright annual.
Leaves fleshy, spoon-shaped, and
broadest near the tip. Flowers
Apr-Nov. Arable land, waste
ground and cultivated soils.

Common Milkwort
Polygala vulgaris
Up to 30cm tall. Delicate trailing
perennial, Flower clusters blue, pink
or white; borne on spikes. Flowers
Jun-Sep. Grassy habitats on all but
the most acidic of soils.

Common Mallow
Malva sylvestris
Up to 1.5m tall. Perennial, upright
or spreading. Stem leaves 5-lobed.
Flowers 5-petalled, pink. Flowers
Jun-Sep. Grassy places such as
meadows and roadside verges.

Hairy St John's-wort
Hypericum hirsutum
Up to 1m tall. Upright perennial.
Leaves hairy, flowers 5-petalled,
yellow, sepals black-tipped. Flowers
Jun-Sep. Damp, grassy areas,
especially along woodland rides.

Common Dog-violet
Viola riviniana
Up to 15cm tall. Perennial.
Leaves long-stalked, heart-shaped.
Asymmetrical flowers blue-violet.
Flowers Mar-May. Woodland rides
and grassy places.

Wild Pansy
Viola tricolor
Up to 40cm tall. Annual, biennial or perennial. Asymmetrical flowers yellow, violet or bicoloured. Flowers Apr-Nov. Cultivated ground and grassland.

Purple Loosestrife
Lythrum salicaria
Up to 1.5m tall. Perennial. Leaves narrow, unstalked. Tall spikes of reddish-purple flowers. Flowers Jun-Aug. Damp ground, typically beside water.

Rosebay Willowherb
Chamerion angustifolium
Up to 1.5m tall. Upright perennial. Leaves spiral up stem. Flowers large, 4-petalled, pink. Flowers Jun-Aug. Wide range of disturbed ground. Forms large clumps.

Enchanter's-nightshade
Circaea lutetiana
Up to 60cm tall. Delicate, creeping perennial. Leaves oval, small white flowers in loose spikes. Flowers Jun-Sep. Woodlands and hedgerows.

Great Willowherb
Epilobium hirsutum
Up to 2m tall. Downy or hairy perennial. Stalkless leaves near stem base. Flowers 4-petalled, pink. Flowers Jun-Aug. Damp soils. Often forms extensive and sizeable clumps.

Cow Parsley
Anthriscus sylvestris
Up to 1m tall. Upright downy perennial. Leaves divided, small white flowers on 'umbrella' heads. Flowers Apr-Jun. Grassy verges, woodland rides and lanes.

Hemlock
Conium maculatum
Up to 2m tall. Upright perennial, poisonous. Flowers similar to those of Cow Parsley. Flowers Jun-Aug. Damp wayside ground, along river margins, on waste ground.

Hogweed
Heacleum sphondylium
Up to 4m tall. Robust perennial. Leaves much divided. Off-white small flowers in large 'umbrellas'. Flowers Apr-Nov. Open, grassy places like meadows and roadside verges.

Scarlet Pimpernel
Anagallis arvensis
Up to 50cm long. Prostrate annual. Leaves in opposite pairs, delicate flowers orange, 5-petalled. Flowers Mar-Oct. Disturbed and cultivated ground. Can become locally abundant.

Cowslip
Primula veris
Up to 25cm tall. Perennial. Hairy leaves form basal rosette. Bell-shaped flowers yellow. Flowers Apr-Jun. Grassland, open woodland rides and scrub on limey/chalky soils.

Primrose
Primula vulgaris
Up to 20cm tall. Clump-forming perennial. Large pale yellow 5-petalled flowers. Flowers Mar-Jun. Woodland rides and margins, shady meadows and hedgerows.

Bell Heather
Erica cinerea
Up to 50cm tall. Evergreen undershrub. Leaves narrow, needle-like. Flowers bell-shaped, purplish. Flowers Jun-Sep. Dry acid soils on heaths.

Heather
Calluna vulgaris
Up to 1.5m tall. Dense under-shrub.
Leaves short, narrow, scale-like,
flowers small, pink or whitish.
Flowers Jul-Sep. Acid soils on
heaths. Can form extensive
ground cover.

Bilberry
Vaccinium myrtillus
Up to 60cm tall. Upright deciduous
shrub. Leaves oval, bright green;
small flowers ripen to black berry.
Flowers Apr-Jun. Localized in
London. Heaths and woodlands
on acid soils.

Common Centaury
Centaurium erythraea
Up to 50cm tall. Upright perennial.
Leaves form basal rosette,
5-petalled pink flowers in loose
cluster. Flowers Apr-Sep.
Dry, grassy places, stony
ground and sand dunes.

Lady's Bedstraw
Galium verum
Up to 1.2m long. Sprawling
perennial. Leaves narrow.
Flowers 4-petalled, yellow, in
dense clusters. Flowers Jun-Sep.
Dry, grassy habitats.

Field Bindweed
Convolvulus arvensis
Up to 2m tall. Creeping, climbing
perennial. Leaves arrowshaped,
flowers white or pinkish trumpets.
Flowers Jun-Sep. Cultivated ground,
roadside verges and disturbed land.

Viper's-bugloss
Echium vulgare
Up to 90cm tall. Hairy biennial.
Leaves narrow, pointed; bright blue
funnel-shaped flowers on spikes.
Flowers May-Sep. Dry, grassy
habitats, especially on chalky or
sandy ground.

Water Forget-me-not
Myosotis scorpioides
Up to 12cm tall. Creeping perennial.
Leaves oblong, flowers 5-petalled,
blue with central yellow eye.
Flowers May-Sep. Watery habitats
on neutral and alkaline soils.

Common Comfrey
Symphytum officinale
Up to 1.2m tall. Upright, hairy
perennial. Bell-shaped white or
pink flowers in curved clusters.
Flowers May-Jun. Damp ground;
often beside rivers or in fens
and marshes.

Wood Sage
Teucrium scorodonia
Up to 50cm tall. Hairy perennial.
Oval, wrinkled leaves. Flowers
greenish-yellow; paired on
spikes. Flowers Jul-Sep.
Woodland rides and heaths
on acid soils.

White Dead-nettle
Lamium album
Up to 80cm tall. Hairy, nettle-like
perennial. Flowers white, tubular
with lip, in whorls. Flowers Mar-
Dec. Roadside verges, hedgerows
and woodland margins.

Yellow Archangel
Lamiastrum galeobdolon
Up to 45cm tall. Hairy, nettle-like
perennial. Flowers like White Dead-
nettle, but yellow. Flowers May-Jun.
Woodlands, hedgerows and
other shady places.

Selfheal
Prunella vulgaris
Up to 20cm tall. Creeping perennial.
Leaves oval. Flowers two-lipped,
blue, in short, dense, heads.
Flowers Mar-Nov. Meadows and
grassy woodland rides, on
calcareous or neutral soils.

Great Mullein
Verbascum thapsus
Up to 2m tall. Robust hairy biennial.
Flowers yellow, 5-petalled, in dense,
unbranched spikes. Flowers Jun-
Aug. Dry, grassy places, roadside
verges and waste ground.

Wild Clary
Salvia verbenaca
Up to 80cm tall. Upright perennial.
Stem leaves purplish. Flowers
usually blue or violet. Flowers
Apr-Sep. Dry, grassy habitats on
lime-rich soils. Rare in London.

Black Nightshade
Solanum nigrum
Up to 70cm tall. Variable annual.
Leaves oval, pointed; flowers
5-petalled, fruit black berry.
Flowers Jan-Oct. Disturbed
ground and cultivated land,
including gardens.

Common Figwort
Scrophularia nodosa
Up to 70cm tall. Hairless perennial.
Leaves oval, pointed, toothed.
Flowers green, brown-lipped.
Flowers Jun-Sep. Damp woodland,
and shady verges and hedgerows.

Common Toadflax
Linaria vulgaris
Up to 90cm tall. Perennial. Leaves
long, crowded. Flowers two-lipped,
yellow with long spurs. Flowers
Jun-Oct. Dry, grassy places, waste
ground, hedgerows and verges.

Foxglove
Digitalis purpurea
Up to 1.8m tall. Biennial. Leaves
form basal rosette. Tall spikes bear
large tubular pink or white flowers.
Flowers Jun-Sep. Woodlands and
waste ground, usually on acid soils.

Heath Speedwell
Veronica officinalis
Up to 10cm tall. Low-growing
perennial. Leaves oval, toothed,
hairy. Flowers blue, 4-petalled.
Flowers May-Aug. Grassy woodland
rides and dry heathland areas.

Brooklime
Veronica beccabunga
Up to 30cm tall. Perennial. Leaves
oval, fleshy. Flowers blue with a
white centre; borne in pairs.
Flowers May-Sep. Restricted to
shallow water and damp soil
beside rivers and ponds.

Common Cow-wheat
Melampyrum pratense
Up to 50cm tall. Upright annual,
semi-parasitic. Leaves narrow,
shiny. Flowers tubular, bright
yellow. Flowers May-Sep. Rare in
London. Grassy woodland rides and
heaths, mainly on acid soils.

Yellow-rattle
Rhinanthus minor
Up to 50cm tall. Annual, semi-
parasitic. Leaves opposite, oblong.
Flowers yellow, on leafy spikes.
Flowers May-Sep. Rough
grassy places.

Common Broomrape
Orobanche minor
Up to 40cm tall. Upright, parasitic
annual. Leaves brownish scales.
Flowers two-lipped, tubular, pinkish.
Flowers Jun-Sep. Wide range of
grassy habitats where suitable
host plants flourish.

Honeysuckle
Lonicera periclymenum
Up to 6m long. Woody, deciduous climber. Leaves oval, dark. Long-tubed yellowish flowers in clusters. Flowers Jun-Oct. Woodlands and hedgerows.

Wild Teasel
Dipsacus fullonum
Up to 2m tall. Prickly biennial. Spiny leaves in rosettes. Purple flowers in spiny conical heads. Flowers Jul-Aug. Grassland on damp, disturbed soils.

Field Scabious
Knautia arvensis
Up to 1m tall. Hairy biennial. Leaves form basal rosette. Small pink flowers in flat-topped heads. Flowers Jun-Oct. Grassy places, usually only on calcareous soils.

Creeping Bellflower
Campanula rapunculoides
Up to 1m tall. Clump-forming perennial. Flowers bell-shaped, bluish-violet; on tall spikes. Flowers Jun-Sep. Grassy places including roadside verges and meadows.

Hemp-Agrimony
Eupatorium cannabinum
Up to 1.75m tall. Upright perennial. Leaves lobed, opposite-paired. Small flowers dull pink, in clusters. Flowers Jul-Sep. Damp ground and marshes; occasionally in drier habitats.

Common Ragwort
Senecio jacobaea
Up to 1m tall. Biennial or perennial. Leaves pinnately divided. Flowers bright yellow; in flat clusters. Flowers Jun-Nov. Dry, grassy places and verges. Often thrives in pastures.

Scentless Mayweed
Tripleurospermum inodorum
Up to 75cm tall. Annual or perennial. Leaves feathery. Flowerheads daisy-like, in clusters. Flowers Apr-Oct. Disturbed ground, cultivated soil, tracks and waste places.

Feverfew
Tanacetum parthenium
Up to 50cm tall. Upright, aromatic downy perennial. Leaves pinnately divided; flowerheads daisy-like. Flowers Jul-Sep. Waste ground, roadside verges and walls.

Colt's-foot
Tussilago farfara
Up to 15cm tall. Perennial. Leaves large, round, with shallow lobes; flowers yellow, daisy-like. Flowers Feb-Apr. Bare and often disturbed ground, usually damp clay soils.

Butterbur
Petasites hybridus
Up to 50cm tall. Perennial herb. Leaves large, heart-shaped. Flowerheads dense, pinkish-lilac; in spikes. Flowers Mar-May. Damp ground close to water.

Common Fleabane
Pulicaria dysenterica
Up to 60cm tall. Woolly perennial. Leaves oblong-lanceolate; flowerheads daisy-like, yellow. Flowers Jul-Sep. Damp meadows, marshes and ditches.

Greater Burdock
Arctium lappa
Up to 1m tall. Robust perennial. Leaves large, heart-shaped. Flowerheads ovoid, purple, fruit spiny. Flowers Jul-Sep. Dry, grassy places and open woods.

Spear Thistle
Cirsium vulgare
Up to 3m tall. Spiny, upright biennial.
Leaves pinnately lobed. Flowerhead
large purple ball. Flowers Jul-Sep.
Disturbed ground such as waste
ground and paths.

Meadow Thistle
Cirsium dissectum
Up to 80cm tall. Upright perennial.
Leaves oval, toothed. Flowerheads
round, reddish-purple. Flowers
Jun-Aug. Damp meadows.

Chicory
Cichorium intybus
Up to 1m tall. Upright perennial.
Lower leaves stalked, lobed.
Flowerheads sky blue.
Flowers Jul-Oct. Dry, grassy
places such as verges.

Lesser Hawkbit
Leontodon saxatilis
Up to 40cm tall. Bristly perennial.
Leaves lobed. Flowerheads with
yellow florets; solitary.
Flowers Jun-Oct.
Dry grassland.

Common Knapweed
Centaurea nigra
Up to 1m tall. Upright hairy
perennial. Leaves narrow.
Flowerheads hold purple florets.
Flowers Jun-Sep. Meadows, verges
and other grassy places.

Smooth Hawk's-beard
Crepis capillaris
Up to 1m tall. Annual or biennial.
Leaves lobed. Flowerheads with
yellow florets in loose clusters.
Meadows, waste ground and
verges. Flowers Jun-Nov.

Common Hawkweed
Hieracium vulgatum
Up to 80cm tall. Upright perennial.
Basal leaves in rosette.
Flowerheads yellow, up to 20 heads.
Flowers Jul-Sep. Woods, verges
and shady hedgerows.

Ramsons
Allium ursinum
Up to 50cm tall. Perennial. Smells
of garlic. Leaves long, oval. Flowers
6-petalled, white, in loose cluster.
Flowers Apr-Jun.
Damp woodland.

Bluebell
Hyacinthoides non-scripta
Up to 50cm tall. Perennial.
Leaves long, narrow. Bluish-purple
flowers bell-shaped, on nodding
head. Flowers Apr-Jun.
Open woodland.

Herb-Paris
Paris quadrifolia
Up to 40cm tall. Upright perennial.
Flower solitary, green-petalled,
black-centred, on long stalk.
Flowers May-Jul.
Damp woodlands.

Yellow Flag
Iris pseudacorus
Up to 1.2m tall. Perennial.
Leaves long, sword-shaped.
Yellow iris flowers up to 10cm across.
Flowers Jun-Jul. Wetland margins
and damp meadows.

Lords-and-ladies
Arum maculatum
Up to 25cm tall. Perennial. Flower
a brown spike concealed in a leaf,
becoming red berries. Flowers
Apr-May. Woodland and shady
hedgerows with damp soils.

Common Spotted Orchid
Dactylorhiza fuchsii
Up to 65cm tall. Upright perennial.
Leaves shiny green, spotted dark.
Flowers pinkish in dense spikes.
Flowers Jun-Aug.
Grassy habitats.

Bee Orchid
Ophrys apifera
Up to 50cm tall. Perennial. Leaves
oval. Flowers on loose spike, dark
with pale 'wings' – bee-shaped.
Flowers Jun-Jul.
Dry grassland.

Yellow Water-lily
Nymphaea lutea
Leaves up to 40cm across. Floating
perennial. Leaves heart-shaped at base.
Flowers up to 6cm across.
Flowers Jun-Sep. Ponds and other
slow-flowing nutrient-rich water.

Arrowhead
Sagittaria sagittifolia
Up to 90cm tall. Upright aquatic
perennial. Leaves arrowhead-spaped,
flowers 3-petalled, white.
Flowers Jul-Aug. Still or
slow-moving waters.

INVERTEBRATES

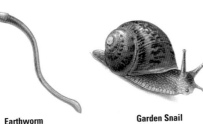

Earthworm
Lumbricus terrestris
Up to 30cm long. Largest worm in Europe. Often has 'saddle' near more tapered head end. Very common in all kinds of soils.

Garden Snail
Helix aspersa
Shell diameter 25-40mm. Brown or yellowish shell has pale flecking and up to five darker spirals. Active at night, and after rain. Parks, woods and wasteland.

White-lipped Snail
Cepaea hortensis
Shell diameter 14-17mm. Shell has up to five dark spirals, but may have none. Lip pale or dark. Active at night, and after rain. Woods, hedges and gardens.

Garden Slug
Arion hortensis
Up to 40mm long. Bluish-black and paler on the flanks, with an orange underside. Active at night, and after rain. Woods, gardens and cultivated land.

Great Grey Slug
Limax maximus
Up to 20cm long. Pale grey, heavily marked with dark spots, appearing striped at the end of the body. Active at night, and after rain. Woods, hedges and gardens.

Pill Millipede
Glomeris marginata
Up to 20mm long. Has 17-19 pairs of legs. Like small, shiny woodlouse. Rolls into a ball. Leaf litter in woodland, hedges and gardens.

Woodlouse
Oniscus asellus
15mm long and 8mm wide. Shiny grey with yellow or cream blotches and pale edges to the plates on the back. Very common, eats rotting wood and other plants.

Centipede
Lithobius forficatus
18-30mm long. Shiny chestnut-brown. Adults have 15 pairs of legs; hatchlings have 7. Abundant in gardens. Predatory, hunting invertebrate prey at night.

Blue-tailed Damselfly
Ischnura elegans
Length 31mm, wingspan 30-40mm. Smallest common damselfly. Male blue on thorax and eighth segment of abdomen. Flies May-Sep. Parks, gardens, meadows.

Common Blue Damselfly
Enallagama cyathigerum
Length 33mm, wingspan 36-42mm. Male blue with black spots, including toadstool shape on first segment. Female variable. Flies May-Sep. Parks, gardens and meadows close to water.

Azure Damselfly
Coenagrion puella
Length 33mm, wingspan 35-44mm.
Male blue with black spots,
including U-shape on first segment.
Female darker. Flies May-Aug.
Parks, gardens, meadows.

Large Red Damselfly
Pyrrhosoma nyphula
Length 36mm, wingspan 38-48mm.
Thorax green. Abdomen red in
male, green in female, with black
longitudinal stripes. Flies Apr-Sep.
Vegetation close to streams,
ponds and lakes.

Emperor Dragonfly
Anax imperator
Length 78mm, wingspan 108mm.
Thorax green, abdomen blue in
male, green in female. Flies May-
Aug. Streams, rivers and lakes.

Brown Hawker
Aeshna grandis
Length 73mm, wingspan 102mm.
Brown with small blue spots.
Wings have distinctive amber
sheen. Flies Jun-Oct. Rivers,
ponds and lakes.

Southern Hawker
Aeshna cyanea
Length 70mm, wingspan 100mm.
Brown with large yellow-green
spots. End segments blue in male.
Flies Jun-Oct. Rivers, ponds
and lakes.

Migrant Hawker
Aeshna mixta
Length 63mm, wingspan 88mm.
Brown with blue spots.
Clear wings. Flies Jul-Oct.
Rivers, ponds and lakes.

Four-spotted Chaser
Libellula quadrimaculata
Length 43mm, wingspan 76mm.
Broad, tapering body. Each wing
has dark spot at tip and at mid-point
on top edge. Flies May-Aug. Rivers
and lakes with plenty of vegetation.

Broad-bodied Chaser
Libellula depressa
Length 44mm, wingspan 76mm.
Broad, tapering body. Male's
abdomen blue, female's brown,
with yellow patches. Flies May-
Aug. Rivers and lakes.

Ruddy Darter
Sympetrum sanguineum
Length 34mm, wingspan 55mm.
Abdomen club-shaped. Male red,
female yellow. Legs black.
Flies Jun-Oct. Streams, rivers,
ponds and lakes.

Common Darter
Sympetrum striolatum
Length 37mm, wingspan 57mm. Abdomen even in width. Male red, female yellow. Legs yellow and black. Flies Jun-Oct. Streams, rivers, ponds and lakes.

Common Field Grasshopper
Chorthippus brunneus
Length 14-25mm. Green, purple or black. Wings extend beyond abdomen. Abdomen tip reddish in male. Adults Jul-Oct. Grassy fields and verges.

Meadow Grasshopper
Chorthippus parallelus
Length 13-33mm. Green, purple, brown or grey. Wings do not reach tip of abdomen (female's very short). Adults Jun-Nov. Grassy fields and verges.

Speckled Bushcricket
Leptophyes punctatissima
Length 10-17mm. Green with fine red spots. Wings very short. Adults Jun-Nov. Favours raspberries and roses.

Oak Bushcricket
Meconema thalassinum
Length 12-15mm. Pale green. Wings extend beyond tip of abdomen. Adults Jul-Oct. Trees, especially oaks.

House Cricket
Acheta domesticus
Length 16-20mm. Brown with black marks on head. Lives in old buildings but becoming scarce due to improved hygiene.

Common Cockroach
Blatta orientalis
Length 18-30mm. Blackish with short brown wings. Lives in buildings, particularly in warm places such as kitchens.

Common Earwig
Forficula auricularia
Length 10-15mm. Pincers measure between 4-9mm. Common in a variety of habitats, especially gardens.

Small Earwig
Labia minor
Length 5mm. Pincers measure between 1.5-2.5mm. Common in a variety of habitats, especially compost heaps.

Forest Bug
Pentatoma rufipes
Length 12-15mm. Brown body with red legs. Adults seen from Jun-Oct. Often found on fruit trees, especially cherry.

Hawthorn Shield Bug
Acanthosoma haemorrhoidale
Length 15mm. Green body with reddish patches. Woodland edges, gardens, parks, hedgerows.

Green Shield Bug
Palomena prasina
Length 10-15mm. Green in summer, bronze in autumn, with brown wingtips. Woods, gardens, parks, hedgerows.

Black-kneed Capsid
Blepharidopterus angulatus
Length 15mm. Plain green with grey-brown wing-tips and black joints on legs. Fruit trees, especially apple.

Common Green Capsid
Lygocorus pabulinus
Length 5-7mm. Plain green with greyish wing-tips. Often seen on potatoes and raspberries.

Common Flower Bug
Anthocorus nemorum
Length 4mm. Shiny brown with black head and spots on forewings. Found on almost any type of plant.

Water Measurer
Hydrometra stagnorum
Length 10mm. Long narrow body and long head. Walks on surface of slow-moving water.

Common Pond Skater
Gerris lacustris
Length 10mm. Moves with rowing action of middle legs. Surfaces of ponds and rivers.

Water Scorpion
Nepa cinerea
Length 20mm. Has strong front legs and elongated breathing tube at tip of 'tail'. Lives under the surface of shallow water.

Common Water Boatman
Nononecta glauca
Length 15mm. Swims with long bristly hindlegs. Lives under surface of still water. Can fly.

Common Froghopper
Philaenus spumarius
Length 6mm. Young coat themselves in white froth known as 'cuckoo spit'. Flies Jun-Sep. Meadows and verges.

Rose Aphid
Macrosiphum rosae
Length 1-2mm. Green or pink with long cornicles not found on other aphids. Feeds on roses in spring and scabious or teasel in summer.

Black Bean Aphid
Aphis fabae
Length 2mm. Can be black or olive. Feeds on dock, beans, spinach and other plants.

Woolly Aphid
Eriosoma langerum
Length 1-2mm. Purplish-brown covered with 'woolly' strands. Sucks sap of fruit trees.

Green Lacewing
Chrysopa pallens
Length 15-20mm. Green body and green veins on transparent wings. Golden eyes. Flies May-Aug. Woods, parks, gardens, hedges.

Scorpion Fly
Panorpa communis
Length 15mm. Head has a 'beak'. Scorpion-like tip to male's abdomen. Flies May-Aug. Shady parks and gardens, woods, hedgerows.

Caddis Fly
Phryganea grandis
Length 20mm. Has 50mm wingspan. Flies May-Jul. Slow-moving streams and rivers.

Small Skipper
Thymelicus flavus
Forewing 14mm. Smaller than Large Skipper. Tawny-orange. Antennae plain orange at tips. Flies May-Aug. Meadows and other grassy places.

Large Skipper
Ochlodes venatus
Forewing 16mm. Tawny orange. Dark veins and margins on upper- and undersides of wings. Flies Jun-Aug. Meadows, grassy banks and woodland edges.

Small White
Artogeia rapae
Forewing 25mm. Wings white with blackish tips and spots, yellowish underside. Flies Mar-Oct. Gardens, parks and hedges.

Large White
Pieris brassicae
Forewing 30mm. Similar to Small White. Black tips extend halfway down edge of forewing. Flies Apr-Oct. Gardens, parks.

Green-veined White
Artogeia napi
Forewing 23mm. Black markings less distinct than previous two. Grey lines along veins on underside. Flies Mar-Nov. Gardens, hedges, woodland edges.

Orange Tip
Anthocaris cardamines
Forewing 23mm. Wing-tips orange (male) or grey (female). Green blotches on underside of hindwing. Flies Apr-Jun. Hedgerows, gardens, damp meadows and woodland margins.

Clouded Yellow
Colias crocea
Forewing 25mm. Orange above with bold black borders. Underside yellowish with dark spots. Flies Apr-Sep. Migrant from mainland Europe in variable numbers. Favours grassland.

Brimstone
Gonepteryx rhamni
Forewing 30mm. Male's wings
sulphur-yellow, whitish tinged green
in female. Each wing-tip pointed.
Flies Feb-Sep. Common in open
woodland, parks and gardens.

Purple Hairstreak
Quercusia quercus
Forewing 19mm. Upperside dark
with purplish sheen. Underside
grey with white line. Flies Jul-Aug.
Oak woodlands or around oaks
in parks.

White-letter Hairstreak
Strymonidia w-album
Forewing 16mm. Brown above.
Short tails and w-shaped marking
on hindwing. Flies Jul. Rare in
suburban woodlands and
hedgerows with elms.

Small Copper
Lycaena phlaeas
Forewing 15mm. Forewing
bright orange with dark spots and
brown edges. Flies Mar-Nov.
Uncommon in gardens and parks
and on waste ground.

Holly Blue
Celastrina argiolus
Forewing 15mm. Male blue above,
female blue with dark border.
Underside of wings pale blue-grey.
Flies Apr-Sep. Common in
woodlands, parks and gardens,
often around Holly and Ivy.

Common Blue
Polyommatus icarus
Forewing 15mm. Male bright blue,
female dark brown. Underside fawn
with black and orange spots.
Flies Apr-Oct. Uncommon and
localized in meadows.

Painted Lady
Cynthia cardui
Forewing 30mm. Upperside mostly
orange; black forewing tip patched
with white. Underside paler. Flies
Apr-Nov. Migrant from North Africa.
Fairly common in all habitats.

Red Admiral
Vanessa atalanta
Forewing 30mm. Dark brown above
with bright red bars on each wing.
Tips of forewings black and white.
Flies May-Oct. Common in
many habitats, including parks
and gardens.

Small Tortoiseshell
Aglais urticae
Forewing 24mm. Upperside orange
and black, with a row of blue
spots on the edges of the wings.
Flies Mar-Oct. Fairly common but
declining in all kinds of habitats.

Peacock
Inachis io
Forewing 29mm. Deep red wings have four large 'eyes'. Underside dark brown, resembling bark. Flies Mar-May and Jul-Sep. Common in many habitats, including parks and gardens.

Comma
Polygonia c-album
Forewing 25mm. Orange, black-spotted wings, jagged-edged. Brown underside with white comma mark. Flies Mar-Sep. Common in parks, gardens, hedges and woodland edges.

Marbled White
Melanargia galathea
Forewing 23mm. Upperwing chequered yellowish-white and black, underside paler. Flies Jun-Jul. Rare and localized in suburban meadows.

Meadow Brown
Maniola jurtina
Forewing 25mm. Dark brown with tawny orange. Upperwing has single black eye with white highlight. Flies May-Sep. Common in grassland.

Ringlet
Aphantopus hyperantus
Forewing 22mm. Upperside blackish-brown. Underside paler with eyespots ringed yellow. Flies Jun-Jul. Uncommon along woodland rides and clearings, and in damp grassy areas.

Gatekeeper
Pyronia tithonus
Forewing 22mm. Smaller, brighter than Meadow Brown, two highlights on each 'eye' on forewing. Flies Jul-Sep. Common in hedgerows and areas of bramble.

Small Heath
Coenonympha pamphilius
Forewing 16mm. Orange-brown with small dark 'eyes'. Underside greyish, forewing has black spot. Flies Apr-Oct. Fairly common in grassy places.

Speckled Wood
Pararge aegeria
Forewing 20mm. Brown wings spotted pale yellow. Flies Mar-Oct. Common in woodland clearings, gardens and parks, tolerates some shade.

Wall Brown
Lasiommata megera
Forewing 22mm. Brown-and-orange lattice pattern with 'eye' on forewing. Flies Mar-Oct. Rare in rough grassland and on waste ground.

Tapestry Moth
Trichophaga tapetzella
Forewing 9mm. Greyish-white wings, brown at base. Flies Jun-Jul. Buildings with high humidity. Larvae feed on animal fibres such as wool.

Leaf-mining Moth
Stigmella aurella
Forewing 3mm. Forewings with yellow bars, underwings pale, feathery. Larva mines Bramble leaves. Flies May-Sep. Woodland, hedges and gardens over most of Europe, except far north.

Raspberry Moth
Lampronia rubiella
Forewing 5mm. Two yellow or cream bars on dark brown wings. Flies May-Jun. Gardens with Raspberries.

Common Clothes Moth
Tineola biselliella
Forewing 5mm. Goldish forewings and silvery hindwings. The larva is white with a pale brown head. Flies all year. Rarely seen outdoors. The most common and destructive clothes moth.

Green Oak Tortrix Moth
Tortrix viridana
Forewing 10mm. Pale green forewings, pale grey hindwings. Green larva will hang on a thread from trees. Flies May-Aug at night. Woods, parks and gardens with oaks.

Codlin Moth
Cydia pomonella
Forewing 9mm. Grey forewing has black and yellowish marks towards tip. White larva with brown head. Flies May-Oct. Orchards, parks, gardens and hedges with apple trees.

Small Magpie
Eurrhypara hortulata
Forewing 15mm. Silky white marked with dark grey, yellowish-gold black-spotted thorax. Larva green. Flies Jun-Aug. Hedgerows, woodland margins and waste ground with nettles.

Gold Fringe
Hypsopygia costalis
Forewing 8mm. Dark brown above, purplish below with gold fringe. Larva whitish, brown head. Flies Jul-Oct. Hedges around grassy places.

White Plume
Pterophorus pentadactyla
Forewing 13mm. White, wings divided into feathery plumes, held rolled at rest. Larva bright green. Flies May-Aug at night. Hedgerows, waste ground and gardens.

Ghost Swift
Hepialus humuli
Forewing 21mm. Male creamy white, female slightly darker. Larva white with dark spots and head. Flies Jun. Downland, meadows and gardens.

Common Swift
Hepialus lupulinus
Forewing 16mm. Brown wings with white marks. Very short antennae. White larva with brown head. Flies May-Aug at dusk. Arable land, gardens, parks and grassland.

Leopard Moth
Zeuzera pyrina
Forewing 20-35mm. White with spotted wings, 6 black marks on thorax. Creamy larva has black spots. Flies Jun-Aug at night. Woods, parks, orchards and gardens.

Goat Moth
Cossus cossus
Forewing 30mm. Greyish-brown, fine dark patterning on forewings. Larva purplish-red. Flies Jun-Aug. Rare in broad-leaved woodland.

Forester
Adscita statices
Forewing 13mm. Upperside forewing metallic green. Larva dull yellow with black spots and small tufts. Flies by day during Jun. Chalk downland, meadows and heaths.

Five-spot Burnet
Zygaena trifolii
Forewing 16mm. Blackish forewings, 5 crimson spots. Hindwing crimson, dark-bordered. Larva as above. Flies May-Jul. Chalk downland, meadows and marshy ground.

Six-spot Burnet
Zygaena filipendulae
Forewing 18mm. As Five-spot Burnet but darker, 6 red spots. Larva similar. Flies Jun-Jul. Meadows, downland and woodland.

Currant Clearwing
Synanthedon tipuliformis
Forewing 8mm. Wings transparent. Black abdomen with yellow rings. White larva has brown head. Flies May-Jul. Rare in woods, gardens and open country with suitable foodplants.

Large Red-belted Clearwing
Synanthedon culiciformis
Forewing 11-14mm. Red band on the abdomen. Wings are bordered black. Flies May-Jun. Rare in open woodland and heathland.

Lackey
Malacosoma neustria
Forewing 13-20mm. Warm brown, paler band down middle of wings. Larva colourful. Flies Jun-Aug at night. Many habitats where scrub grows.

Oak Eggar
Lasiocampa quercus
Forewing 29-45mm. Small, dark-ringed white spot on brown forewing. Female larger, paler. Larva hairy, dark. Flies May-Jun. Woodland and hedgerows, as well as heathland.

Lappet
Gastropacha quercifolia
Forewing 28-42mm. At rest, brown or purplish wings resemble dead leaves. Larva fleshy, dark brown-grey. Flies May-Aug at night. Open woodland, hedges, orchards and gardens.

Fox Moth
Macrothylacia rubi
Forewing 20-30mm. Reddish, two narrow, pale stripes on forewings; females are paler. Larva velvety, dark. Flies May-Jul. Heathland, open countryside and woodland margins.

Drinker
Philudoria potatoria
Forewing 25-35mm. Orange-brown, double dark lines and white spots. Female paler. Larva hairy, blue-grey. Flies Jul. Open woodland, often in damp habitats.

Emperor Moth
Saturnia pavonia
Forewing 34-42mm. Furry, large eyespots on all wings. Larva tufty, green, banded black, with tufts. Flies in spring, laying eggs in May. Heaths and woodland.

Peach Blossom
Thyatira batis
Forewing 15mm. Forewings brown with pink blotches. Larva dark brown with slanting white lines. Flies May-Aug at night. Woodland and woodland edges.

Large Emerald
Geometra papilionaria
Forewing 25-32mm. Pale blue-green with faint white lines and spots. Larva yellowish-green, warty. Flies Jul. Woodland, heathland and marshes.

Winter Moth
Operophtera brumata
Forewing 15mm. Greyish-brown, faintly patterned wings; female almost wingless. Larva green, loops. Flies Oct-Feb. Abundant wherever there are trees and shrubs.

Garden Carpet
Xanthorhoe fluctuata
Forewing 14mm. Greyish-white wings, dark triangle where forewings join thorax. Larva brown looper. Flies Apr-Oct from dusk. Common in cultivated areas.

Small Emerald
Hemistola chrysoprasaria
Forewing 18mm. Pale grey-green with fine white lines. Larva pale green with white dots, brown head. Flies May-Aug at night. Downland, hedges and woodland edges.

Brimstone Moth
Opisthograptis luteolata
Forewing 18mm. Sulphur-yellow with brown flecks on outer forewing. Brown looper larva. Flies Apr-Oct at night. Woods, hedges and gardens.

Lime-speck Pug
Eupithecia centaurearia
Forewing 12mm. Pale grey with dark marks on forewings. Green or yellow larva often has red spots. Flies May-Oct from dusk. Rough areas and gardens throughout Europe.

Magpie Moth
Abraxas grossulariata
Forewing 20mm. Variable black-and-white pattern, with yellowish-orange line. Green looper larva. Flies Jun-Aug. Woods, gardens and hedges.

August Thorn
Ennomos quercinaria
Forewing 17mm. Pale yellowish with two narrow brown stripes. Abdomen fluffy. Greyish looper larva. Flies Aug-Sep at night. Woodland, parks and gardens.

Large Thorn
Ennomos autumnaria
Forewing 12-25mm. Yellow with purplish-brown speckling. Larva slender, twiglike. Flies Sep. Woodland and bushy areas.

Swallowtailed Moth
Ourapteryx sambucaria
Forewing 30mm. Wings are bright lemon, rapidly fading to pale cream or white. Larva a brown looper. Flies Jun-Aug at night, often coming to light. Forest edges, woods, gardens and parks.

Peppered Moth
Biston betularia
Forewing 20-30mm. Variable. White with fine dark marks, or sooty black. Green or brown looper larva. Flies May-Aug, coming to lighted windows.Woods, gardens, scrub and parks.

Mottled Umber
Erannis defoliaria
Forewing 18-25mm. Upperside creamy-brown, forewing darker. Female wingless, larva dark green. Flies mainly Oct-Dec. Woodland.

Poplar Hawkmoth
Laothoe populi
Forewing 30-46mm. Brown. Orange patches on hindwings. Green larva with yellow horn and stripes. Flies May-Sep. Woodland margins, river valleys and parks.

Eyed Hawkmoth
Smerinthus ocellatus
Forewing 36-44mm. Pale with large 'eye' marks on hindwings. Green larva, yellow stripes, greenish horn. Flies May-Jul. Open woodland, parks and gardens.

Pine Hawkmoth
Hyloicus pinastris
Forewing 35-41mm. Dark grey, wing edges chequered black and white. Larva green, darkens with age. Flies Jun-Jul. Pine forests throughout Europe.

Hummingbird Hawkmoth
Macroglossum stellatarum
Forewing 20-24mm. Grey forewings, orange hindwings, abdomen dark with white spots. Hovers to feed. Migrant, reaches UK in varying numbers in summer. Parks, gardens and flowery banks.

Privet Hawkmoth
Sphinx ligustri
Forewing 41-55mm. Brown, black markings. Body striped with pink and black. Larva green, white-striped. Flies Jun-Jul, Woodland edges, hedges, parks and gardens.

Elephant Hawkmoth
Deilephila elpenor
Forewing 28-33mm. Olive-brown and pink. Larva greenish or brownish, tapering, with eye-spots. Flies Jun. Woodland clearings, meadows, gardens, river valleys and waste ground.

Buff-tip
Phalera bucephala
Forewing 30mm. Silver-grey with orange head and wingtips, at rest like broken twig. Larva yellow. Flies May-Aug. Woods, parks, orchards and gardens.

Puss Moth
Cerura vinula
Forewing 31-40mm. White with fine black pattern. Hindwings grey. Larva large, green with colourful 'face'. Flies May-Jun. Woods and hedges.

Figure of Eight
Diloba caeruleocephala
Forewing 15mm. Brown-and-grey forewings with figure-of-eight marking. Grey-blue larva. Flies Sep-Oct. Woodlands, scrub and gardens.

Common Footman
Eilema lurideola
Forewing 15mm. Pale grey forewing is fringed with yellow. Hindwings pale yellow. Larva hairy, grey. Flies Jun-Aug. Hedges, woods and orchards.

Yellow-tail
Euproctis similis
Forewing to 20mm. White with yellow-tipped abdomen, furry. Larva black, very hairy. Flies Jun-Aug. Woods, gardens, parks, orchards, tree-lined streets and hedges.

Brown-tail
Euproctis chrysorrhoea
Forewing to 20mm. White with brown-tipped abdomen, furry. Larva black with yellow tufts. Flies Jul-Aug. Woods, hedges, parks and gardens.

Vapourer
Orgyia antiqua
Forewing 17mm. Chestnut with a white spot on each forewing. Female wingless. Larva grey with tufts. Flies Jun-Oct, Woods, parks, gardens, hedges and tree-lined streets.

Great Prominent
Peridea anceps
Forewing 26-36mm. Greyish-brown with darker markings. Hindwings yellowish-white. Larva yellow-green. Flies Apr-Jun. Widely distributed, especially in woodlands.

Garden Tiger
Arctia caja
Forewing 28-37mm. Brown and cream; hindwings orange with black spots. Larva brown, very hairy. Flies Jun-Aug. Open habitats, including gardens and scrub.

Buff Ermine
Spilosoma lutea
Forewing 19mm. Pale buff to creamy, broken dark line on forewing. Larva has tufts of long brown hairs. Flies May-Aug. Most habitats, but especially on waste ground and in gardens.

White Ermine
Spilosoma lubricipeda
Forewing 17mm. White with sparse black spots. Yellow, black-spotted abdomen. Larva brown, very hairy. Flies May-Aug, in 1-2 broods. Hedgerows, gardens, waste ground and other habitats.

Cinnabar
Tyria jacobaeae
Forewing 18mm. Blackish with red streaks and spots; hindwing red. Larva banded black and yellow. Flies May-Jul. Waste ground, roadsides, meadows and heathland.

Garden Dart
Euxoa nigricans
Forewing 18mm. Upperwing with grey-brown forewing and pale whitish hindwing. Larva brown. Flies Jul-Aug. Farmland, gardens, marshy areas, commons and waste ground.

Heart and Dart
Agrotis exclamationis
Forewing 20mm. Wings have vaguely heart-shaped and dart-shaped markings. Larva dull brown-and-grey. Flies May-Sep at night, in 1-2 broods. Almost any habitat, especially if it is cultivated.

Large Yellow Underwing
Noctua pronuba
Forewing 25mm. Brown; hindwings deep yellow with a black border. Green larva with black markings. Flies Jun-Oct. Well-vegetated habitats.

Setaceous Hebrew Character
Xestia c-nigrum
Forewing to 20mm. Greyish-brown to chestnut with a purplish tinge. Larva green, becoming paler. Flies May-Oct. Lowland areas including cultivated regions, woodland and marshes.

Mouse Moth
Amphipyra tragopoginis
Forewing 15mm. Dark brown with three dark spots. Underwings pale. Larva green with narrow white lines. Flies Jun-Sep. Widespread in woods, hedgerows, gardens and open country with scrub.

Cabbage Moth
Mamestra brassicae
Forewing 18mm. Mottled greyish-brown with rusty scales. Plump larva brownish-green. Flies all year, but mainly May-Sep. Almost any habitat, commonest on cultivated land.

Clay
Mythimna ferrago
Forewing 15mm. Straw to reddish-brown, white mark in middle of forewing. Pale brown larva. Flies May-Aug. Common in grassy places across Europe.

Green Arches
Anaplectoides prasina
Forewing 20mm. Greenish forewings have variable black markings. Larva is brown with darker markings. Flies mid-Jun-mid-Jul at night. Deciduous woodland.

Common Wainscot
Mythimna pallens
Forewing 15mm. Pale with creamy forewing and white hindwing. Larva yellowish with three white lines. Flies Jun-Oct. Grassland including meadows and marshes.

Old Lady
Mormo maura
Forewing to 35mm. Dark brown and black. Greyish-brown larva with dark smudges and white line. Flies Jul-Aug, often coming towards light. Woods, hedges, gardens, parks.

Burnished Brass
Diachrisia chrysitis
Forewing to 20mm. Two metallic marks on forewings. Tuft on thorax. Larva bluish-green with white streaks. Flies May-Oct, in 1-3 broods. Gardens, parks, hedges and waste ground.

Mullein
Cucullia verbasci
Forewing 20-25mm. Pale brown with streaks, twig-like. Larva creamy white, with yellow and black spots. Flies Apr-Jun. Woodland edges, scrub, river banks, gardens and parks.

Merveille du Jour
Dichonia aprina
Forewing 23mm. Forewing green with dark speckles. Larva variable with broken white line down centre. Flies Sep-Oct. Parkland and oak woodland.

Angle Shades
Phlogophora meticulosa
Forewing 25mm. Greyish with distinctive V-shaped markings. Wings rolled at rest. Larva plump, green. Flies most of year, but mainly May-Oct. A migrant found in almost any habitat.

Silver Y
Autographa gamma
Forewing 20mm. Variable grey-brown with a silver Y-mark on forewing. Green larva. Flies throughout the year. A migrant found in all habitats, sometimes very common.

Grey Dagger
Acronicta psi
Forewing to 20mm. Grey with dark, dagger-shaped marks. Hairy grey-black larva with yellow line. Flies May-Sep. Woodlands, commons, parks and gardens.

Red Underwing
Catocala nupta
Forewing to 35mm. Grey with red underwings. Pale brown larva has warty, bud-like lumps on its back. Flies Aug-Sep at night. Woodlands, hedges, gardens and parks.

Herald
Scoliopteryx libatrix
Forewing to 25mm. Purplish to orange-brown, bright orange near head. Larva slim, green. Flies Aug-Oct, and in spring after migration. Woods, gardens, parks, open countryside.

Snout
Hypena proboscidalis
Forewing 19mm. Dark grey with paler hindwing. Head with long 'snout'. Larva green with white lines. Flies Jun-early Aug and Sep-early Oct. Gardens, waste ground, woodland, hedgerows.

Common Crane-fly
Tipula paludosa
25mm long. Long, narrow brown abdomen and wings, very long legs. Larva leathery, burrowing. Flies all year, especially autumn. Common in all open, grassy habitats.

Spotted Crane-fly
Nephrotoma appendiculata
15-25mm long. Like Common Crane-fly but abdomen yellow, black-spotted, and wings clear. Flies May-Aug. Farmland, parkland and gardens.

Gall Midge
Jaapiella veronicae
2mm long. Wings longer and broader than abdomen. Larva forms galls on speedwell plants. Flies in summer, often forming swarms and entering lit windows. Open areas.

Chironomid Midge
Chironomus plumosus
8mm long. Abdomen longer than wings. Male antennae bushy. Larva red, aquatic 'bloodworm'. Flies in spring and summer. Common near water.

Common Gnat
Culex pipiens
6mm long. Wings longer than abdomen. Male antennae bushy. Larva aquatic. Flies in summer at night, hums. Common in all habitats near water.

Mosquito
Theobaldia annulata
6mm long. Like Common Gnat but wings brownish, legs with white banding. Flies in spring and summer. Common near sources of stagnant water.

St Mark's Fly
Biblio marci
12mm long. Stocky, hairy, black. Clear wings, legs dangle in flight. Larva large-headed, burrows. Flies Apr-May. Gardens, woodland edges and well-vegetated open countryside.

Fever-fly
Dilophus febrilis
4mm long. Like miniature, hairless St Mark's Fly. Larva burrowing. Flies Mar-Oct. Common in most open habitats.

Cleg-fly
Haematopota pluvialis
10mm long. Dull grey, abdomen blunt-tipped, head triangular with green eyes. Larva burrowing. Flies May-Oct. Damp woodland.

Large Bee-fly
Bombylius major
12mm long. Fluffy brown, bee-like. Long proboscis. Wings bicoloured. Larva parasitic on bees. Flies Apr-Jun. Woodlands.

Window-fly
Scenopinus fenestratus
7mm long. Stocky, blackish with blunt-tipped abdomen. Larva predatory. Often seen indoors, especially at windows in old buildings.

Dance-fly
Empis tessellata
11mm long. Long-legged, broad-winged hairy fly. Hunts other flies, carries prey on wing. Flies Apr-Aug. Woodland edges, hedgerows, gardens and scrub.

Hover-fly
Scaeva pyrastri
12-15mm long. Broad black abdomen with 6 yellow crescent markings. Larva hunts aphids. Flies May-Nov. Flower-rich habitats including gardens and parks.

Hover-fly
Syrphus ribesii
10mm long. Resembles wasp, yellow and black stripes on abdomen. Larva green, slug-like. Flies Mar-Nov. Habitats rich in flowers.

Hover-fly
Volucella zonaria
15-25mm long. Hornet-like but plump, with orange and black bands on abdomen. Flies May-Nov. Woodlands, woodland edges and gardens.

Hover-fly
Melanostroma scalare
6-9mm long. Very slim black and yellow abdomen, broad wings. Larva eats aphids. Flies Apr-Nov. Flowery or herb-rich habitats.

Drone-fly
Eristalis tenax
10-15mm long. Like male Honey Bee, blackish with orange markings. Larva a 'rat-tailed' maggot. Flies all year. Parks, gardens, woodland edges and other flowery habitats.

Flesh-fly
Sarcophaga carnaria
12-20mm long. Hairy, grey and black chequers on abdomen, red eyes. Larva flesh-eating maggot. Flies all year. Common around houses.

Narcissus-fly
Merodon equestris
10-15mm long. Like carder bee, brown and fluffy. Larva burrowing, eat plant bulbs. Flies Mar-Aug. Gardens, parks, woods and hedgerows.

Fruit-fly
Drosophila funebris
3mm long. Reddish with very large wings. Larva eats decaying fruit or vegetable matter. Flies all year, commonest in summer and autumn. Common in gardens and orchards.

Bluebottle
Calliphora vomitoria
12-15mm long. Blackish with blue sheen, red eyes, hairy. Larva pale tapered maggot, eats carrion. Flies all year. Common around houses.

Common House-fly
Musca domestica
8mm long. Dark brownish with paler marks on abdomen. Larva a pale maggot. Flies all year, especially Jun-Sep. Common around houses.

Greenbottle
Lucilia caesar
8-15mm long. Strong metallic green sheen, reddish eyes. Larva a maggot, eats carrion. Flies all year. Common around houses and most other habitats.

Cabbage Root-fly
Delia radicum
5-7mm long. Bristly, blackish. Larva eats roots of brassica plants. Flies Mar-Nov. Common in flowery habitats.

Yellow Dung-fly
Scatophaga stercoraria
8mm long. Furry, yellowish (females greyer). Larva eats horse and cow dung. Flies most of the year. Pastures where cows or horses graze.

Hawthorn Sawfly
Trichiosoma tibiale
20mm long. Black with yellow legs, hairy body and leathery wings. Larva green with brown head. Flies May-Jun. Scrubby habitats where Hawthorn grows.

Gooseberry Sawfly
Nematus ribesii
10mm long. Plump and squat, yellow (female) or black (male) abdomen. Larva caterpillar-like. Flies Apr-Sep. Gardens where Gooseberries and currants are grown.

Horntail
Urceros gigas
40mm long. Wasp-like, yellow and black, female has long ovipositor. Larva almost legless. Flies May-Oct on sunny days. Coniferous woodland.

Yellow Ophion
Ophion luteus
15-20mm long. Very long, slender yellow legs, abdomen and antennae, black eyes. Larva parasitic. Flies Jul-Oct. Woodlands and other well-vegetated habitats.

Ichneumon wasp
Pimpla instigator
10-24mm long. Black with long yellow legs. Parasitizes Snout Moth. Flies all summer. Most habitats where host species occurs.

Brachonid wasp
Apanteles glomeratus
10mm long. Black with yellow legs, long black antennae. Parasitizes Large White Butterfly. Flies all summer in two broods. Common wherever host species occurs.

Rubytail Wasp
Chrysis ignita
7-10mm long. Black, lustrous, with crimson abdomen. Parasitic. Flies Apr-Sept. All kinds of open habitat.

Robin's Pincushion Gall Wasp
Diplolepis rosae
4mm long. Black with yellowish abdomen and legs. Whitish larva forms galls on wild roses. Flies Apr-June. Open countryside with flowers.

Currant Gall Wasp
Neuroterus quercusbaccarum
2.8mm long. Black with yellow legs. White larva forms round galls on oak leaves. Flies from early spring. Oak woodlands.

Oak Apple Gall Wasp
Biorhiza pallida
1.7-2.8mm long.
Yellowish, abdomen
darker. Forms round galls
('oak apples') on oak
twigs. Flies from January.
Oak woodlands.

Black Garden Ant
Lasius niger
5mm long. All-black,
small ant, some with
wings in summer. Active
all year (winged ants
Jul-Aug). Common in
gardens and other
open habitats.

Yellow Meadow Ant
Lasius flavus
4mm long. Yellow all
over, with winged
individuals in summer.
Forms anthills. Active
year-round. Rough,
mature grassland.

Yellow Lawn Ant
Lasius umbratus
4-5mm long. Slightly larger
and stockier than Yellow
Meadow Ant. Active year-
round. Lives underground
in grassland.

Red Ant
Myrmica rubra
4-5mm long. Reddish,
with dark eyes and
abdomen tip. Winged
adults appear in summer.
Active year-round,
winged ants in late
summer. Found in
open habitats.

Mason Wasp
Ancistrocerus parietinus
10-14mm long. Slim, mainly
black with yellow bands
on abdomen. Flies
Apr-Aug. Common
in all habitats.

German Wasp
Vespula germanica
12-16mm long. Abdomen
mainly yellow with narrow
black bands and spots.
Builds paper nest.
Flies from spring to
autumn. Common in
most
habitats.

Common Wasp
Vespula vulgaris
11-14mm long. Slightly
smaller than German
Wasp with subtly different
pattern. Flies from spring
to autumn. Common in
most habitats.

Hornet
Vespula crabro
18-25mm long. Large,
brownish rather than
black with mainly yellow
abdomen. Flies from
spring to autumn.
Woodland and
sometimes gardens.

Mining Bee
Andrena haemorrhoa
10-12mm long. Black
abdomen with yellow tip,
furry reddish thorax and
legs. Flies in early spring.
Woodland edges, scrub
and gardens.

Tawny Mining Bee
Andrena fulva
10-12mm long. Tawny,
fluffy with black head and
legs. Male is darker. Flies
Apr-June. Open habitats –
burrows in lawns and
bare ground.

Flower Bee
Anthophora plumipes
14-16mm long. Blackish
(male with red-brown
thorax); hairy body and
legs. Flies Mar-Jun.
Dry open habitats,
including gardens.

Wood Carder Bee
Anthidium manicatum
11mm long. Blackish with yellow legs and marks on abdomen sides. Flies Jun-Aug. Common in flowery habitats.

Mason Bee
Osmia rufa
8-13mm long. Black and reddish, somewhat Honey Bee-like, hairy. Flies Apr-Jul. Common in open flowery habitats.

Leaf-cutter Bee
Megachile centuncularis
10-12mm long. Dark, with subtle fine yellowish stripes on abdomen. Cuts sections from leaves. Flies May-Aug. Woods, gardens and parkland.

Honey Bee
Apis mellifera
12-15mm long. Brownish or orange, slimmer and less furry than bumblebees. Flies from spring to late autumn. Ranges widely in search of nectar.

Common Carder Bumblebee
Bombus pascuorum
18mm long. Buffish brown thorax, abdomen, head and legs a little darker. Flies from March. Common in sheltered, well-vegetated habitats.

Meadow Bumblebee
Bombus pratorum
16-18mm long. Like a slim Buff-tailed Bumblebee with a red-brown abdomen tip. Flies from March in gardens, woodlands and meadows.

Garden Bumblebee
Bombus hortorum
20-24mm long. Like White-tailed Bumblebee but more yellow on thorax. Flies from spring. Common in gardens and other well-vegetated habitats.

White-tailed Bumblebee
Bombus lucorum
20-22mm long. Plump, black with yellow stripes at top of thorax and centre of white-tipped abdomen. Flies from February. Common in well-vegetated habitats.

Buff-tailed Bumblebee
Bombus terrestris
20-22mm long. Similar to White-tailed Bumblebee, but abdomen tip pale brownish. Flies from March. Common in gardens, woodland edges and other flowery habitats.

Barbut's Cuckoo Bee
Bombus barbutellus
20mm long. Like Garden Bumblebee but less hairy. Parasitizes Garden Bumblebee nests. Flies from mid-spring. Gardens and other habitats where its host occurs.

Field Cuckoo Bee
Bombus campestris
15-17mm long. Blackish with yellow on thorax. Parasitizes nests of Common Carder Bumblebee. Flies from spring. Similar habitat to its host species.

Furniture beetle
Anobium punctatum
2.5-5mm long. Long-bodied, brown with striations down wing-cases. Larva is woodworm. Occurs May-Jul. Dry wood in deciduous woodland, and in buildings.

Larder beetle
Dermestes lardarius
7-9.5mm long. Black with fawn band across top of wing-cases. Larva short-bodied, hairy. Seen all year. In houses and in birds' nests.

Violet Ground Beetle
Carabus violaceus
20-35mm long. Oval, long-legged, black with purple sheen. Larva shiny, dark. Nocturnal. Woodlands, hedgerows, gardens, scrubland.

Carabid beetle
Carabus nemoralis
20-30mm long. Oval, long-legged, bronzy sheen, striations down wing-cases. Nocturnal, found in most habitats.

Rove beetle
Oxytelus laquaetus
6mm long. Short orange wing-cases, orange legs, otherwise black. Damp places with rotting vegetation, such as compost heaps.

Rose Chafer
Cetonia aurata
14-18mm long. Oval, small-headed, bright shiny green all over. Larvae eat rotting wood. Seen May-Aug. Woodland edges, hedgerows and gardens.

Devil's Coach Horse
Staphylinus olens
20-30mm long. Black. Long segmented body, exposed by very short wing-cases. Large head. Nocturnal. Damp, sheltered habitats including outbuildings.

Black Beetle
Feronia nigrita
16mm long. Oval, shiny with striated wing-cases. Long bristly legs. Nocturnal. Woods, gardens, parkland.

Stag Beetle
Lucanus cervinus
25-75mm long. Black with reddish wing-cases
and mandibles (very large and antler-like in male).
Seen May-Aug, males fly in search of mates.
Mature woodlands and gardens.

Churchyard beetle
Blaps mucronata
18mm long. Oval with broad thorax and
small head. Black, wing-cases pointed at
tips. Nocturnal. Found in dark, sheltered
places such as cellars.

Wasp Beetle
Clytus arictis
7-14mm long. Long-legged,
mostly black with yellow bands
on abdoment. Seen May-July.
Woods, parks, gardens and
similar habitats.

Cardinal Beetle
Pyrochroa coccinea
14-18mm long. Scarlet with black
head and legs. Abdomen widens
towards tip. Seen May-Jul.
Woodland edges and
flowery places.

Soldier Beetle
Cantharis rustica
11-14mm long. Black with buff
thorax (with black central spot),
thighs and front of head. Seen May-
Aug. Damp woodlands and other
sheltered countryside.

Click Beetle
Athous haemorrhoidalis
7-10mm long. Slim, long
with black head and
thorax, otherwise
brownish, striated wing-
cases. Seen May-Jul.
Open grassy habitats.

Wireworm Beetle
Agriotes lineatus
7-10mm long. Similar to
Click Beetle but pale
brown all over. Seen all
year, especially May-Aug.
Grassland and farmland.

Potato Flea Beetle
Psylliodes affinis
2.8mm long. Oval, red-
brown with black head
and thick black thighs.
Seen from spring. Common
around potato patches,
also eats nightshades.

Two-spot Ladybird
Adalia bipunctata
3.5-5.5mm long. Circular, scarlet wing-cases each with a black central spot, white marks on thorax. Seen from spring to autumn, common in gardens and other similar habitats.

Seven-spot Ladybird
Cocinella septpunctata
5-8mm long. Like Two-spot Ladybird, but larger with seven black spots. Seen from early spring to autumn. Well-vegetated habitats including gardens.

Whirligig Beetle
Gyrinus natator
6-7mm long. Oval black swimming beetle, yellow legs, often spins on surface. Seen through most of the year. Still and slow-moving water.

Pea Weevil
Sitona lineatus
4-5mm long. Grey-brown, striped darker and lighter down wing-cases. Seen mainly in spring and autumn. Found wherever peas or related plants grow.

Nut Weevil
Curculio nucum
6-9mm long. Brown, round, with thick thighs and long sucking mouthparts. Seen Apr-Jul. Woodlands and other habitats where Hazel and oaks grow.

Water beetle
Hydrobius fuscipes
6mm long. Black, shiny. Legs paler. Wing-cases striated. Dives and crawls over underwater plants. Scavenger.

Garden Spider
Araneus diadematus
Female 10-13mm long; male 4-8mm. White cross on abdomen. Varies from pale yellowish-brown to very dark brown. Common in gardens, hedges, woodland and heathland. Builds large round web.

House Spider
Tegenaria duellica
11-16mm long. Dark brown, with pale markings. Male smaller than female, but has longer legs. Widespread near human habitation. Builds a triangular web.

Nursery-web Spider
Pisaura mirabilis
10-15mm long. Male smaller, slimmer. Colours vary from yellow to brown, with subtle markings. Widespread across northern Europe. Hunts prey on food in daylight.

BIRDS

Mute Swan
Cygnus olor
152cm. Adult all white with orange bill and
black knob at base, juvenile grey-brown.
Common resident.
Ponds, lakes, rivers, streams.

Canada Goose
Branta canadensis
97cm. Brown body with a black head and
neck, and a white chin-strap.
Introduced resident.
Common on lakes and ponds.

Greylag Goose
Anser anser
83cm. Grey-brown plumage with orange
bill and pink legs. Introduced resident.
Common on lakes and ponds.

Egyptian Goose
Alopochen aegyptiaca
70cm. Pale brown with green, rufous and
white on wings. Dark eye-patch in adults.
Introduced resident.
Uncommon on lakes and ponds.

Shelduck
Tadorna tadorna
61cm. Large with mostly white body, green head and red, knobbed bill. Immature greyer. Locally common resident on Thames marshes, gravel pits and reservoirs.

Mandarin Duck
Aix galericulata
45cm. Breeding male unmistakeable. Female speckled grey with white eye-ring. Introduced resident. Locally common on lakes and ponds surrounded by trees.

Mallard
Anas platyrhynchos
58cm. Male distinctive. Female speckled brown with dark bill and deep blue speculum. Common resident around most wetlands.

Gadwall
Anas strepera
51cm. Male grey with a blackish rump and bill. Female brown with white speculum. Fairly common resident on lakes and ponds.

Wigeon
Anas penelope
46cm. Drake has chestnut head, yellow forehead. Female red-brown. Bill blue, speculum green. Locally common winter visitor from Oct-Mar on marshes and gravel pits.

Common Teal
Anas crecca
35cm. Small. Drake has a chestnut head with a green eyestripe, female brown. Speculum green. Common migrant and winter visitor to wetlands fringed with vegetation.

Shoveler
Anas clypeata
51cm. Large, spatulate bill. Drake has dark green head and chestnut flanks, female brown. Fairly common resident and common winter visitor to lakes and reservoirs.

Tufted Duck
Aythya fuligula
43cm. Drake black with white sides, drooping crest; female brown. Eyes yellow. Common resident on lakes and rivers.

Pochard
Aythya ferina
46cm. Drake grey with chestnut head, black breast and tail. Female grey-brown with a pale face. Uncommon resident and common winter visitor to large ponds and lakes.

Ruddy Duck
Oxyura jamaicensis
40cm. Small with raised stiff tail. Male dark reddish, white cheeks, female brown with striped cheeks. Introduced resident. Fairly common on ponds and lakes.

Common Pheasant
Phasianus colchicus
Male 85cm; female 60cm. Male chestnut with green head and red wattles. Female paler buff-brown. Locally common resident in suburbs and beyond. Favours woods, scrub and farmland.

Great Crested Grebe
Podiceps cristatus
48cm. When breeding has crest and reddish ruff. In winter head white with black cap. Common resident on lakes, ponds, rivers and canals.

Little Grebe
Tachybaptus ruficollis
27cm. Chestnut cheeks and throat in summer,
brown and grey in winter. Fairly common
resident on lakes, ponds and rivers.

Cormorant
Phalacrocorax carbo
90cm. Adult all black with white patches on
throat and thigh. Juvenile brown. Common resident
on lakes and rivers.

Grey Heron
Ardea cinerea
95cm. Large, tall, mainly grey, with black-and-
white markings and yellow bill. Common resident
around ponds, lakes, streams, rivers and canals.

Little Egret
Egretta garzetta
60cm. Small white heron with blackish bill and
legs and yellow feet. Uncommon but increasing
resident on marshes, lakes and reservoirs.

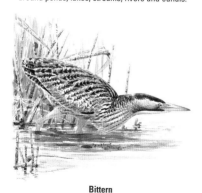

Bittern
Botaurus stellaris
75cm. Cryptic brown heron, perfectly camouflaged
against reedbed habitat. Rare winter visitor. London
Wetland Centre or Lee Valley are the best sites.

Sparrowhawk
Accipiter nisus
28cm (male), 38cm (female). Wings blunt and
broad. Breast barred red in male, brown in female.
Eyes yellow. Fairly common resident in parks
and gardens.

Kestrel
Falco tinnunculus
34-38cm. Long tail, pointed wings. Russet-brown,
male with grey head and tail, eyes dark.
Fairly common resident in various habitats
including the city centre.

Peregrine Falcon
Falco peregrinus
40-50cm. Blue-grey with moustache and barred
(adult) or streaked (juvenile) underparts.
Uncommon resident around tall buildings,
reservoirs and Thames marshes.

Hobby
Falco subbuteo
32cm. Small, swift-shaped. Dark greyish above
with black cap, white cheeks and red thighs.
Uncommon summer visitor from May-Sep.
Found around gravel pits and marshes.

Moorhen
Gallinula chloropus
30cm. Black with white undertail, red bill tipped
yellow and green legs. Juvenile brown.
Common resident. Ponds, rivers, lakes and
marshy places.

Coot
Fulica atra
38cm. All-black water bird with white bill and
shield on forehead. Juvenile greyish.
Common resident. Ponds, lakes,
rivers and streams.

Ringed Plover
Charadrius hiaticula
19cm. Black mask and breast band, narrow
white wing-bar and orange bill and legs. Uncommon
resident with local movements. Thames marshes,
reservoirs and gravel pits.

Little Ringed Plover
Charadrius dubius
16cm. Like Ringed Plover, but has yellow eyering,
duller legs and bill, no white wing-bar. Uncommon
summer visitor from Mar-Sep to marshes, lakes
and gravel pits.

Golden Plover
Pluvialis apricaria
28cm. Spangled yellow and brown all over.
Breeding birds have black throat and belly.
Uncommon winter visitor to marshes and
large open fields.

Lapwing
Vanellus vanellus
30cm. Dark greenish above and white below
with black breast and long fine crest.
Uncommon resident and fairly common winter
visitor to marshes, lakes and fields.

Dunlin
Calidris alpina
19cm. Small with decurved bill. Grey in winter.
In spring rufous above with black belly. Passage and
winter visitor from Aug-May. Regular only
on Thames marshes.

Redshank
Tringa totanus
28cm. Grey-brown. Orange-red bill and legs;
white rump and trailing edges to wings.
Fairly common. Breeds marshes and gravel
pits, winters mainly on Thames marshes.

Greenshank
Tringa nebularia
32cm. Pale grey, legs greenish, rump and
tail white. Uncommon passage migrant.
Marshes, shallow rivers, reservoirs.

Green Sandpiper
Tringa ochropus
22cm. Blackish above and on breast with
white undeparts. White rump shows in flight.
Uncommon late-summer passage migrant,
rare winter visitor. Marshes, reservoirs.

Common Sandpiper
Actitis hypoleucos
20cm. Small. Brown above, white below, with
white wing bar. Bobs tail. Uncommon passage
migrant. Rare winter visitor.
Lakes, reservoirs, rivers.

Curlew
Numenius arquata
54cm. Large, streaked brown with very long,
decurved bill and white rump. Passage and
winter visitor from Aug-May. Regular only
on Thames marshes.

Black-tailed Godwit
Limosa limosa
41cm. Long straight bill, white rump and
wing-bar. Neck and breast rufous except in winter.
Passage and winter visitor from Aug-May.
Regular only on Thames marshes.

Snipe
Gallinago gallinago
27cm. Small with cryptic plumage and very
long bill. Locally common passage and winter
visitor to marshes and reed-fringed lakes.

Black-headed Gull
Larus ridibundus
37cm. Red bill and legs. Dark brown hood in
summer and small black marks on head in winter.
Common (except in mid-summer) on lakes,
parks and playing fields.

Common Gull
Larus canus
41cm. Like small Herring Gull, but legs yellowish,
no red bill-spot, eyes dark. Common winter visitor
from Aug-Apr. Lakes, parks and playing fields.

Herring Gull
Larus argentatus
61cm. Silver-grey wings with black tips, red
spot on yellow bill, pink legs. Immature brown.
Common resident and winter visitor to a
variety of habitats.

Lesser Black-backed Gull
Larus fuscus
55cm. Like Herring Gull but wings and back
dark grey, legs yellow. Immature darker.
Common resident in many habitats.

Great Black-backed Gull
Larus marinus
72cm. Larger and darker than Lesser Black-
backed with pink legs. Immature has pale head.
Fairly common winter visitor to Thames and
large reservoirs.

Common Tern
Sterna hirundo
35cm. Black crown, red legs and bill and long,
forked tail. Forehead white in winter. Common
summer visitor from Apr-Sep. Lakes,
rivers, canals.

Feral Rock Dove
Columba livia
33cm. Variable – grey, black, white or reddish,
often with black wingbars and a white rump.
Common resident in parks and gardens and
around buildings.

Stock Dove
Columba oenas
30cm. Grey rump and black trailing edges and
tips to otherwise plain grey wings. Dark eyes.
Fairly common resident in parks and open woodland
with mature trees.

Woodpigeon
Columba palumbus
41cm. Large, waddling. Adult has neck patches
and a white bar across each wing. Common
resident in parks, gardens and woods.

Collared Dove
Streptopelia decaocto
32cm. Small, long-tailed, plain brown-buff with
black collar and white in tail. Common resident in
suburban parks and gardens.
Absent from city centre.

Ring-necked Parakeet
Psittacula krameri
40cm. Bright green with long tail, black chin and
red bill. Has loud screeching call. Introduced.
Now common and increasing in most of London.

Cuckoo
Cuculus canorus
34cm. Raptor-shaped in flight with long wings
and tail. Grey with a pale, barred breast.
Scarce, declining summer visitor from Apr-Aug
in suburban parks and open woodland.

Tawny Owl
Strix aluco
38cm. Large tawny-brown owl, dark eyes.
Nocturnal and more often heard than seen.
Fairly common resident in woodland, parks
and large gardens.

Little Owl
Athene noctua
22cm. Small brown-and-white owl with
yellow eyes. Uncommon resident in suburban
parks and tracts of farmland.

Swift
Apus apus
17cm. Long, narrow wings, forked tail. Plumage
blackish with pale throat. Screaming call. Often
around buildings or wetlands. Common summer
visitor from May-Aug.

Kingfisher
Alcedo atthis
18cm. Fairly small. Bright blue above and orange
below; long bill, short tail. Uncommon and localized
resident on rivers, streams, ponds and lakes.

Green Woodpecker
Picus viridis
33cm. Green with yellow rump and red cap.
Juvenile greyer and speckled. Has 'laughing' call.
Fairly common resident in woods and parks.
Often feeds on ants on the ground.

Lesser Spotted Woodpecker
Dendrocopos minor
16cm. Small – only sparrow-sized. Finely barred
black and white on back. Rare resident.
Occurs in some London parks.

Great Spotted Woodpecker
Dendrocopos major
24cm. Blackbird-sized, pied with white shoulder
patches and red under the tail. Common resident in
parks, large gardens and woods.

Skylark
Alauda arvensis
18cm. Streaked brown above with short crest and white outer tail. Has hovering song flight. Localized resident around suburban meadows and farmland, grassland.

Swallow
Hirundo rustica
15cm (not including tail streamers). Glossy blue above, cream underparts and red throat. Common summer visitor from Apr-Sep. Favours open country, often seen near water.

House Martin
Delichon urbica
14cm. Dark blue-black above with white rump and underparts. Common summer visitor from Apr-Sep. Breeds in colonies on buildings.

Meadow Pipit
Anthus pratensis
15cm. Streaked brown above and spotted below with pink legs. Common winter visitor to open meadows and marshes from Sep-Mar. Localized breeder.

Grey Wagtail
Motacilla cinerea
19cm. Grey above with yellow rump and underparts. Bobs very long tail. Fairly common resident, especially close to tall buildings or running water.

Pied Wagtail
Motacilla alba
18cm. Black or grey above with white face, underparts and outer tail feathers. Common resident in many habitats. Often seen on lawns and in car parks.

Wren
Troglodytes troglodytes
10cm. Tiny, short tail often held cocked. Reddish-brown plumage, faintly barred. Common resident in gardens, parks and other habitats.

Dunnock
Prunella modularis
14cm. Streaky brown above with blue-grey underparts. Common resident in gardens, parks, open woodland and hedgerows.

Goldcrest
Regulus regulus
9cm. Tiny; greenish back, yellow crest bordered black. Face plain, paler around dark eyes. Common resident in coniferous and mixed woodlands; often seen in Yew trees.

Blackbird
Turdus merula
25cm. Male black with yellow bill and eyering,
female plain dark brown, juvenile spotted.
Common resident in woodland, parks
and gardens.

Fieldfare
Turdus pilaris
26cm. Grey head and rump, rufous back, dark
spots below. White underwings show in flight.
Fairly common winter visitor (Oct-Mar) to
woodland, parks, fields and gardens.

Mistle Thrush
Turdus viscivorus
28cm. Large, sandy brown, spotted below.
In flight shows white tail corners and underwings.
Fairly common resident in woodlands, parks
and gardens.

Song Thrush
Turdus philomelos
23cm. Medium-sized, warm brown with black spots
below. In flight, underwings yellow-orange. Common
resident in woodlands, parks and gardens.

Redwing
Turdus iliacus
21cm. Smaller than Song Thrush with white
eyebrows and red patch under wing. Common
winter visitor from Oct-Mar. Fields, open woodland,
parks and gardens.

Reed Warbler
Acrocephalus scirpaceus
13cm. Plain brown warbler with rounded tail and
chugging song. Fairly common visitor from Apr-Sep.
Mostly in reedbeds, but in bushes on migration.

Willow Warbler
Phylloscopus trochilus
11.5cm. Greenish above with pale yellow eyebrow and breast. Legs usually pale. Cascading song. Fairly common summer visitor from Apr-Sep. Parks, open woods.

Common Chiffchaff
Phylloscopus collybita
11cm. Very similar to Willow Warbler but legs usually dark, simple two-note song. Common visitor from Mar-Oct. Rare in winter. Parks, open woods, scrub, hedgerows.

Sedge Warbler
Acrocephalus schoenobaenus
13cm. Streaked above with pale eyebrow, rufous rump and rounded tail. Fairly common summer visitor from Apr-Sep. Found around wetland vegetation.

Common Whitethroat
Sylvia communis
14cm. Rufous wings and white throat. Long tail edged white. Male has grey head. Common summer visitor from Apr-Sep. Open woodland, hedgerows and scrub.

Lesser Whitethroat
Sylvia curruca
13cm. Duller grey-brown above than Common Whitethroat, with no rufous tones. Fairly common visitor from Apr-Sep to hedges, woodland edges, scrub and parks.

Blackcap
Sylvia atricapilla
14cm. Plain grey, with black cap in male, red-brown in female. Common summer visitor from Mar-Oct. Rare in winter. Woodland, parks, large gardens.

Garden Warbler
Sylvia borin
14cm. Plain unmarked brown. Blackcap-like warbling song is best characteristic. Fairly common summer visitor from Apr-Sep. Woodland and scrub.

Stonechat
Saxicola torquata
12cm. Male has black head, white neck-patches, orange below. Female duller, streaked brown. Uncommon winter visitor to marshlands and rough fields.

Robin
Erithacus rubecula
13cm. Orange-red breast fringed pale grey. Juvenile heavily spotted brown and buff. Common resident. Gardens, parks and woodlands.

Black Redstart
Pheonicurus ochruros
14cm. Grey or black with bright
orange-red rump and tail in all
plumages. Rare resident. Favours
factories, building sites and
waste ground.

Long-tailed Tit
Aegithalos caudatus
14cm (including 7cm tail). Black and
white with pink on wings and belly.
Common resident. Parks, gardens
and other places with
bushy undergrowth.

Blue Tit
Parus caeruleus
12cm. Blue crown, wings and tail.
Black stripe through eye. Yellow
underparts. Common resident in
gardens, parks and woods. Often
visits bird-feeders.

Great Tit
Parus major
14cm. Blue-and-green above, yellow
below. Black head and belly-stripe;
white cheeks. Common resident in
gardens, parks and woods. Often
visits bird-feeders.

Coal Tit
Parus ater
11cm. Black cap, grey back, buff
underparts, long white patch
running down nape. Uncommon
resident. Woodlands, parks and
gardens, especially with conifers.

Marsh Tit
Parus palustris
12cm. Plain brown above and buff
below with shiny black cap and
small black bib. Rare and localized
resident in suburbs. Mainly
deciduous woodland.

Nuthatch
Sitta europaea
14cm. Short tail, long bill. Blue-grey
above, orange below, descends
trunks head-first. Uncommon
resident. Woods, parks and large
gardens with mature oaks.

Treecreeper
Certhia familiaris
13cm. Streaky brown above, white
below. Decurved bill. Creeps mouse-
like up trees. Uncommon resident.
Woodland, parks, large gardens.

House Sparrow
Passer domesticus
15cm. Male has grey-and-chestnut
cap, black bib, female plainer with
buff eyestripe. Resident. Gardens
and parks. Common in suburbs,
now uncommon in city centre.

Jay
Garrulus glandarius
34cm. Pinkish with black moustache, wings and tail, white rump and blue wing patch. Fairly common resident. Woods, parks and gardens.

Magpie
Pica pica
44cm (including 25cm tail). Black with metallic sheen, long tail and white on wings and body. Common resident. Gardens, parks, woods.

Jackdaw
Corvus monedula
33cm. Small crow with grey nape, pale eye and distinctive 'kya' call. Absent from city centre, but common resident in fields, woods and gardens in suburbs.

Carrion Crow
Corvus corone
46cm. Large, all-black crow with stout bill. Common resident. Many habitats including parks and gardens.

Rook
Corvus frugilegus
46cm. Glossy black with bare white face accentuating long bill. Juvenile has dark face. Not found in city, but common resident in farmland just beyond outer suburbs.

Starling
Sturnus vulgaris
21cm. Glossy black with yellow bill, pink legs, white spots and metallic sheen. Common resident. Wide variety of habitats.

Chaffinch
Fringilla coelebs
15cm. Male pink and blue, female brown and buff. White wing bars and outer tail. Common resident. Parks, gardens, woodland edges.

Bullfinch
Pyrrhula pyrrhula
16cm. Black cap and tail, grey back and white rump. Male pink below, female brown. Uncommon resident. Mixed woods, parks, large gardens.

Linnet
Carduelis cannabina
13cm. Brown back; white in wings and tail. Forehead and breast red in breeding male. Fairly common resident. Fields, scrub, wasteland.

Lesser Redpoll
Carduelis caberet
12cm. Brown with dark streaks, red forehead and black bib. Male has pink breast. Uncommon winter visitor: Sep-Mar. Often in Alder and birch.

Goldfinch
Carduelis carduelis
13cm. Golden-brown with black-and-gold wings. Rump white. Adult has red face. Common resident. Gardens, parks, waste ground.

Greenfinch
Carduelis chloris
15cm. Green or brown (juvenile streaked) with yellow patches on wings and tail. Common resident. Woodland edges, parks, gardens.

Siskin
Carduelis spinus
12cm. Streaked greenish-yellow, pale wing-bars, male with black cap and bib. Winter visitor in variable numbers from Sep-Mar. Often in alder and birch.

Reed Bunting
Emberiza schoeniclus
15cm. Streaked brown, white outer tail feathers. Summer male has black head. Fairly common resident. Marshes, rough fields, scrub.

OTHER ANIMALS

Smooth Newt
Triturus vulgaris
Length 7-11cm. Lizard-shaped, smooth-skinned.
Breeding male colourful with wavy crest along back.
Hibernates. Active day and night. Damp habitats,
usually in ponds or ditches in spring.

Common Toad
Bufo bufo
8-15cm long. Females are larger than males. Warty
skin, large long bulge behind eye. Tadpoles blackish.
Usually walks slowly. Hibernates. Mainly nocturnal.
Found in most damp and shady habitats.

Common Frog
Rana temporaria
6-8cm long. Smooth skin with dark markings.
Tadpoles have golden sheen. Hops strongly.
Hibernates. Active day and night. Widespread
in moist, shady habitats.

Common Lizard
Lacerta vivipara
Total length 10-16cm; tail up to twice the length of
the body. Dull grey-greenish with subtle dark markings.
Sunbathes; runs and climbs rapidly. Diurnal, hibernates.
Open habitats – woodland edges, heathland.

Grass Snake
Natrix natrix
70-150cm long. Females bigger than males.
Dark green with yellow collar and small black
marks down sides. Has distinct head. Active day
and night. Hibernates. Well-vegetated habitats,
usually near water.

Hedgehog
Erinaceus europaeus
Body 20-30cm long; tail 1-4cm. Stocky, covered in
brownish spines. Rolls into spiny ball when threatened.
Nocturnal, hibernates. Gardens, parks, woodland
and hedgerow.

Mole
Talpa europaea
Body 11-16cm long; tail 2-4cm. Blackish, velvety, short-legged. Tiny eyes and ears, large shovel-shaped forepaws. Active all year, all day and night but rarely above ground. Fields, parks, woods, gardens.

Wood Mouse
Apodemus sylvaticus
Body 8-10cm long; tail 6.9-11.5cm. Warm brown, whitish on underside. Large ears, eyes and very long bare tail. Nocturnal, active all year. Gardens, parks, woodlands, occasionally in buildings.

House Mouse
Mus domesticus
Body 7-10cm long; tail 6.5-10cm. Relatively small ears and eyes. Brownish-grey, scaly tail. Mainly nocturnal, active all year. In buildings (including London Underground).

Grey Squirrel
Sciurus carolinensis
Body 23-30cm long; tail 19-24cm. Grey with yellow tinge, bushy tail. Fast runner, agile tree-climber. Often very confiding. Diurnal, active all year. Woodlands, parks and gardens.

Common Pipistrelle
Pipistrellus pipistrellus
Body 3.5-4.9cm long; wingspan 27-30cm. Tiny, small-eared bat with narrow wings and fast and jerky flight. Nocturnal, hibernates. Found in all habitats.

Fox
Vulpes vulpes
Body 56-77cm long; tail 28-49cm. Reddish, black ears and legs, white chin, chest and tail-tip. Bushy tail, pointed ears. Shy. Mainly nocturnal, active year-round. Found in all habitats.

Index